LIKE A TRAMP, LIKE A PILGRIM

HARRY BUCKNALL

Harry Bucknall was born in London in 1965 and brought up in Dorset. Travel has been an indelible part of his life since early childhood summers spent exploring the Poole Harbour archipelago in a Mirror dinghy. Educated at Harrow and the Royal Military Academy, Sandhurst, he served as a regular officer in the Coldstream Guards. After, Harry worked in the oil and mining industries and as a consultant in the Middle East. He has also produced theatre on the London Fringe, sat on the Olivier Awards Panel and acted as a reviewer for Arts Council, London. As a freelance travel writer, he has contributed to both the national and international press. Harry's first book, *In the Dolphin's Wake,* about his journey from Venice to Istanbul through the Greek Islands, was published in 2011.

Like a Tramp,
Like A Pilgrim

On Foot, Across Europe to Rome

HARRY BUCKNALL

BLOOMSBURY
LONDON • NEW DELHI • NEW YORK • SYDNEY

First published in Great Britain 2014

Cover by Chris Wormell
Illustrations by Louise Sheeran
Maps and chapter-end designs by Lachlan Campbell

A Continuum book

Bloomsbury Publishing Plc
50 Bedford Square
London WC1B 3DP

www.bloomsbury.com

Bloomsbury is a trademark of Bloomsbury Publishing Plc

Bloomsbury Publishing, London, New Delhi, New York and Sydney

A CIP record for this book is available from the British Library.

ISBN 9781408187241
10 9 8 7 6 5 4 3 2 1

Typeset by Fakenham Prepress Solutions, Fakenham, Norfolk
NR21 8NN
Printed and bound in Great Britain by CPI Group (UK) Ltd, Croydon
CRO 4YY

Also by Harry Bucknall
Published by Bene Factum
In the Dolphin's Wake

It is the road that teaches us...and the road that enriches us...
Paulo Coelho, *The Pilgrimage*, 1987

Contents

Note

*

Denotes passage of a day or more in the narrative.

Acknowledgements

EVERY DAY THAT I sit at my desk looking out over the Dorset Downs, I never forget what a great privilege it is to write. Working on *Like a Tramp, Like a Pilgrim* has brought me such joy, not only because of the adventure itself but for all the people I met along the way. This was a journey which started five years ahead of that May morning in 2012 when I set out from St Paul's Cathedral. Countless friendships were made and a number rekindled in the process, in some cases after 30 years or more – the experience was worth it for that alone. But it took the efforts of many, before, during and after the enterprise, to help get the book to completion. The majority appear in the pages that follow; one or two have had their names changed either for my or their own sakes, while a host of others, in the shadows, selflessly leant their shoulder to the wheel on my behalf.

Through two long winters and a glorious summer as I typed my manuscript, these special people, whose kindness and generosity helped bring the pages to life, have rarely been far from my thoughts.

My parents, Robin and Diana, for putting up with my flights of fantasy; my brother, James, for letting me stay hidden away from the distractions of the everyday, and Tessa, his wife, who has lived with every stage of the *Tramp* these past two years; my sister, Kate Benson and James and Azucena Keatley for being the diligent guardians of every draft; my readers, Peter and Anne Williams, Alan Ogden, David Prest and Nicholas Armour who gave so much of their time to challenge, cajole and bully the text into some semblance of form and forewarn of howlers.

Anthony Weldon and Christopher Lee for nurturing the scheme; Phillip Sturrock, for his counsel; Artemis Cooper, George Waud, Barnaby Rogerson, Stephanie Allen, Anthea Gibson Fleming, Ben and Tessa Fisher for their introductions; Mark and Alexandra James for their words of encouragement; Annie Maguire for her timely reminder; William and Bronwyn Marques and Joe Paterson of the Confraternity of Pilgrims to Rome for their invaluable briefings; Edmund Hall, Lucy Dichmont, Philip Noel, Christopher Page, Cassian Roberts, Sergio Gimenez, Graeme Moyle and Martha Bofito for their invaluable assistance in getting me under way; Rose and Andy Keir in the village for looking after my dog, Sam; Canon Mark Oakley, the Reverends Ewen Pinsent and Darren A'Court for their blessings and prayers; Vishal Raghuvanshi, Michael Harm, Sue Quinn and Henrietta Green for their farewell; Captain Billy Matthews at Regimental Headquarters, Coldstream Guards for his jovial support; Keith and Sandra Robinson, Scott Veitch and Guy Cholerton, Edward and Wheezie Cottrell for their hospitality, and Robert Woods of P&O Ferries for getting me across the English Channel.

Generalmajor Carsten Jacobson of the Bundeswehr, Max Arthur and William Horstmann-Craig for their research on Arras; Charles Goodson-Wickes, Charles and Sarah Daireaux, Emmanuel Barbaux and Jean-Baptiste de Proyart who helped my passage through France.

Claudio Sebasti for his welcome in Geneva and my dear friend, Raúl Santiago Goñi, for turning up quite unannounced; Mark Ridley for making me so at home in Italy and John Gibbons for advice over the odd brick in Pavia.

The Prince and Grand Master Fra' Matthew Festing, Lucia Virgilio and Rebecca Chalmers of the Sovereign Military Order of Malta for their joyous reception in Rome and clean clothes; Tim Baxter for his poetry; Hugh McKenna for feting my return home; Abbot Timothy Wright, Father Andrew Cole, the late Father Gerard Hughes and Father Matthew Power, who gave spiritual comment on pilgrimage; Monsignor Philip Whitmore of the Venerable English College in Rome for his findings and the Very Reverend Dr Robert Willis, Dean of Canterbury Cathedral, who was so generous and helpful on numerous occasions.

David Anderson, Joan Witts, Alfredo Tavares, Salvatore Cantanzaro, Alfred Kelp, Joaquin Santos, Lucca San Martino, Djaffar Namane, Lukasz Pyra, Chris Pineda, Antonio Silva, Michal Pyra and Tomasz Naporski, who kept the coffee flowing while drafting at the best-kept secret in London; Martin Morrisey for his wisdom; Rosemary Etherton for her subtle harangue whenever she guessed my output was slowing; Nick and Kim Hughes and their leviathan photocopying machine; Alan Titchmarsh for his enquiring and ever-cheery words that meant so much; Justine 'Freds' Hardy, my eternal muse, for keeping the ship afloat with copious quantities of laughter during the odd squall that inevitably rocked the boat from time to time. Not forgetting Nick Edmiston and his now rather frayed hat, which is still a cut above the rest, and Jools Holland, whose music never fails to make me smile – Chapter 7 refers.

I cannot finish without thanking Robin Baird-Smith, my long-suffering publisher at Bloomsbury, for his gently guiding hand, faith and fun throughout; Nicola Rusk, Joel Simons, Jamie Birkett, Kim Storry, Dawn Booth, Tristan Defew, Adam Smart and Jane Tetzlaff, who gave order to my script in double-quick time; Ros Ellis, Helen Flood and Maria Hammershoy for shouting my name from the rooftops of Bedford Square so expertly; Lachlan Campbell for Venus 'without', his marvellous maps and the end chapter designs; Louise Sheeran for such evocative illustrations crafted with her beloved exploding pen; Clive Chalk for his patient photography; Chris Wormell for creating such a wonderful cover and the special Μιχάλημου … never fail to remember that 'three' is greater than 'too'. Always.

Finally, Ernest Brown, please now eat your hat!

HCB, Everley, Dorset
St. Patrick's Day,
17th March, 2014

Illustrations

1

Waiting for the kettle to boil...

'Nothing happens unless first a dream.'
Carl Sandburg, *Washington Monument by Night*, 1922

WAITING FOR THE KETTLE to boil, I picked up the newspaper; the inside page instantly caught my eye – emblazoned across it was a large medieval map of Europe tracing a route, in red, from Canterbury to Rome, the Via Francigena. It was Tuesday, 31 July 2007.

Minutes earlier, I had just typed the last full stop of *In the Dolphin's Wake*. Satisfied, I leant back in my chair and looked out of the window; the horses grazed in the paddock, Sam, my Jack Russell, was lazing in the sun, the chickens fussed about the hedges and overhead a lark sang. My view.

Then, quite without warning, the sky turned leaden grey, a rush of wind forged up the valley and within seconds the tranquil scene was turned to mayhem as chickens, dog, birds and horses variously scattered in every direction chased by torrents of rain. From the sanctuary of my desk, I watched curiously removed as this turbulent tableau unfolded before me, until, overhead, an explosion of shattering magnitude transformed my look to one of utter disbelief as the cable linking my computer to the outside world momentarily glowed an iridescent blue and, in seeming slow motion, a spark struck at the heart of the machine with the accuracy of a guided missile. The screen went black.

This has not happened, I tried to convince myself – except that it had. Eighty-eight thousand words had, quite literally, just gone up in a puff of smoke. A small cloud dissipated in the beams above. For a moment, I sat there numb. To scream would have been futile, so instead I went downstairs to make myself a cup of coffee.

That map, instantly evocative, led my mind to wander as I traced a finger down its line: a 1,400-mile journey through England, France, Switzerland and Italy until it reached the Eternal City, Rome itself – an adventure of Elizabethan proportion that would carry me off into lands steeped with history, culture and, no doubt, incident and escapade. It was the sense of future that made the idea of pilgrimage so exciting – a chance to shake free once more from the chains of reality: offices, meetings, budgets, in short the everyday bureaucratic theatre that we all get caught up in, which seems so important, yet, more often than not, is so very unimportant. Or was it perhaps the last hurrah of youth? One final carefree outing before I finally gave in to the serious business of middle age and set course for my twilight years.

The Via Francigena, the route that has linked Canterbury to Rome since the earliest of times, is a virtual straight line in a south-easterly direction – as you might expect any journey between two points, especially when, for much of the past two millennia, a round trip, undertaken on foot or horseback, lasted the best part of six months. The Francigena was never an established road as such; it was more a corridor of movement along which merchants traded, armies marched, embassies moved and pilgrims travelled. It is incredible, however, that despite the invasion of Britain by Julius Caesar in 55–54BC, St Augustine's arrival from Rome in AD595 or the thousands of others who must have travelled up and down it for whatever reason, the first recorded itinerary of the Via was made by Sigeric the Serious, King Æthelred the Unready's Archbishop of Canterbury from 990 until his death in 994. Sigeric was luckier than one of his predecessors, Ælfsige (or Elfsy), who froze to death in the Alps while making the same journey.

Forgotten for his significant role in attempting to save the country from repeated invasion by the Danish King, Sweyn Forkbeard, Sigeric is remembered almost solely today for the fact that he just happened, probably out of boredom, to write down the 80 or so places where he stopped on his return to England from Rome after being officially invested with the pallium, the scarf-like vestment worn around the neck and effectively the Archbishop's badge of office, by the

Pope. His account is nothing more than a list – no year, no date, not so much as a remark; indeed, some of the places he recorded confound historians tucked away on the shelves of the British Library in an Anglo-Saxony Miscellany to this day. Nonetheless, it is on this unremarkable document found in the pages of an Anglo-Saxon Miscellany in the depths of the British Library that the present route of the Via Francigena is based.

The popular image of the Christian pilgrim dates back to the Middle Ages, celebrated most notably by Chaucer's fictional story of a band of everyday characters on their way from Southwark to visit the tomb of St Thomas à Becket, England's premier shrine, in *The Canterbury Tales*. To give an idea as to how popular the pilgrimage was around that time, over two million people were believed to have flocked to Rome from all over Europe in 1300 and, in 1450, it was estimated an astonishing 40,000 people a day were pouring into St Peter's Basilica.

St Wilfrid of Hexham was the first named English pilgrim to make the journey, in the mid-seventh century; others included Alfred the Great, sent by his father, and King Canute. The rich would make the journey on horseback, passing from bishop's palace to bishop's palace, while the poor would travel on foot from monasteries and convents to hospitals run by religious orders. Despite the renewed popularity of the Camino de Santiago, never since has the Christian pilgrimage on foot enjoyed such a following as it did in the latter half of the Middle Ages – perhaps due to war, time, the effort required or the inescapable fact that nowadays the Church, in general, plays an ever smaller role in Western society. By comparison, today, less than a handful of Britons walk to Rome every year.

However, pilgrims had been travelling to far-off places well before the Middle Ages, in search of saintly relics – including many fakes too – to pay homage to holy bits of finger, skull and other obscure pieces of this and that which they believed, in visiting, brought them closer to God either by touching or – worse – drinking, in the hope of making a prayer come true, curing sickness and disease or plain bolstering up virtue. To die a saint meant almost immediate dismemberment, as your various parts were scattered across Christendom, like new exhibits at the Royal Academy – a piece of Becket's bone even ended up at the Venerable English College in Rome. The only others who suffered a similar fate were criminals after execution.

Such was the clamour to get sight of these relics, like the Veil of Veronica – the cloth that the saint is said to have wiped Christ's face with – that people were frequently crushed to death in the mêlée. Pilgrims, effectively religious tourists, were good for business; the enormous numbers of the devout on the move all needed to be housed, fed and watered – revenue from pilgrim dues helped rebuild Canterbury Cathedral after it burnt down in the twelfth century. And, at a time when Christianity was the framework for everything, to go on pilgrimage was to embark on the journey of a lifetime and a much sought-after opportunity to earn, in the process, a few bonus points (in the form of Indulgences) to present at the Gates of Heaven to forego temporal punishment due on sins forgiven. This was all the more important, given that the ghastly prospect of Hell, as peddled from the pulpit every Sunday, was worth avoiding at all costs.

Another compelling reason for anyone to go specifically to Rome was the reward of forgiveness from all sin; this sounded particularly attractive to me – the chance to wipe the slate clean after a not entirely angelic 42 years on this earth had a special appeal all of its own.

But it would be another four years before anything of consequence happened. The idea smouldered away and life rolled along until one day, my publisher, over lunch, dropped into the conversation that 'it would be a pity if that Rome book didn't get written …', his voice tailing off suggestively. A throw-away comment that resulted in a swift email exchange and, three days later, it was agreed that I would set out for Italy in early April, after Easter, on what was for me, at that stage, a 'romantic adventure'.

At a friend's dinner party later in the week, I announced my news. There was an awkward silence.

'Have you got God?' someone asked.

No, I replied, I was walking to Rome for the hell of it. No cars, no taxis, no buses. I would do it the old way, on foot. But, I added that I didn't believe anyone could embark on an undertaking of such length and be at the behest of one's own devices for so long without some form of spiritual reflection either.

'What will you do about your luggage?' came another.

The more I explained, the more the consensus around the table was that to travel to Rome by any means other than an aeroplane was, in this day and age, frankly unhinged.

Back at home, I consulted the map again: it was indeed a very long way. The French bit alone was two hands and Italy almost three – never mind the English or Swiss sections. As I was walking to a great capital it seemed meet that I should set out from a great capital, and so I decided to leave from London, adding another five days and nearly 100 miles to my journey. In the last 20 years, I hadn't walked so much as ten miles in one day, let alone 20 miles every day for three months non-stop.

And then there was the business of 'my luggage', which of course would be a rucksack – the cumbersome modern version of the 'scrip' or leather pouch, which held my medieval counterparts' every need, transforming me into an unseemly beast of burden. I had a matter of weeks to get ready. The April departure quickly became early May. The weather, I reassured myself, would be better then.

The more I went about my preparation, the more it became apparent that this was no ordinary endeavour; in fact, it would be a momentous event in my life, as the familiar would be exchanged for the unfamiliar. Almost monastic in its execution, the nature of the undertaking, I fast learnt, was just the same now as I suspected it had been in the Middle Ages or earlier and no less hazardous. My life pared down to a time-liberated and materially limited existence, as I rid myself of my flat, my job, my dog and my possessions, enabled me to embark as unencumbered by the trappings of the everyday as possible, free to wander, free to wonder and free to muse. As custom once dictated, but sense still demanded, I renewed my will and put my jumbled affairs in some sort of order – long-lost tradition in parts of Europe having it that, should I not return within a year and one day, I would be declared dead and my assets dispersed accordingly.

But ridding myself of everyday adjuncts and comforts that could reasonably be taken for granted was painful and loaded with emotion; it felt like I was tearing the skin from my back.

I learnt once again to pack for weight over elegance, a skill long lost since military days; my only nod to fashion being the purchase of a thumbstick while staying with my eldest brother, Charlie, in Northumberland, which I fancied would make me look a bit more authentic, even rugged, and a bottle of Murdock's 'Black Tea Aftershave' – a scented reminder that I was only absconding from the real world temporarily; at least, I would only stink like a tramp by day.

Alice Warrender, Andrew Bruce and Brian Mooney – veterans of the road to Rome – coached me in the intricacies of what would lie ahead. Andrew warned me to watch out for my boots in hostels, Brian discussed wolves in the woods around Radicofani, while Alice could talk of nothing but feet hurting like they had been caught in a vice.

Andrew dragged me off to Cotswold Camping in the most unlikely location of central Knightsbridge. I was handed over to Tamzin Norbu, the son of a Ladakh yak herder and no stranger to the Himalayas. My feet were measured this way and that, I was made to stand up, sit down, walk on the flat, walk around and even walk over a little bridge while the mountain man considered his new charge. And then, from behind a velvet curtain, an enormous pair of boots was produced with some ceremony. Grey and covered with lace-holes and rivets, they looked horrible. I was assured, however, that these monsters would get me to Rome with no problem. 'Nooo problem!' Andrew echoed, beaming with joy as if he had just delivered a baby.

Rucksacks followed in all shapes and sizes – contrary to memory, they were actually quite comfortable; once chosen, my newfound home was duly filled with socks, water bottles, glowy things to make me shine in the dark, blister kits and, finally, a set of reassuringly expensive bright red waterproofs, the latest thing in breathable clothing – 'to make you stand out in the rain so the lorries don't hit you', Andrew hushed at me as I questioned the colour.

Back in Dorset, I was accosted by my old friend Mike Marshall in the Village Shop: 'You'll need a key to take with you as a symbol of your pilgrimage.'

I looked at him quizzically.

'It's a key for St Peter, you know, just like they take a scallop shell to Santiago. I'll make you one.' A business-like conversation as to design and aesthetics followed and the retired schoolmaster-cum-steam engine builder left with a wave and sloped away to his comprehensively equipped lair of workbenches, tools, lathes and oily rags like Caractacus Potts to a new invention. Two weeks later, I was summoned to Mike's kitchen where a large steaming mug of tea was thrust into my hand and a package the size of a book, wrapped in ripped sheets, was waiting for me on the table. I opened it, the peppery musk of *Brasso* wafting about me as I unwound the binding to reveal two handsome keys, golden in colour; the robust bow handles were scored with the cross and cut with holes at each diagonal large enough for my finger to fit through. They glinted in the afternoon sun. The shafts were engraved with my name while the bit was castellated and carved on both sides with the crucifix. Keys fit for the Gates of Heaven and, being made by a locomotive man, about the right size too.

'Why two?' I hadn't the heart to add that they weighed a ton.

'Well, I figured, you'll need one for the Vatican and the other to put up in church when you get back. Not every day we have someone in the village walking to Rome after all.'

In the Post Office, Rose stamped the first page of my Pilgrim Passport, a document issued to me by the Confraternity of Pilgrims to Rome – the organization established to help like-minded souls reach St Peter's – setting me apart from the everyday traveller. The simple card entitled me to the three basic pilgrim privileges: the right to hospitality, safe passage and exemption from the payment of tolls. It would render me a ward of the Church and act as proof of passage as I made my way across Europe. The daily stamp would be my routine from now on at every place I stopped for the night until I reached Vatican City. Unfolded on the wooden counter, the shiny new Passport appeared bare and empty. Andy the taxi man looked on with a sombre face and in his gentle Dorset burr, wished me 'all the best for your walk then 'Arry. You take care now, and mind you'm do come back in one piece an' all.'

And so, unwittingly, once again, I found myself catching up with ancient custom as not only I, but my stick and the enormous keys were blessed at the altar in church with much hoo ha, like a Knight departing on Crusade. We sang *To be a Pilgrim* and I was sent on my way with the exhortation that God keep me in the palm of his hand until I return. He who would valiant be...

1,411 miles to Rome.

Part 1
England

...This precious stone set in the silver sea,...
William Shakespeare, *King Richard II*, c. 1595

2

St Paul's Cathedral to Chilham Castle, Kent

When April's fruitful rains descend
And bring the droughts of March to end...
Why, then folks go on pilgrimages
And pilgrims yearn for foreign strands
And distant shrines in foreign lands.

Geoffrey Chaucer, *The Canterbury Tales*,
late fourteenth century

ST PAUL'S CATHEDRAL LOOMED over me, when at 8 o'clock the bells began to sound in deep toll to summon the few to early communion that 7 May. We were ten, huddled together in a whitewashed side chapel: my godmother, some close friends and a lady from Nigeria who just happened to be there. The canon blessed me, my Passport was stamped and, after an obligatory photograph on the steps, we set off like an itinerant troupe for Millennium Bridge; as we did so, I noticed a blackbird high up on the grand portico. There was silence and, in that moment, the little bird sang, his joyous call ringing out a farewell for all to hear.

We breakfasted in the lee of Southwark Cathedral. Everybody else, save me who was in shorts and t-shirt, was sensibly wrapped up in overcoats and scarves; for some reason that morning – perhaps it was the nerves – I was oblivious to the cold. We ate bacon sandwiches with mugs of tea, some bottles of champagne were produced and I was just settling in when Andrew Bruce looked at his watch and, being very sensible, reminded me that I had 20-plus miles to go to reach Dartford that evening.

It was a ramshackle path that I traced down the Thames, through a maze of back streets and alleyways, past darkened warehouses and workshops, once home to cargoes of wool or timber, the barge-builder or the sail-maker; now gentrified residences for materially minded office workers in nearby Canary Wharf, stripped of purpose and the hustle of yesteryear, there was a melancholic feel to them. I headed east for Greenwich, over swing bridges and lock gates and past docks where the water hung idle, until Deptford, the King's Yard, 600 years earlier the most important dock in England and later the principal victualling store for the Royal Navy's Home Fleet – today, a silent memorial to the great adventurers of a maritime past long gone. Drake set sail from here around the globe in the *Golden Hind*; it was in Deptford that Raleigh laid his cape before his Virgin Queen, Cook departed for the Southern Seas and much of Nelson's fleet was built.

In the spring of 1698, on his 'Grand Embassy' to rally support against the Ottoman Empire, a young Peter the Great, Tsar of Russia, spent three months in Deptford. At King William III's request, the diarist John Evelyn rented Sayes Court, which no longer exists, to Peter and his extensive retinue who evidently enjoyed all the neighbourhood had to offer, prompting Evelyn's servant to write, 'there is a house full of people, and right nasty'. Come departure in April, the place was wrecked – Russia was sent a bill that included the replacement of 300 windows, 12 broken doors, several pieces of walnut furniture, bedlinen that had been torn to shreds, a blown-up kitchen floor and family portraits that had been used for target practice.

At Blackheath, I joined Watling Street, the ancient road from London to Dover, that would take me to Dartford; first established by the Ancient Britons, it was improved by the Romans, and is better known as the A2, a horrible road, ruled over by lorries in headlong charge to the coast.

I was welcomed to Bexley with a wolf whistle – 'dainty boots mate!' the couple shouted as they swung along arm in arm, spitting on the pavement. But Bexley, to my mind, which was beginning to wander a bit, the excitement of departure having worn off, was a remarkable place. I reckoned you could buy a house in an estate agent at the top of the High Street and by the far end have kitted the place out from top to bottom – bathrooms, kitchens, the lot – finishing the afternoon off with a manicure in one of the many nail bars and buying a takeaway to eat in the evening from the local Balti House or Polish restaurant in front of your newly delivered TV; in short, a wonderland...until I noticed British National Party posters hanging off the streetlights.

Dartford, now little more than lots of lanes of traffic, an oversized bridge and some superstores, remains the first stop on the way to Canterbury for pilgrims. Peter Longbottom, a retired teacher, committed St John's Ambulance worker and steam enthusiast, but to me a total stranger, had called out of the blue a week earlier after reading a notice put out by his parish priest, to say that I could sleep that first night in his spare bedroom.

He was a welcome sight when I knocked on his door late in the afternoon. My spirits were high, feeling none the worse for the distance I had walked. That evening the kindly Peter offered me game pie and hot cherry tart for supper; I ate the lot at an alarming rate, quick to learn that one of the perks of my undertaking was that sugar, cream, chocolate and sweets were back on the menu in abundance. I could eat what I wanted, when I wanted – I needed it.

Dressed in dazzling red like a garden gnome escaped from its rockery, the following morning I ventured into the rain and back to the wretched A2. I felt pretty chipper – I had walked 20-odd miles the previous day without incident, not an ache, not so much as a twinge; then I stopped for a sit-down by a bridge. All was fine until I tried to get up – I couldn't. It was as if my knees had been locked. After a lot of unseemly grunting, I rolled onto all fours, crawled to the bridge, pulled myself up using the handrail and wobbled off into rustic Kent, where I soon found myself in a verdant landscape of poplar-lined lanes, tumbledown farmyards, rape in full bloom and fields filled with lambs and foals.

*

By the end of that third day, the feeling that someone had strapped a pair of heated cannonballs to the back of my legs was beginning to ebb; in turn, however, the soles of my feet began to complain bitterly, just as Alice had said they would – although, to my embarrassment, earlier than I had imagined. As the day drew to a close, so my pace slowed until by the time I arrived at my destination, I was as good as finished. My constant ally in all this was my thumbstick; the fashion accessory that I had bought for effect was now my crutch. It was the first indication as to how much I would rely on it.

I am still not quite sure how I reached Challock that night; it lay on a map square I didn't have. Amanda Cottrell, my hostess and an old family friend, who, given her good works, is to all intents and purposes the Queen of Kent, wasn't quite sure either. But oh the joy of release, when I dropped my rucksack on the ancient oak flooring in her hall – an act which rendered me temporarily weightless and had me, momentarily, bouncing about like I was playing football on the moon.

After her dogs had stopped jumping all over me, I was sent upstairs to luxuriate in an enormous bath with a glass of whisky – baths were important at this stage, I had only three days left before the Continent. My wet clothes were taken from me and, restored, I was called down to join friends exiled from Zimbabwe in her large kitchen where plates of venison stew were produced, followed by bowls of Sissy Heath's home-made Gypsy tart thick with double cream fresh from the dairy. By coffee, as talk veered to the murk of European gloom and François Hollande's victory in the French presidential elections, I grew reflective – ten years earlier, sitting at the same table, Amanda's American mother, Gracia, whom we all called 'Granny Hotdog', had discussed an unusual invitation to tea.

'My father had just died and my mother decided we should go on a tour of Europe', she told me; 'it was 1936, before the Anschluss. Well, I wanted to see what all this National Socialism was about and so I went to one of their rallies. I tell you, the atmosphere was *a-mazing*, and Hitler so rousing.'

'Harry', she continued in her Southern lilt, 'I could so easily have become a Nazi that day. So, anyway, at the end of the

afternoon, just after Hitler left, one of his officers came up
and asked me if I would care to join the Führer for tea. Well,
of course, I said, yes!', her eyes bulging with excitement. 'We
arrived there before him. My boyfriend was not invited and so
he waited in the car. I was put into a lift that took forever to
get up to the main quarters, which had the most stunning views
right across the whole Tirol through enormous plate-glass
windows. The room was boiling I remember...', she paused,
looking to an imaginary point somewhere up on the ceiling,
'when, in walks Hitler himself surrounded by important-
looking officials and aides. He was a little man compared to
everyone crowding round him. A screen was produced, he
went behind, changed jackets and came and sat next to me at
the head of the table. You know, he had these piercing electric
blue eyes, he was captivating and, boy, so interesting. He asked
me if I was too hot and when I said, yes, he flicked a button
in the arm of his chair and the windows lowered automati-
cally. We'd never seen that before', she added wistfully, 'and
then we started to talk. For about 45 minutes, maybe an hour,
we had the most, and, Harry, I mean the *most*', she drew her
finger across the place mat and tapped each word in emphasis,
'fascinating, engaging and informative conversation. At the end
of which, I turned to him and said, "Herr Hitler, we have just
had the most incredible discussion about art, literature and the
theatre; how come the papers say you're such a nutter?" Well,
another switch was flicked, the guards came and my feet didn't
so much as touch the ground until I was down that lift and back
in the car and, as the SS officer so succinctly advised, hightailing
it for the Austrian border...'

It wasn't quite so wet in the woods as it was outside them, when
I set forth for Chilham; the towering beech trees in King's Wood
were resplendent and fresh in their new leaf, bluebells abounded
and in the silence, apart from a passing fox and the scowl of a
jay, there was an ancient mystical feel, as if the place was my
sole preserve to the exclusion of everybody else and I could run
through the forest unhindered, shouting 'mine, mine, mine!'
     The rain persisted and, as I came to the ridgeline that
leads down to the banks of the river Stour, I got caught in

an impenetrable thicket of bramble. I tried to wade through, but in the ensuing foray I ended up being catapulted into a deep furrow that straddled the spur – even upside down, it was apparent that on top of a hill the ditch served no obvious agricultural purpose. I had fallen straight into the earthwork that Hilaire Belloc in his book, *The Absence of the Past* described as where '*...began the great history of England*'. In 54BC the earthwork I now found myself in was the site of the Britons' last stand before being routed by Julius Caesar's Tenth Legion; it would, however, be almost another century before Claudius established Londinium in AD43.

Mud-spattered, stung by nettles and definitely *mouillé*, I slid down the hill towards the turreted elegance of Chilham Castle, first built in the fifth century. Home to Saxon and Kentish kings, it was lived in by William the Conqueror's illegitimate half-brother, Odo, Bishop of Bayeux and Earl of Kent. King John found time to hunt here and Capability Brown had a hand in the design of the gardens. I arrived via the croquet lawn. Otto, a handsome tiger-striped lurcher, bounded out to greet me, futile attempts to curb his enthusiastic advances emanating from the kitchen window.

Tessa Wheeler, dressed in leather trousers and cowboy boots, was pretty cool. I felt self-conscious by comparison, a stream of explanations that I didn't normally look like this followed, while I was led, bumping and grinding my rucksack behind me, down flagstoned passages, up winding staircases, along tapestry-lined corridors and past yawning drawing rooms to a bedroom the size of a small house. It had a fireplace that looked like it had once been the portico of a Georgian mansion and a four-poster bed camouflaged under a mass of eiderdowns and pillows fit for minor royalty. Chilham was a magical place. Tessa, however, was apologetic too, as she explained – between barked orders to Otto to 'leave Harry alone will you!' – that she had to go to the theatre in London; a delicious supper, however, had been laid on for me, and Otto, in the kitchen.

The next morning, I bade Tessa farewell and walked down the drive; the horses were being led across the park to the fields.

It was a glorious day as I headed through the rose-embowered village to the river Stour whose swollen course I would follow all the way to Canterbury and the start of the Via Francigena.

1,332 miles to Rome.

3

Canterbury, Dover and crossing the English Channel

O Thomas, return,...return to France.
You come with applause, you come with rejoicing,
but you come bringing death...
A doom on the house, a doom on yourself, a doom on the
world.

T. S. Eliot, *Murder in the Cathedral*, 1935

THE COBBLED STREETS THAT late afternoon were cramped to bursting with folk as I walked into Canterbury; the old buildings peered over me as if to enquire who I might be. Making my way towards the crested eminence of the Christchurch Gate, I jostled past tourists and students who were crowding around a bearded and bowler-hatted Irish busker playing a ukulele. I felt no more out of place than if I were a traveller in the thirteenth century and that this was some God-given right of passage due to me.

'Pass, Pilgrim!', the bespectacled man at the barrier announced as he took one look at me, in my grimy state. After such acknowledgement, my pace quickened and I strode purposefully under the sandstone arch; rounding the corner, Canterbury Cathedral rose up before me like a solitary oak, unmistakably English; Bell Harry's Tower reaching into the sky, framed by trees, it was a glorious sight.

I leant forward, resting my full weight on my stick and stared up at the great building. It was founded by St Augustine, a Benedictine monk and later the first Archbishop of Canterbury, over 1,400 years ago after he was sent to England by Pope Gregory the Great to convert Æthelberht, the Anglo-Saxon King of Kent. The Cathedral took 500 years to complete.

Augustine's journey was remarkable. He set out from Rome in 596AD with 40 followers but by France his band had grown disheartened; the anticipated reception in England did not appeal. The hapless Augustine was sent back to Rome to reason with his papal master. Gregory, however, saw matters differently and the monk was ordered to return to his brothers with renewed zeal and further letters of authority to continue to England. Landing on the Isle of Thanet, Augustine was met by the pagan Æthelberht who, married to Bertha, the Christian daughter of Charibert I, the Merovingian King of Paris, converted almost immediately. Indeed, so effective was the Saint's ensuing ministry that on Christmas Day that same year it is believed that 10,000 people were baptized in the River Swale.

Weary, I slept in the sun for a good hour until woken by the minute bell. I tried to blank it out, but it played with my conscience like a notice for Sunday morning communion in the *Parish Magazine* and so, despite my seizing joints, I hobbled into the cathedral – it was freezing.

Robes flowed everywhere as a multitude of clerics and officials darted one way or another, forever smiling at the disorientated and the curious who were being politely but firmly marshalled into the confines of the quire – a darkened carved Gothic complex topped with pillars and archways that lead the eyes to gaze up at coroneted ceilings hovering loftily above, which in turn were illuminated by shafts of kaleidoscopic light from the stained glass windows that looked on.

The choir led the procession, filing into candlelit stalls. They were presided over by an enthusiastic director who conducted in wild flailing movements of the arm, while his groomed charges joined in sublime vocal union with the organ's boom; treble, alto, tenor, bass rang out across the aisle as hymns, versicles and responses, psalms, Magnificat and Nunc Dimittis were all played out until Evensong drew to a close.

At the door to my room, I was caught fumbling for my key. Covered in side pockets, ticket pockets, map pockets, a little sleeve pocket that fitted my compass, breast pockets and inside pockets, I was host to a myriad of opportunities to lose things and, at that particular moment, my key had escaped me. The homely Louise – who was not short, with a dense thatch of auburn on top – was 'just visiting from Dundalk'; passing, she me gave a knowing look.

'Oh, don't be telling me now, you've gone and lost yer key for sure, haven't you?' she said. 'Honest to God, I tell you, I've lost mine three times already today.'

I admitted I had.

'Well, not to worry. I always pray to St Anthony in these situations and he *never* lets me down.'

'Who's St Anthony?' was not the best, but honest, response from this novice pilgrim.

'The saint of lost things…c'mon with yer now!' Louise chided, at which she closed her eyes in prayer. And, from nowhere, my key appeared in the folds of my handkerchief.

'He *never* fails, I swear to you', her face straightening, 'but saints can be funny souls at times, be sure to give him some money now or else he'll never find anything for you *ever* again!'

Canterbury, where Chaucer's pilgrims turned around and headed for home, marks the official start of the Via Francigena and so I shouldn't have been surprised when I arrived in the darkened crypt just before 8 o'clock the next morning for communion, to find a well-built shaven-headed man sitting opposite me, dressed almost identically. We whispered hellos. After, I learned that Alain Boucher, a recently retired photographic engraver from outside Paris, had walked to Santiago de Compostela four times, but, like me, this was his first outing to Rome. We were joined by Canon Clare, a gentle no-nonsense woman and experienced pilgrim, who led us a circuitous route to the main door out of the cathedral; the conversation was cheery, blister remedies mostly, the consensus being that to thread them with needle and cotton was 'without doubt' the best and most satisfying solution. It was then that we started to talk about Thomas à Becket, England's most famous saint.

Introduced to Henry in 1154 by the then Archbishop, Theobald, Thomas became a close friend of the King, who appointed him Chancellor. He was instrumental in Henry's expedition to Toulouse in 1159 when the province of Quercy was captured, it being recorded that he fought courageously. Not long after his return in 1161, when Theobald died, Henry

Canterbury Cathedral
…where Chaucer's pilgrims turned round and headed for home…

persuaded Thomas to become head of the Church, despite the latter's misgivings. Over two days in June 1162 he was ordained a priest and consecrated a bishop, threw off the flamboyant garb of a senior adviser at Court, resigned as Chancellor and embraced the spiritual lifestyle of a humble cleric with vigour – a role which Thomas warned Henry would force him to oppose the King's ambition to reduce Church authority and influence.

Within two years, as a result of his resolute opposition to Henry's designs, Thomas was forced to flee to France, in disguise, and seek the sanctuary of Louis VII and the Pope, Alexander III, then resident in Sens. By December 1170, following a reconciliation between King and Archbishop, Thomas felt able to return to Canterbury, but he steadfastly refused to absolve the Bishops of London and Salisbury for their role in supporting the coronation of Henry the Young, as King of England, by the Archbishop of York – an attempt by Henry II to overcome the disputes of succession that he had suffered as a young man; a stance that would cost the Archbishop dearly.

Canon Clare grew sombre as we neared the spot where, on 29 December 1170, Thomas was cut down by Reginald FitzUrse, William de Tracey, Hugh de Morville and Richard le Breton – four knights from the court of King Henry II who, taking their monarch's word at face value, determined to rid the world of 'this meddlesome priest'. Beckett's head was cleaved in two, one of his assailants' blows so strong that the blade of his sword broke on the stone, leaving the pieces of his spattered brains to be kicked around the cathedral floor by an aptly named sub-deacon, Hugh the Evil.

'He knew he was going to die', Canon Clare said, pointing to the door that the monks had urged Thomas to lock. 'It was here the murderous party made good their entry into the hushed atmosphere of evensong that cold winter's night. "It is not proper that a house of prayer, a church of Christ, be made a fortress"', she said, quoting Thomas. 'Becket's death created an enormous stir and not just in England; he challenged the unchecked authority of the Crown over the Church and, as a consequence of his martyrdom, his stature as a saint spread across Europe – many miracles were attributed to him and

Canterbury became one of the greatest shrines in Christendom', she told us, pointing to worn steps where for centuries the devout had made their way to pray at the site of the original shrine, now marked with a lone candle; at that moment, Bell Harry rang out in mournful tone above.

'The shrine', she went on, 'was destroyed in the Reformation for being too "Rome-ish" – not the right word, but you know what I mean', she added, 'and since then no one has ever been entirely sure of the whereabouts of the saint's remains.'

Out in the early morning sunshine, the wind biting, Clare led us to a small piece of lawn. In the middle was a paving stone, carved with a blue roundel within which was a bearded and robed figure with a staff and swag bag slung over his shoulder; the surrounding inscription read 'La Via Francigena. Canterbury–Rome'. Clare bid Alain and I to kneel; she said a prayer for our safe protection on the journey ahead. We all shook hands and went our ways – I for Dover and Alain to unlock the secrets of Canterbury, which he had never visited before.

I continued down an ancient network of footpaths, bridleways and rides, where yellowhammers, corn buntings, larks and linnets filled the sky with song, cuckoos announced their arrival, hares ran and mares grazed. Heading for the coast, I passed through villages like Bekesbourne and Adisham in the Hundred of Eastry and stopped at the Norman church of Barfreston to marvel at its stone carvings and the bell that hangs in the yew nearby.

Coming off the Downs, I was covered in a thick dusting of pollen where I had walked along field after field of rape, like everything else, in full flower. This magical spell of rustic perfection was broken, however, as sinister weasel-faced types, in ill-fitting leather jackets lurking on dusty street corners, greeted my arrival in Dover. Their presence made the once-elegant Victorian town feel seedy and unwelcoming. Boarding *The Pride of Burgundy* nevertheless brought a frisson of excitement, as engines vibrated noisily throughout the ship and the unmistakable smell of oil mixed with sea air hung over the deck. As we left the breakwater, I looked at my phone and switched off the data. No more emails. I was gradually being drawn into a secret pilgrim world, exclusive to but a select few, a special place far removed from the fetters of time and the everyday. Cold, I turned my back and, going inside, bid England farewell.

1,292 miles to Rome.

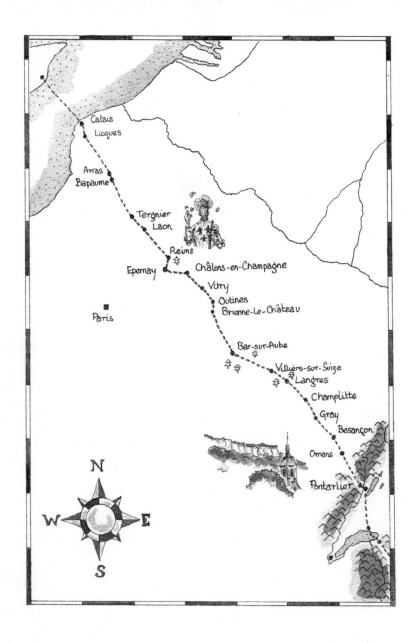

Calais
Licques
Arras
Bapaume
Tergnier
Laon
Reims
Epernay
Châlons-en-Champagne
Vitry
Outines
Brienne-le-Château
Paris
Bar-sur-Aube
Villiers-sur-Suize
Langres
Champlitte
Gray
Besançon
Omans
Pontarlier

N
W   E
S

Part 2

France

First to follow Truth and last to leave old Truths behind –
France beloved of every soul that loves its fellow-kind!
Rudyard Kipling, France, 1913

4

Pas de Calais to Camblain l'Abbé

A thousand knights have rein'd their steeds
To watch this line of sand-hills run,
Along the never silent Strait,
To Calais glittering in the sun...
Matthew Arnold, Calais Sands, 1850

DICK WHITTINGTON WAS TWICE Mayor of Calais in the fifteenth century, or 'the Staple' as it was also known – a shrewd move on the businessman's part who, as a mercer or trader in fine silks and linen, amassed considerable wealth supplying the Crown. The port, which fell to Edward III in 1347 following an 11-month siege, after the Battle of Crécy, was England's last possession on French soil and for over 200 years the country's centre for trade with Europe. 'The Company of the Staple at Calais' controlled all exports of tin, lead, lace and wool – 'staples' which were subject to taxation and an important source of revenue for the Crown. The Company, in return for the monopoly, was responsible for the town's defence, until the Duc de Guise recaptured it in 1558.

Just as in Dover, however, on every corner there seemed to lurk the same shifty out-of-place characters, presumably bent on escape across the Channel. I could but imagine the pitiful tales of flight that had lifted these poor souls from privation, torture, poverty and war, delivering them within sight of those white cliffs that were so close...yet so far.

The cold weather had done little to encourage people to think of summer. In the village of Licques, the following night, I was 'upgraded' from a caravan to a chalet when I arrived at a popular stop with pilgrims, recommended to me by Alice Warrender before I left London, the Trois Poissons Camping.

After a night under two duvets clutching the heater, I stumbled into the campsite café and breakfasted on a bowl of coffee and a croissant. Catherine, my châtelaine, asked me to sign the Livre d'Or, in this instance a large green exercise book filled with page after page of French, English, Canadian, American, Italian, New Zealand and Australian pilgrims' comments; some confident, some less so. It was still an early stage on the road to Rome. I wondered if they had all made it. The wall, covered with postcards from St Peter's, seemed to indicate that in all probability they had; all the same, the Vatican felt very far off indeed.

'It's the Pilgrims who find us, not the other way round', Denis, Catherine's bear of a husband, said as he passed through with a hammer in his hand. 'I guess that's how it always was, word of mouth. After all, Alain warned us you were coming', referring to my Canterbury companion, now ahead of me after I had taken a rest day.

'Every now and again, people need to pause at life', Catherine said in her soft French accent, 'they need to enjoy some calm and reflect. Pilgrimage is all about the simple pleasures we too often forget.'

At the top of the steep ridge, leaving the village of Journy behind me, something caught my eye: in the wood line was a large slab of toppled masonry like a tumbled piece of Stonehenge, but three, maybe four times the size. Odd and out of place, I was drawn to it, siren-like. Pulling myself up onto the bank, I dropped my rucksack off and ran across the sharply undulating field.

A few hundred yards on, I found an enormous piece of concrete, below which was a bunker of some sort. I tried to dismiss the twisted remains, but something about them didn't feel right. Despite the tranquillity of the woods around me, the huddle of cattle grazing nearby, there was an eeriness fuelled by the curious structures that lay dormant and mangled all about. I walked further on and at the edge of some beech trees I came across two ramped walls, in perfect parallel. I stood in between them and looked back down the escarpment. I could almost see Calais. I didn't need to look at my compass to know I was in direct line of sight to London, 112 miles away – or 30 minutes' flying time for the V1 rockets that launched from here, wreaking havoc on our capital in the summer of 1944. It all made sense then; the 'sharp undulations' I had run across were in fact craters left by the bombers that had silenced the place.

A car stopped abruptly next to my rucksack. I leapt over the fence and sprinted across; the driver, seeing me, sped off. It was a lucky escape. I didn't fancy walking to Rome without any kit. The ramps were the first scars of war that would stalk me for the next three weeks.

Come 16 May, ten days and 161 miles since leaving London, I was settling into the somewhat monastic routine of my pilgrim existence. It always seemed, however, that the last hour of the day, as I neared my billet for the night, was the longest; that no place to rest a weary head could be reached without trial: a reward for hard work done, or was it just that no day would ever be restful until that final arrival in Rome?

The Benedictine Abbaye de Notre Dame at Wisques was no exception; the hill that led up to it went on and on and then a bit further. I thanked my lucky stars I wasn't staying at the Monastère de St Paul, a mile further on. The Abbaye, when I finally walked down its gravelled drive, was a large nineteenth-century encumbrance in pale brick with an oversized chapel hanging off its right side. I rang the bell and listened to its rasp somewhere within.

Soeur Lucie met me at the door. She had a weathered face, fixed grin and teeth as white as her wimple. She put her finger to her lips and beckoned me into Vespers where the rest of the nuns were celebrating the start of the Feast of the Ascension; there was a sense of anticipation in the air.

The congregation, mostly middle-aged ladies from the village, sat in gloom behind the marble altar at one end of the chapel; we were separated from the nuns, who were seated in the distance at the opposite end, by a stout cage-like screen that ran the width of the nave. Their singing, clear and sweet, was a welcome relief from the rigours of the day. Cold, I clutched myself, cursing the warm fleece that was in my rucksack on the wrong side of the door.

Vespers over, Soeur Lucie led me out into to the grounds where, in a corner, was a doll's house of a building – guest quarters that had once been a hunting lodge. As we walked,

I couldn't help noticing how at peace the old nun seemed and no less well-informed despite her cloistered existence from the world; she wanted for nothing and only saw good in everything, telling me that when she joined the Abbaye in the early 1960s, she was one of 65 sisters; now, only 25 remained. But there was a great sense of timelessness about Soeur Lucie as she shrugged the decline off; for her, this was just a turn of the wheel and, in the greater scheme of things, one day, maybe a hundred years hence, maybe less, the Abbaye would thrive as a community again.

Inside the guest house, my room was plain, whitewashed with a basin in one corner, a table and a crucifix made of sticks on the wall above the bed which, piled high with blankets under a bedspread, looked as if someone was already asleep in it.

When the nun asked where I came from – the easy answer always London – I replied: 'From the South, near Salisbury; the cathedral has the tallest spire in Europe.'

She fixed me, like I had said something wrong: 'How tall is the spire?'

'Er, well, I don't know to be honest, but it is very tall.'

She giggled. Soeur Lucie was not without mischief.

'Dinner will be at 7 o'clock', she said, placing a gold sticker in my Passport, 'we will be in the same room but separated.'

'Of course', I replied, 'you are behind a grille.'

She smiled: '*We* like to think it is *you* who are *behind* the grille.'

At supper, I was joined by Melanie, a divorcee, who had been having a bad time of it and had sought out the tranquillity of the Abbaye for a few days; wrapped in a large quilted coat with fur-lined collar and cuffs, she looked like her mind was elsewhere. She was bemused by the idea of my walking to Rome – her bemusement gave way to amazement, however, when she witnessed the speed with which I descended on the food, after Soeur Lucie had said grace. Hardly pausing for breath, I grabbed at the bread, stuffed two eggs into my mouth, wolfed down a bowl of soup and, without remorse, asked if there were second helpings. The risotto got the same treatment, a bottle of wine disappeared, as did cheese and pudding after – Soeur Lucie burst out laughing when I brought my plates into the pantry: 'Are these for washing too?' – I had wiped them clean of any food, such was my ravenous state.

I stopped in Thérouanne the following morning for a cup of coffee. Sitting in the café window, the sun beginning to warm the day at last, I couldn't help thinking to myself how solitary an experience the walk was becoming; there was no one else about. I was ever on the move, a constant being only to myself, but to anyone else who met me just a moment of transience, here one minute, gone the next. I went to pay.

'You're a pilgrim?' the old lady asked.

'Yes', I replied, 'on my way to Rome.'

'Oh, we get many of you lot through here', she replied.

'You do?'

At which she pointed at the unmistakable silhouette of a man with a pack momentarily obscuring the window. I ran out to catch him.

'*Vous allez où M'sieur?*' I bellowed across the street.

'Can you speak English please, I don't have very good French you see!'

It only took one car to realize that the middle of a busy road was not the safest place to exchange pleasantries. Alfredo was a tall, thin, grey-bearded doctor from Turin. In time I would learn to distinguish the different nationalities by the way they stowed their kit – Italians, for example, don't put things *inside* their rucksacks, they prefer to hang as much off the outside as possible; boots, towels, waterproofs would all be festooned from loops and buckles or plain tied on, lending them the appearance of an itinerant tinker who had something for every occasion. Alfredo, who was going to Rome because he liked to walk, was no exception. He too had stayed the night before in Wisques, but with the monks. "Ow much you pay?" he demanded with a nod of the head.

'Twenty euros, I think' – a bit taken aback by his directness.

'Twenty euro?! Twenty euro?!' he exclaimed. 'I paid no-thing', he replied, making an 'O' with his fingers to emphasize the victory, 'and I ate *gratuit* too...'

But Alfredo's reaction, I was to discover, was not uncommon among my fellow pilgrims, many of whom seemed to pride themselves in getting as much for as little as possible; it felt somehow wrong, given the hospitality we were being shown.

Alfredo was, however, in a rush; he had another 30 kilometres to do that day, whereas I only had 20 to reach

Amettes, so he decided to take off down the Brunehaut, which was now a frantic highway. I advised him to follow the back routes.

'No', he snapped, 'I 'ate the Pas de Calais, it's so depressing. I just wanna get through it as quickly as I can', so we parted, no hard feelings, no contract broken. I watched Alfredo disappear into the distance, stick in one hand, guidebook in the other and chaotic rucksack swinging at his back. I never saw him again.

A car suddenly shot past – I didn't look at it with envy, but with pity; the driver in such a hurry, for what, I wondered? A meeting that was so important? I knew where I would rather be.

Frère Jo told me that Camblain l'Abbé was a small place, 'You will have no trouble finding us.' I walked twice around the village and asked three people before I found L'Ecole Jean-Baptiste La Salle which to the uninitiated, with its flagpole, parade ground and profusion of single-storey buildings, looked just like an army camp. At the centre of this picture of military precision was a bungalow with an Italianate portico attached crudely to the front, the pillars wound with wisteria; 20 years earlier it was a familiar formula to me – this had to be 'headquarters'.

I opened the door with trepidation and crept in; the dark blue *fleur-de-lys* papered hall was like a spiritual salvage yard, littered with statues of the Virgin, sculptures of Christ and portraits of popes, cardinals and archbishops. There was a strong smell of floor wax. I found a ship's bell and rang it...'ding ding!'

Without a sound, a slight man in a black habit appeared from behind a double life-size Christ holding the Sacred Heart. He wore a scarf around his neck and a cardigan to guard from the cold. 'I am Frère Jo', he smiled, 'did you find us okay?'

I lied.

Passing yet more marble busts and rescued carvings, Frère Jo took me to the Infirmary, my room for the night. On the way, he explained that the school was on break, but normally the place would be alive with over 200 children aged nine to 19.

The Infirmary was a curious place – clean to a clinical standard, as the name might suggest, its two beds were laid out as for inspection: blankets stacked, towels folded. There was a desk, fastidious in its tidiness, with a pot of finely sharpened pink colouring pencils in one corner; it was flanked by a pair of grey lockers with model tanks and a collection of army hats on top. The walls were decorated with sensible health posters admonishing me, through fear mostly, to good health – in the one above my bed, a large man was sneezing into a handkerchief. 'Got a cold? See your doctor!' it screamed, like Kitchener invoking national service. My favourite, though, was *ANIOS* – a wonder cure that had figures from the early twentieth century lined up on clifftops, proclaiming 'Microbes, here's the enemy!' Soldiers, cooks, housemaids and businessmen all poured, and in some cases fired, buckets of the 'disinfectant without odour' onto scarpering bugs and beasties who looked as if they had jumped straight out of a picture by John Anster Fitzgerald – among them was the plague, malignant pustules (yuk), galloping consumption (eeugh), typhus, cholera, mildew and, of course, foot and mouth disease. I felt short-changed – this was hardcore; the best we ever managed when I was at school was impetigo.

By my bed was a large bucket of seed; outside in the enclosed courtyard canaries and parakeets flitted about the walls – sweet little creatures, so endearing and adorable when they sang too. Then, on a table, I noticed someone had thoughtfully left a bottle of claret and a glass; things were looking up.

The Common Room, where we assembled for dinner later, was a wood-panelled utopia of leather sofas lined with books. There was a log fire in the grate and the smell of home cooking drifted from the kitchen next door; the room had a baronial feel that belied the concrete exterior. While Frère Jo busied in the kitchen, Père Robin, a young priest who had once been a lawyer, welcomed me – he now taught Latin and English. Frère Jean, a softly spoken man whose domain was design, joined us – he had served with distinction in Lebanon with the Chasseurs Alpins, the elite mountain infantry of the French Army.

After Robin had said grace, we sat down to cheese fondue and wine from Alsace, the room soon filling with laughter and the growing bonds of friendship. I couldn't help but feel I was in the company of good people whose love for their vocation in life was so tangible. For them, teaching was a privilege, as if singled out from all humanity for a special task.

As we ate, so I began to describe the mysteries of the Infirmary in great detail; Frère Jean, looking on with interest, began to smile, until finally he could contain his hysterics no longer, especially at the mention of the colouring pencils; he was, of course, the school medic. But it was Frère Jo who held sway at dinner, not the priest, as he deftly steered the conversation this way and that like his lessons in catechism or the Gregorian chant; quietly ensuring that a convivial night didn't turn contentious as the conversation veered to the finer points of religious belief, such as the existence of the Archangel Michael. Well fed, I went to bed content.

I wish, however, that I could say I woke in the same frame of mind. The canaries were up at 4.30 a.m. They were not nearly so sweet, endearing or adorable at that unearthly hour; if only I could have got a hand through the mesh on the windows. I reported my experience to Frère Jean over breakfast, who smiled knowingly, adding that it was an appropriate penance for my report the previous evening – small wonder he slept so far away. My Passport duly stamped with a large baroque crest that filled the page, it was time to depart.

Leaving was by now becoming something of an emotional wrench; every night somewhere new, a friendship born of a few intense hours, only to be thrown like scraps to the dogs in the morning. In most cases, I would never meet my hosts again. At the portico, I waved goodbye, walked down the drive and turned right for Arras.

1,204 miles to Rome.

5

Arras to Frières-Faillouël

> *'Good-morning; good-morning!' the General said*
> *When we met him last week on our way to the line.*
> *Now the soldiers he smiled at are most of 'em dead,*
> *And we're cursing his staff for incompetent swine.*
> *'He's a cheery old card', grunted Harry to Jack*
> *As they slogged up to Arras with rifle and pack.*
> *But he did for them both by his plan of attack.*
>
> Siegfried Sassoon, *The General*, 1918

I DIDN'T GO DIRECTLY to Arras that morning as my route suggested; instead I set out across fields of freshly mown hay, startling coveys of partridge in my path and ducking through woods until eventually reaching the gates of Neuville-St Vaast Cemetery – not, as might be expected, La Targette or Roclincourt. St Vaast is the resting place for nearly 45,000 German war dead.

Inside, tended lawn stretched out before me in every direction, tacked down by rank upon rank of dark Teuton crosses; in comparison to the white, almost jaunty headstones of the Allied cemeteries with their rose bushes and flowers, these glades of sorrow felt stark, almost out of the way and forgotten – maybe that was why I made the point of going there. Down the rows I went, past *Ersatz Reservists, Unteroffiziers* and *Kanoniers; Reinhards, Hermanns* and *Johanns*; Jew and Christian, until eventually I found whom I had come in search of: Gregor Hämmerling, *Musketier*.

It doesn't matter how Gregor died; I, you, we can but imagine. It was the date he died that mattered – 3 May 1917. I knelt down on the grass in front of his grave and thought of the telegram boy opening the gate to go up the garden path bearing the news of a child's death to an unsuspecting family; at first disbelief and then grief, in an instant, ripping through the house, tearing at walls, banging on doors and beating at windows, screaming, shouting and wailing, 'my son is dead, my beautiful son is dead!' – 3 May 1917, the date my Great Uncle Walter was killed, perhaps yards from Gregor, possibly in the same attack. We will never know.

Walter, a Captain in the Northumberland Fusiliers, was just 20 years old when he died. His story is no different from many of that generation except that, unlike Gregor, he has no grave, just a name lost high among countless others on the memorial in Arras; his memory, like a distant ship gone over the horizon, now little more than a few creased photographs in an album.

I pulled a bundle of papers out of my pocket; a photograph of Walter stared out at me – a picquet cane under his arm, he looked so smart in the service dress uniform of the Fighting Fifth, as his regiment was known. Beneath, my great grandmother had written his war record in neat rounded script: wounded aged 18 in the Second Battle of Ypres, fought at the Bluff, took the trenches in the Battle of St Eloi and then, shell shock. He was 19 years old.

At the end of 1916, back at the front, Walter was wounded again, this time by a bursting bomb, but come March the following year, he returned to France to command 'Y' Company, in the First Battalion, celebrating his twentieth birthday just two weeks earlier.

'*Quo Fata Vocant*' or '*Whither the Fates Call*' is the Northumberland Fusiliers' motto and, in the dawn of that 3 May, the Fates did indeed call; attacking the Bois des Aubépines, '*your brother...was shot through the head by a sniper just after entering the wood*', so Lance Corporal Parker wrote in pencil to my grandfather, then a Captain in the Middlesex Regiment, serving 'up the road' on the staff of 114 Brigade. In his diary that evening, on hearing the news of his younger brother's death, he wrote '*rode out on my horse, to have a think*'. Nothing else.

Nearly a hundred years later whether victor or vanquished is irrelevant; time has moved on, thankfully, and those headstones are now the beacons by which '*lest we forget*'. A car raced by, breaking the peace for a second, and then nothing, just silence; my hand stretching out across the generations, I ran my thumb gently over Gregor's name, the letters sharp to the touch and the metal warm in the sun. For a moment, I clutched the cross bar in the cup of my hand, and shut my eyes.

I said a prayer, folded the papers and made to leave. Heading towards the gates, I passed the grave of a Jewish soldier and, as is the custom, I placed a single stone on it.

Arras is remarkable because, given the destruction it suffered in both World Wars, it has been almost completely rebuilt without mark or blemish. It is a majestic town of broad boulevards, secret squares, elegant courtyards and intimate streets, reminiscent of parts of Paris. That afternoon, it was busy and I was excited at the prospect of my first Saturday night in France; all the more as Sunday was a rest day for me. The first stop was to get my Passport stamped; I never felt I had arrived anywhere properly until that was done.

It had been a long day, the first really hot day in fact, by the time I walked up the steps of St Vaast Cathedral. Finding no one about, I grew a little frustrated – you tend to easily become so by the end of the day when carrying all you possess on your shoulders – so I looked around until I came across a little shop tucked away in a former side chapel. The lady behind the counter was in deep conversation with an old French queen in search of a souvenir. Patiently, I waited my turn, leaning forward and resting the full weight of my rucksack over my thumbstick.

There followed a protracted conversation about the many publications on the shelves – which were good value, which had the best pictures and so on; the comments greeted with gasps of 'oh *really*' and 'how *beautiful*'. At first I listened patiently but, as the load on my back began to dig into me and time wore on, so my thoughts became progressively less Christian. I kept my calm, offering a few evil looks instead. Eventually, some cards were bought and the lady put them in a bag, which she then stamped.

'Qu'est-ce que c'est?'

'*That*', she announced, 'is the *timbre* for the Pilgrims' Passports; Arras is on the road to Compostella.'

I groaned as then came a short lecture on Santiago after which, with a fey hand gesture, the man left.

'What do *you* want?' madame asked, looking at me in disdain.
'A stamp'.
'A *what?*'
'A stamp in my Passport', I snapped, 'I am a pilgrim!'
'*Ah oui, Compostella?*'
'*Non, Rome*', omitting to add 'it's twice as far'; she suddenly softened, smiled, stamped my papers and gave me a free guide; I felt rather ashamed.

But my rest day proved to be anything but; by early Sunday afternoon I was possessed with an insatiable urge to get back on the road. It was as if the Via Francigena was now my very life and soul, without which I felt naked, vulnerable. Everything else an irrelevance, the road called to me like a distant voice, whispering gently in my ear, 'Rome...Rome...Rome!'

The grey and the cold returned on the Monday morning when I left. Good walking weather, the best even, I mused as I stepped out into the street, my breath catching on the air. Outside Arras, the countryside was plunged into thick fog, the temperature fell and a fierce northerly whipped at my back. Visibility less than a hundred yards, I took to the main road, speed the object, to be buffeted by the spray of oncoming lorries. Chilled, wet and caught in a ghoulish landscape of muffled sound, save the spectral whoosh of vanishing TGVs, there was little to focus on than the few yards around me. The day became dark, filled with black thoughts as if I was trapped in an inescapable requiem as each of the pitiful cemeteries and lone memorials that I saluted as I passed tore at my heart. Depression swiftly settled on my shoulders as solitude, which had been stalking me for days, finally caught up and taunted my soul.

Hooded, like a cowled monk, I made my way at best pace through the Artois – a barren void seemingly bereft of life, where humanity had turned its face to the wall.

The Château de Morchies, near Bapaume, was my saviour that night. Soaked to the bone, by the time I walked through its newly built palatial gates, I was in an increasingly confused and muddled state, not fit to see or be seen by anyone, the onset of early hypothermia doing its utmost to take a hold. A nodding retainer let me in. Ushered through boot rooms and down corridors lined with family citations for the Légion d'Honneur, portraits of kings, queens and politicians and through enticing smoke-scented dining rooms whose walls were hung with engravings of Napoleon, I was shown to a cosy bedroom with a *lit bateau* sleigh-bed tucked in one corner.

But, despite this image of timeless heritage, the château was, like most buildings in the area, a relative imposter. Built on a ground-floor plan only, there was a rather gentlemanly, understated feel to the place. The Kaiser's Army destroyed the original, a many-storeyed turreted affair of nineteenth-century creation, as it withdrew to the Hindenburg Line in 1917.

Tired from a day that had thrown itself at me, after the retainer left, I soaked in a bath until a semblance of normality returned. I had the place to myself; my host, who was ironically walking in Spain at the time, later telephoned while in a downpour to joke that he was enjoying equally pleasurable conditions.

While cooking supper, I scoured the kitchen for a drink. I needed one. It was not possible, I reasoned, to be in a French château that was dry. As the worst of guests, therefore, I began to search every cupboard, nook and cranny I could find for alcohol. I was just about to give up all hope when eventually, tucked away at the back of a drawer, I spied an ancient bottle of cooking brandy. I set upon it like a child in a sweet shop, but my enthusiasm to get at the liquid within was such that I pulled the cork out with so much force that it broke. Disaster. So then I rummaged through every drawer for a spare cork. None. I blushed like a schoolboy caught in the act; the cork was broken and my trespass couldn't be covered up. I poured myself a large glass followed by a liberal shot in my tea and an equally generous slurp in my soup. I felt better almost instantly. My spirit lifting, I then covered the bed with every blanket I could muster and sought the sanctuary of sleep.

*

The Château de Frières-Faillouël, 286 miles into my journey, was a handsome red-brick building with sandstone facings and a pitched roof, neat but not fussy, its lines measured and tasteful. It stood opposite the war memorial between the villages of Frières and Faillouël, framed by a pair of tall pillars, above which hung a large family crest.

Passing through the gates down the gravel drive made for a rather magnificent entrance; malodorous and ill-dressed for the grandeur of my setting, I headed for the back, rather than the front, door, which presided over this Gallic idyll at the top of a long flight of steps like a haughty butler. I was uncharacteristically early; I rang the bell repeatedly, but to no avail, until at last a head poked around a large beech hedge to the side.

'Are you the *pèlerin*?' the girl asked, 'Charles Edouard is out campaigning'; but before my imagination could conjure up images of sabres, cavalry and drums on the march, she was quick to remind me of yet more national elections to come in ten days' time; the French must get so bored with voting, I commiserated. Thus it was Nathalie, the groom, and Fouquet, a wire-haired Jack Russell, who welcomed me; Fouquet thought I smelled just perfect.

We walked down to the stables and between the pair of them, I was given a tour of the kitchen garden – Fouquet forever disappearing into hedges. It was not long, however, before the yard was echoing to the sound of hooves as Cecilia, Charles Edouard's wife, rode in from the woods like Artemis from the hunt, her bay gelding polished and steaming; picturesque and elegant, she showed no sign of the evident long gallop.

Jumping off, she left her horse to Nathalie and we strolled back to the château to sit under a spreading plane tree and drink fresh lemonade. I couldn't help noticing how new the brickwork looked.

'New-ish', Cecilia replied, 'it is actually the third château on this site; the original was burnt down by the Prussians in 1870. Then, in 1917, the Germans packed the second château with explosives, parked a pair of howitzers outside the gate, just where the war memorial is now, and blew it to smithereens. Charles Edouard's grandmother rebuilt the place in the 1920s and, remarkably, it survived the Second War despite the Luftwaffe using it as an airbase.' I looked out over the terrace at paddocks and fields thick with wheat to distant woodland; it was hard to imagine any aeroplane landing anywhere near here.

I was shown to an airy bedroom papered in red Toile du Jouy with a bathroom the size of an engine shed leading off. The doors and polished floorboards creaked reassuringly, while water trickled from the tap as if summoned from Hades; it took a good 15 minutes for the tub to fill.

There was nothing pretentious about the château. It had the feel of a much-loved home; everything had a story to tell. I was admiring a marble bust of a Maréchal de la Grande Armée at the top of the staircase when Charles Edouard bumped into me; he was tall, with an unruly head of grey hair and a face that was home to a permanent smile.

'My ancestor, Alexandre', he said. 'He had quite a life – a celebrated officer in the Artillery, he saved the day for Napoleon at Wagram, fought the British in the Peninsular War and was our Ambassador to Russia. He was also captured by the Prussian, Blücher, at Leipzig. But his shrewdest move, unlike the others who flocked back to Napoleon, was to remain loyal to Louis XVIII during the Hundred Days – within two years the King created him Marquis de Lauriston.'

Charles Edouard invited me to join him in the garden, his way of relaxing from the exertions of the hustings. As we walked and talked, so I realized that people were all the Marquis really thought or cared about; he bore his title with a great sense of responsibility, living and breathing for the community of which he had been Mayor for over 30 years.

'We have been here for more than three centuries; this is our home', he said when I asked if he had ever contemplated moving back to his family's estates in Normandy where the risk of being overrun, however remote it might be now, was surely less. 'But you know, Harry, the people here are very scarred by war; it runs so deep in our memory...', the conversation interrupted by a crashing through the trees as two boys broke cover from heavy branches and shot past on their bicycles in a blur of pedal and chain. '*Bonsoir, Papa!*' screamed his son, Erik. Charles Edouard shouted after him, but the pair had already disappeared into a maze of hedges; '...and perhaps only now that his generation is growing up' – he pointed in the direction the children had disappeared – 'will the scars be finally behind us'.

Cecilia's cry announced dinner was ready and in a wide circle we slowly turned back towards the château. In the antler-filled hall, looking around him, Charles Edouard smiled wistfully. 'At the end of the First War, a German Colonel crated up the contents of our house and shipped them to his home, but he didn't pay the two soldiers who did the actual work. My mother found them, tracked him down and brought all our possessions back. For this, the Colonel was sentenced to death, "in absentia" because he had already fled to Africa. He survived.' There followed, like a private museum tour, quirky illustrations of what had travelled afar against its owner's wishes – clocks, bronzes, portraits, tables and chandeliers; the Colonel had been diligent in his shopping.

Before we sat down to eat, Charles Edouard produced an old black-and-white photograph; about the size of a playing card, it was creased in one corner. The picture was of a dashing young German officer in a black leather flying jacket with the Knight's Cross around his neck. He wore his service cap at a rakish angle; oozing style, it instantly reminded me of Marlon Brando in *The Wild One*.

'This is Major Theodor Weissenberger. One of the Luftwaffe's greatest fighter aces, he celebrated his two hundredth kill of the Second World War with his brother officers here in our dining room.'

We ate in splendour under candlelight at one end of the long dining table, paintings of cuirassiers, serious-faced ancestors, shooting parties and defiant stags looking on while Charles Edouard, with his courteous manner and friendly ease, apologized that his family had traditionally been at loggerheads with the English. 'We are really of Scottish descent, my ancestor were bankers, Law of Lauriston, where we owned estates. It was John Law, perhaps a little too supportive of the Jacobites for his own good, who settled in France. In 1694, he was challenged to a duel in Bedford Square by a fellow called Wilson over the affections of Elizabeth Villiers, who had been for a time King William's mistress. He killed his challenger with one thrust of his sword, was sentenced to hang for murder, but escaped to Amsterdam. Eventually, he fell in with Philippe d'Orléans who, as Prince Regent, appointed him Controller General of

Finances to restore the national wealth after it was bankrupted by the war-mongering of Louis XIV. He did pretty well, to be fair. He was one of the early proponents of quantitative easing and printed a lot of paper money, until he came up with the idea of the Mississippi Company, which overtraded wildly and whose collapse was simply *énorme*. The riots in Paris were so widespread and violent he had to escape dressed as a woman. Bankrupted, my family then settled and prospered for some time in India at Pondicherry, the French-held territories, until Jacques, whom you met on the stairs, came back to France – in a roundabout way. But, Harry', he laughed, 'these days are all well behind us now!'

Just before we turned in, Charles Edouard announced he had to go to Laon the following morning. 'I could give you a lift perhaps?' It was a genuine offer, well meant and, if anything, it underlined how bizarre the idea of walking any distance was in this modern age.

'You are very kind', I replied, 'but I really do have to walk all the way to Rome.'

1,125 miles to Rome.

6

Laon to Villiers-Franqueux

I never weary of great churches.
It is my favourite kind of mountain scenery.
Mankind was never so happily inspired as when it made
cathedrals.

Robert Louis Stevenson, *An Inland Voyage*, 1877

I AM STILL NOT quite sure what went wrong that following day – it took forever to complete the 29 miles to Laon. I shuffled into the town like a pathetic vagrant, exhausted, parched, sunburnt and wrung out. Had I been shown a ticket home there and then, I would have taken it; I cursed the cathedral on the hill above me.

Safe within the sanctuary òf a mildew-ridden hotel room, I took to the shower, where emotion finally relented and I crumbled into a mess on the floor. What on earth had I got myself into? I had never felt so lonely, so weak – and yet, to confess to such after the hurrah of departure three weeks earlier would have been an inconceivable admission of weakness. Alone I had set out and alone I had to reconcile the fact that I had no alternative other than to continue to Rome; premature return was not an option.

As the warm water coursed over me, so life began to seep back into my drained soul. I must have stayed there for an hour or more until I felt the confidence to emerge. I tended to blisters, dressed cuts and massaged my body back to some sense of being; gradually, my will returned. Again I looked up at the cathedral; damned if I was going to be beaten by the building, however imposing it may have appeared at that moment, I grabbed my stick, launched out of the room and made for the steps that led up the 300-foot ridge.

Such was the fervour for Christianity in France during the Middle Ages that there were roughly 200 people to every church built; between the eleventh and fourteenth centuries, the French quarried more stone in pursuit of their adoration of Christ than in the entire history of Ancient Egypt.

Laon Cathedral, or Notre-Dame de Laon, begun in 1160, was one of the first cathedrals built in the Gothic style. These complex structures, whose towers seemed to touch the heavens, with ornate windows, vaulted ceilings and flying buttresses, were the Wembley Stadia, the Melbourne Cricket Grounds and the LA Memorial Colisea of their day – soaring temples to the worship of God designed to accommodate thousands, as awesome to behold then as they are today.

Reaching the top of Laon's plateau that evening, it was as if all Picardy was laid out before me. As far as the eye could see stretched railways, roads and fields – a panorama so great that you felt you could almost see the curvature of the Earth itself. I had watched the cathedral grow ever larger as I snaked my way through the countryside that afternoon, but it wasn't until I turned a corner that I was assaulted by its sheer size; only then did I realize what an amazing piece of architecture Notre-Dame de Laon was, its beauty stopping me in my tracks.

It was a defining moment. The pilgrimage, the sole purpose of my life at the time, suddenly became clear; this cathedral, a monument to the glory of God in all His forms, exuded the power of the Church – to any pilgrim in the Middle Ages, no matter his station, it must have been an overwhelming sight. Christianity in those days was not the emasculated sideshow of today – it dictated the cycle of the day, the pattern of the week and the change of the seasons like some all-encompassing computer program; it was the tool by which monarchs ruled, ensuring their subjects paid their taxes and toed the line. In short, Christianity was life, and vast buildings such as Notre-Dame de Laon were powerful and lasting statements on the landscape in case anyone dare forget. So to be presented for the first time with this gargantuan building on top of a hill that reared up from Picardy's plain like a leaping stag would have been in those far-off days a special moment for any pilgrim, let alone one who had walked all the way from London. I also stood there in its

vast shadow and stared up in awe for, even cen.
was bowled over and speechless at the stark beaut)

Sir Nikolaus Pevsner, the celebrated scholar of ar
wrote that the exteriors of the Gothic cathedrals of
twelfth and early thirteenth centuries were designed to   .i
perfect harmony with their interiors – except that few were
completed to plan, save Notre-Dame de Laon, the only one
that gives a true idea of what a cathedral was intended to look
like. Probably because Laon, started at the beginning of the
great cathedral-building period in the late twelfth century, was
fortunate enough to be completed before the Hundred Years
War, which resulted in a shortage of funds, skilled labour and
the closure of a large number of workshops and ateliers.

For a good hour I circled the cathedral, marvelling at its
magnificence. On every side there was a huge array of stained
glass. At each elevation was something new to marvel at:
gargoyles in the shape of winged hippopotami and rhinoc-
eroses, foxes, jaguars, lions and tongue-lolling grotesques.
Goblined and beastied corbels dressed towers in which cows
and goats poked out from layer upon layer of pillared galleries
and, finally, three large doors with massive sculpted surrounds,
which were set with knights, bishops, angels, saints, apostles
and Christ Himself at the centre, drew in the passerby like the
gaping mouth of some monstrous whale.

But what made me reflect all the more was that if I was so
taken by this great edifice now, then what would my medieval
forebears have thought? I began to imagine how, on their
return, they would sit in smoke-filled hostelries, inns and house-
holds recounting with rapture their experiences across the land
and that this cathedral, of all they had seen, would be up there
on a special pedestal of its own. Notre-Dame de Laon was quite
possibly the most wondrous building I had ever seen.

I turned around and almost immediately limped into a fellow
sporting a curled moustache that was much too wide for his
face; perhaps noticing I was in need of a sit down, he ushered
me into his restaurant to a table that looked out over the
cathedral, the whole now floodlit standing proud against the
night sky.

Didier, without recourse to the menu, set about plying me with food, starting with *une pelle Thiérachienne*, a plate of local allsorts – a dollop of cassoulet, potatoes, lardons and a *tarte maroille* which, despite being sharp and flavoursome, smelt like it should be left well alone. *Roti du porc moelleux à la bière du garde* followed (appropriately, roast pork steeped in the Guardsman's beer), accompanied by copious carafes of red wine. It wasn't long before all the other guests had left and Didier, giving the odd furtive glance to check the coast was clear, started to play bagpipe music at full blast which, blaring out across the little square, for some unfathomable reason felt wholly appropriate. Despite 20 miles on the agenda the next day, my host was adamant that I could not leave until we had toasted each other with his home-made *eau de vie* which was dispensed from a large apothecary-shaped Hendrick's gin bottle; I hesitated at first until chided by a shout of *'chacun à sa croix!'* The cathedral was in darkness when I finally left; a pharmacist's neon sign read 21 degrees. I have no recollection of my descent back to the bottom.

I was up early the next morning; from now on, the only way to get the work done would be to break the back of the day well before noon. I made my way up the hill for one last visit to the cathedral.

Reaching the top, the sun barely risen, the air was already warm. Again, I walked around the leviathan building. There was not a soul about and, with some trepidation, I pushed the great red door, which, to my amazement, opened. I had the place to myself.

Inside, all was still. Not a sound, the air cool and unmoving. I looked down the length of the nave to the distant choir and then, in a far-off corner, I heard a faint clatter. Eager for my Passport stamp, I followed it and found a wizened old man wearing a cloth cap, carrying a beautiful polished cane, a golden Malacca brown, with a fist head. He busied himself changing the candles in the side chapels. His breath sweet with wine even at that early hour, he greeted me in a soft whistled tone, *'Venez m'sieur, voyez cette cathédrale magnifique! Je vous montrerai ses secrets'*, and with that he led me to a corner.

Notre-Dame de Laon
…I stood there in its vast shadow and stared up in awe…

'Look at this column', he instructed as he struck it and the stone replied with a deep resonant bell-like clang.

I looked at him in disbelief…'it's hollow?'

'*Non, m'sieur*, it's solid; one piece.' This time I struck it and again it boomed out in the silence. 'It has been quarried in the direction of the grain and, because it is one piece, it rings like a bell – it is not hollow, I assure you', he laughed.

He took me across the aisle to another column, which he also struck – nothing, just a dull thud. 'You see, it has been cut in two, but here' – he took his palm to another larger pillar … 'bonggg!' The stone rang out louder and deeper with a rich bass note.

At the far end of the chancel, he pointed to the square apse, 'just like they have in York and Cologne; all the other cathedrals have rounded ends and here, see the bright colours'. Like Merlin with his wand, he thrust his cane skyward, highlighting the remnants of frescoes that once surrounded the Great Rose Window. 'In the old days, the whole church would have been decorated like this and, where not, it was hung with tapestries.'

We stepped over marble tombstones, smoothed by time, until we reached a little side chapel tucked away from the world – '*Regardez*!' He motioned me to look up into the corner of the ceiling where a mason had carved a tiny figure, '*une sirène*' – his voice soft and musical, almost emphasizing the beauty of the curled-up medieval mermaid. As we stepped into bright sunshine, so the bells tolled the hour; the old man smiled, patted me on the arm and said '*Bonne route à Rome, eh*!'

Leaving Laon, the country took a step change; plain gave way to hill, red brick to white limestone, grey slate to Roman pantile, and the ferocious dogs that had barked at me ever since Calais now seemed content to doze in the sun. Life felt less manicured and altogether more relaxed.

Vineyards began to pop up with increasing regularity and I encountered the first mosquitoes of summer in the woods outside Corbeny, once a place of great significance to the newly crowned Kings and Queens of France. The day after their coronation in nearby Reims, they would make pilgrimage to the shrine of St Marcoult and there give thanks to him for the 'royal touch', which, it was believed, could cure scrofula.

It was by now late May and the land, like a giant market stall for all to wonder at, was at its finest. Crossing the River Aisne, however, I became aware of a new phenomenon – latter-day cathedrals that now punctuated the countryside. No smaller, the towering grain silo, in comparison to its ecclesiastical counterparts, was a brutal, ungainly interruption and worse, now everywhere to be seen.

*

When Hélène Spanneut, or rather 'LN' as she styles herself, is not putting up dusty pilgrims in her house at Villiers-Franqueux, she can, more often than not, be found thousands of feet up in the sky, indulging her passion as a world record-holding hot air balloonist. It was hard to imagine this little sparrow of a figure wrestling guy ropes, lugging gas canisters and hauling bulky passenger baskets at 60-odd, but beneath her smiling veneer there lurked a gutsy character with a will of iron.

LN's approach to everything is founded on discipline and so, once I had been welcomed by her dogs, Djinn and Shannon, I was summoned into the kitchen with a *'Venez, pèlerin'* that would have been the envy of any Sergeant Major. She was not to be trifled with – well, not at that stage of the journey anyway.

For LN, pilgrimage represented a challenge in the same way that ballooning did. She swapped altitude for weight, wind planning for route planning and, as you would expect of a world record-holder, was encyclopaedic in her knowledge and meticulous in her research. She knew everything, which was just as well for me as, south of Reims, I was in unfamiliar territory.

After I had showered, LN appeared with an armful of her own books, maps and waysheets: 'Follow the GR 654, the legs are not so long and the country nicer and, look, plenty of places to stay – I told Alain the same yesterday'. So, my friend from Canterbury, whom I had not heard of for some time, was still a day ahead and apparently in good heart; word of mouth was still the timeless method by which pilgrims learned of each other's progress.

There was a crunch of gravel in the drive, as LN's husband, Alain, returned from Reims, where the couple helped run the desk that registered and tended the needs of pilgrims as they visited the cathedral. A large bearded man, he poured me a glass of home-made walnut wine to drink, while we sat in the garden. LN emerged from the kitchen with a large casserole and, as she served us, she explained that she was due to meet friends in Lausanne in four weeks' time to complete her own journey to Rome; talking of their current progress from Canterbury, they were travelling at speed and, with no rest days, had planned an early August arrival in Rome.

In the morning, LN set out with me towards Reims, Djinn and Shannon forever disappearing in pursuit of rabbit, pheasant or deer. Curious, I quizzed her about ballooning; at the very mention of the word '*Montgolfier*', her eyes lit up.

'It began over 40 years ago, at a small balloon gathering near here and for me, it was the "*coup de foudre*", how you say, "love at first sight". I started off as a navigator for the balloon designer, Jacques Bernardin. Together we won the French National Championships and worked with Don Cameron, the British balloonist. Then I found a wonderful ballooning partner in Michel Arnould – he had such spirit, such character', she said. 'With him, we decided to go for records not the races.' My mind wandered back to her study: walls of trophies and photos of a gorgeous Farrah Fawcett lookalike with a handsome bearded *sportif* type surrounded by certificates and mementoes; pride of place on her mantel-piece was the helmet which Michel had worn while winning the altitude record in an open basket balloon. Not stopping to draw breath, she went on: 'It was so exciting, we were ground-breakers; fêted as pioneers of aviation, we lived for the sport, crossing the Mediterranean, the Channel and setting distance and endurance records too. But funnily, the most famous was one morning in 86, when my balloon got caught in the towers of Reims Cathedral. That was a lucky escape – we just climbed out of the basket and walked down the staircase but *oh la la*, they even read about it in New York!'

Then her spirit faded. 'We were at a festival one day. Michel said he wanted to fly these new microlites which were just appearing on the scene. He was an experienced pilot, he had licences for balloon, glider and fixed wing, I mean, he knew what he was doing. He said to me, "hold my whisky, I am just going to take this little machine for a test flight, nothing more than a quick five minutes".' I knew what was coming – her trembling voice, the change in tense and the ghostly visage of that empty helmet. 'I watched him take off and never saw him again; he got caught in a downdraft, hit high-tension cables and…boff! Michel was killed instantly. Ha! Not six months after the death of my ballooning partner, and then my troubles really began. Oh boy! We had just set up a balloon manufacturing company, but without Michel I had no idea how to run it. Everything changed; my marriage broke up and with it went my social life and my firm. As I was the owner, I had no redundancy, no unemployment benefit and, all of a sudden, here I was in this big house, children, dogs and not a penny to my name. Then you find out just who your real friends are – it is easy in the good times, huh? So I drew up a list of people and rang the first name on the top of the page. He gave me a little job in Paris and day by day, I began to rebuild. Somehow we managed. I kept the house and then, some years later, I met my Alain', at which she smiled again. '*Voilà*, your path to Reims is straight ahead 'Arry.'

1,063 miles to Rome.

7

Reims to Epernay

Gentil Roy,
Or est éxécuté le plaisir de Dieu,
Qui voulait lever le siège d'Orléans
Et vous amener en cette cité de Reims,
Recevoir votre saint sacré,
En montrant que vous êtes vrai roi
Et celui auquel le royaume doit appartenir.
     Joan of Arc, at the coronation of King Charles VII, 1429

ON 17 JULY 1429, Joan of Arc, or *La Pucelle*, the Maid, having routed the English Army after breaking the siege of Orléans, delivered the Dauphin to Reims Cathedral where he was presented with his spurs and sword as First of the Knights, received the symbols of Royalty and was crowned Charles VII – one of the most charged moments in France's story. It is ironic that, less than a year later, Joan would be captured by the Burgundians, purchased by the English, tried in a sham court at Rouen and, at 19, sentenced to death by burning on trumped-up charges of heresy. It would take another 600 years before she was sanctified.

The cathedral's limestone bulwarks were curious variations of beige. The leviathan structure is a constant work-in-progress as weather and exhaust take their toll; its 2,300 sculptures and embellishments, perpetually in differing stages of decay, keep an army of artisans in work. Hence at any one time, parts of the building look brand new while others seem near to ruination.

I was enjoying a glass of champagne in a bar around the corner when Jacques Bolelli swept in and ordered *encore deux coupes*. He apologized that congestion on the road from Paris had held him up. Traffic, I replied with some relish, was rarely an issue for me nowadays.

Jacques is a *Maître-Artisan de France* with a passion for maintaining his country's most ancient and individual manufacturing traditions. From drawbridges and sporting rifles to urns in the gardens at Versailles, he now included Atelier Simon Marq in his quiver – the family-run company which, since 1640 and for the last 12 generations, has been responsible for the creation and maintenance of the cathedral's stained glass windows.

Entering the hushed nave, the vaulted ceilings echoing to the chatterings of the many tourists and pilgrims alike, Jacques turned on his heel and pointed up at the West Rose Window. 'A cathedral cannot be a monument to times past; it is a living thing in a constant state of evolution. It could fall to Benoît and Stéphanie Simon to restore this magnificent window in two years' time, just as Benoît's grandfather, Jacques, restored the South Rose 80 years ago.'

As we walked down the nave, Jacques explained how, in the Middle Ages, stained glass was designed to complement a cathedral's decoration, to inspire worshippers to prayer through the beauty of light and to help tell the story of Christianity to those who could not read.

'But of course', he went on, 'it was also to do with the Cult of Relics, uh?' I nodded. 'With thousands of people flocking to the cathedrals on Feast Days and Festivals they had to be built large enough to take everybody. Yet they also had to be light enough so that the faithful could see the antiquities and remains satisfactorily. Here in Reims, for example, they had in their possession the Sainte Ampoule, the Holy Ampulla, used by Bishop Remigius – St Rémy to you and me – to baptise Clovis, the first ruler of all the Franks and the first Christian King of Gaul. The Sainte Ampoule was used to anoint every French ruler from then on. The chrism, or ointment inside, was said to be divine – no one knew how or where it came from, other than God himself. The sacred phials, sadly, were crushed during the Revolution.'

Jacques paused for a moment as if to reflect and then, looking at the bare walls, continued: 'They destroyed a lot in those times but not nearly as much as the ravages the churches suffered in the seventeenth and early eighteenth centuries.

Christians in those days simply could not believe that medieval works permitted a dignified glorification of God – strange how we Catholics didn't have the stomach even for our own catholic tastes at that moment in history. Churches, consequently, became demolition yards, we can only imagine their beauty before. Abbot Suger, the driving force behind the building of these great structures, would be rolling in his grave if he could see the drab austerity of these fantastic places of worship today.'

Reaching the apse, we arrived at the unmistakable blue wash of the Chagall windows which, when they were installed in the early 1970s, attracted much criticism. Now they look conservative when compared to the abstract kaleidoscopic shards of strident colour that make up the neighbouring windows created by the German artist Imi Knoebel to mark the cathedral's eight-hundreth anniversary in 2011.

'I like them', Jacques declared, as if seeking to draw me on the issue, 'and, on a technical point, these windows are very difficult to make. Both artists' designs are complex and as for Chagall, well, he was a pioneer of modernism, the absolute perfectionist – everything had to be just right; there could be no room for inaccuracy whatsoever. He started these windows by gluing pieces of cloth to a scale model. You have to admire him.'

I looked at the new with the old, the bright theatrical hues, the Crucifixion picked out in white, shining like a beacon at the heart of the creation – the whole demanding attention as if the onlooker was held hostage until an opinion was formed. I watched as people paused at both sets of windows. For me, perhaps because these were the works of a major Jewish and a major German artist, the designs simply sent out a powerful message of forgiveness and reconciliation. For that timeless value alone, I liked them.

We lunched in style at the nearby Café du Palais under an art deco canopy of more stained glass – the ecclesiastical exchanged for greys and blues, forming a sky in which swallows dived and swooped. This was the work of Jacques Simon years earlier. We drank bottles of refreshing Bouzy rouge and ordered plates of *jambon de Reims*, salads of *foie gras* and smoked quail breasts, finishing with freshly picked strawberries and an obligatory *digestif*.

Thus fortified, we made our way through the backstreets to an ungainly stone building with a three-storeyed glass window at its front, Atelier Simon Marq. Inside, the ground floor was a labyrinth of little rooms. One in particular caught my attention: a bare cell with nothing more than a wooden shelf and a large drain. Bleached spotless, it was perfect for the disposal of a body. It was the acid shop where glass is etched to bring out colour. Passing humming kilns, Jacques led me upstairs where the patterns are cut, a difficult job, the benches riddled with holes where nails hold the panes in place.

Alain, a lean wiry sort, came over; he was working on an order for Russia, and so we represented a welcome break for him from some intricate lead mitring which had to be formed just so. He had worked in the Atelier for over 37 years. Old offcuts, purples, blues and maroons were picked from a dusty wooden box. 'These', he said, 'are thirteenth-century; they have gone opaque. In the Middle Ages, they used a lot more potassium to make glass, it was easier to fashion – see the bubbles and the way it is wavy?' He pointed with his finger. 'The trouble was that the glass was also more porous in those times, it absorbed soot and dirt, grew mould and would eventually be rendered useless. We work with over a thousand colours here so we can replace pretty much anything and hold stock in the store rooms that is, in some cases, over 200 years old.' He cast a disciplined eye in the direction of a young man in deep concentration as he marked out a design. 'My son Eric, he is studying at Chartres Cathedral for his apprenticeship.'

We were led through a door that was a curious Dali-esque mélange of ears, eyes, hands, faces and noses. 'Scraps, rescues and throw-outs. This was made in the 1930s, from pieces that go back 800 years', Alain muttered, as it swung open into a large airy room that was a good two floors high. 'This building was specially built for Atelier Simon Marq. Here, we lay out the windows to full size to make sure everything is correct. The *maître-verrier* has to marry his work with that of the *maître-maçon*, there can be no room for error. It has to be *exacte*.' He gave a nod of acknowledgement across to the studio where

Chagall worked for years on his detailed compositions, not only for Reims but other great institutions like the cathedral at Metz, the United Nations Headquarters in New York and the Abbell Synagogue in Jerusalem.

A black cat slept on a sofa, next to which was a large glass-fronted bookcase whose shelves were lined with a set of substantial gold-embossed leather volumes. 'Those', Alain said as he rolled a cigarette, 'are the company reference books' – he slipped the roll-up behind his ear – 'the 28-volume *Diderot et d'Alembert Encyclopédie*, one of only 200 still in use from an original print run of 4,250; the rest are in museums. It was based on your *Ephraim Chambers's Cyclopaedia*. You know it?'

I nodded.

'Well, here in France', Alain continued, 'the authorities considered the work dangerous because it gave people knowledge and encouraged free thinking that could question the rules of the established order. But, any time we need to know something, we still check here first; it was the internet of its day, full of information – a remarkable *oeuvre*.'

Indeed such was the concern of the ruling classes that in 1752, a year after Denis Diderot released the first volume of his *Encyclopédie*, publication was suspended by the courts. He was held by the authorities for his references on religion and the laws of nature while his house was searched for any further scandalizing drafts, all of which had been hidden in the residence of Guillaume-Chrétien de Lamoignon de Malesherbes, at the time Directeur de la Librairie, who sanctioned the action but was secretly in favour of the idea. Voltaire, Rousseau and Montesquieu, arguably the finest minds of the period, contributed at the beginning, helping to create a body of work that many consider was ahead of its time. But for Diderot, who lived not far away in Langres and was widely fêted as one of the prominent figures of the Enlightenment alongside Jefferson and Newton, editing the *Encyclopédie* became a considerable labour of love, as society increasingly saw the books as unorthodox and seditious. His fellow contributors, including the co-editor d'Alembert, deserted the project, leaving completion of this enormous task virtually to Diderot alone.

In 1759 publication was again blocked by decree and, while the work doggedly continued, Diderot lived under permanent threat of police harassment. It took nearly 22 years to complete the *Encyclopédie*, and it was only when the last volume was produced that the final twist in the tale was revealed – Diderot's publisher and bookseller, André LeBreton, had been arbitrarily removing any passages from the final proofs that he felt were contentious. After all Diderot's efforts, the published volumes were emasculated and incomplete.

Reims was a major milestone. Three weeks since my departure and I was now making appreciable progress. Leaving the clutches of England and the Pas de Calais behind me, the weather was improving by the day and I had settled into a routine and rhythm rather than merely being the clumsy participant in a daily progression southward.

Sitting in a café, I was listening to an accordionist playing 'Lara's Theme' from *Dr Zhivago* when the peace was abruptly broken by a waitress spilling a tray of glasses.

'Uh-oh!' said the old lady sitting at the table next to me with her husband.

Anne and Bert, from Melbourne, were on a driving holiday to Holland. In 1944, it transpired, Bert's father had been the owner of a shop by the ill-fated bridge at Arnhem, 'and then we found ourselves right in the middle of it. When the Paras landed and the shelling started, Dad said, we're moving out, and had it not been for that, Anne and I would never have met because we ended up in the same air raid shelter'.

'Well, it's kinda spookier than that really', Anne said. 'I was one of nine sisters and had a habit of sleep-walking, so the others used to tie me to a bed. One day we got a direct hit; how we survived I don't know, except that we were all saved by the bed which overturned and saved us all from the blast!'

'So, you see', Bert chipped in, 'good can come from war. We've been married 54 years now. I reckon this is gonna be the last road trip though – our daughter's going to join us in a day or two. It may seem strange but, for all her years, she's never been to Holland before, even though she's Dutch through and through.'

Before I said goodbye, I was intrigued to find out the fate of the shop. 'Incredibly the place survived', Bert said, 'but Jeez, it was terrible, you wouldn't want to live through that – but you know what? When we moved back in, the black marketeers had sold our front room carpet to our neighbours – they were so embarrassed. We got it back straight away.'

Back in my room, the space was soon transformed into a scene of much ripping and shredding as I tore into the contents of my rucksack. Nothing was spared scrutiny as a sleeping mat, spare socks, packaging, the covers and end papers of guide books, a knife, a corkscrew, enough antiseptic wipes to clean a hospital and finally, my one luxury, a copy of Iris Origo's *War in Val d'Orcia*, all got the hoof in an attempt to lighten the load of my rucksack further, leaving a small pile of debris at the foot of my bed. But what really niggled was one canvas bag that was tiny in size yet weighed over a kilo. It was filled with all the leads and adapters for the necessities of a twenty-first-century pilgrimage and any plug between London and Rome. But, no way could I ditch my iPod – without that I would have gone insane within days of setting out.

In the mirror, I noticed I had now turned an odd shade – a brown left wrist, a matching right forearm, a mahogany neck, a red tip to my nose and beautiful golden knees and shins that stopped well short to reveal, just like the entire rest of me, feet and ankles preserved in perfect ivory white.

I left Reims for Epernay along the Aisne Canal at 6 a.m. Vineyards abounded; everywhere, workers pruned while awkward sputnik-like machines steered down the rows blowing out white sulphurish clouds to protect the grapes from pest and pestilence. Picking up the Reims-Epernay railway line, I climbed up to the *Forêt de la Montagne de Reims*, a 200-square-mile swathe of oak and beech.

I loved the woods, not only for the tranquillity and respite they offered from the road but for the privacy they afforded too. It was Dustin Hoffman who once said that 'music is the spine of everyone's life' and in the forests, without embarrassment or concern, I could dance. Often I could be found

Forêt de Reims
...a 200 square-mile swathe of oak and beech...

prancing away like it was 11 p.m. on a Friday night out. In the beginning, the routines were pretty tame, the odd shuffle, bit of a jig, nothing too flamboyant, but as the journey wore on, so my confidence grew – with arms spread wide, thumb-stick swinging in the air, I swooned, swayed and strutted my pilgrim stuff in a bliss-like trance not dissimilar to some obscure rain dance. My iPod transported me to far-off musical plains where played everything from Barry White to Amy Winehouse, Mozart, Louis Prima, Chet Baker, the Kings of Leon or Black Sabbath; ten kilos of rucksack at my back adding a decidedly forward momentum.

Little was spared from my choreographical and choral inter-pretations as the hapless flora and fauna of France's forests were routinely subjected to falsetto screams, tenor moans and bass groans while number after number belted out at full blast with my earphones firmly implanted. One day, waltzing down a track, with all the grace and panache of a Teletubby on ice, such was my carefree delight that while singing Abba's 'Dancing Queen' I nearly speared myself onto the forks of an oncoming tractor.

But perhaps my favourite time, at this stage, was lunch when, with nothing around save the stillness of the afternoon, I would find a spot on the edge of a clearing, take my boots off, lay out on my coat and eat *sauçisson sec*, *baguette*, fruit and cheese; a chance to take stock and count my good fortune – the essence of pilgrimage.

'What on earth is that?!' I exclaimed as I recoiled at the foul stench.

'Oh, Harry, it is very French!' replied Hubert de Billy, my comfortably built host. It was a novel way to sum up sausages made from hogs' colons. In France the *andouillette* is considered comfort food. They are vilified the world over for their pungent aroma and questionable flavour, commented on variously by non-Gallic food writers as 'The Dish of Death', 'smells like a *pissoir*' or more tactfully as an 'acquired taste... even for adven-turous eaters', leaving one 'a little traumatized'. No matter how well this crudely made medieval peasant fare is seasoned, how slowly it is cooked or what rich and imaginative sauces it is disguised with, there is no escaping the indisputable fact that the prime ingredient comes from the wrong end of a pig.

To the French, however, this particular variety of sausage remains a delicacy with such a following that a trade guild, the *Association Amicale des Amateurs d'Andouillette Authentique*, has been established to ensure standards are maintained. To me, at that gag-inducing moment, there was little amicable in the act of consuming a plate of steaming *andouillette*.

Hubert, a Pol Roger in all but name, was treating me to a bottle of his family's Blanc de Blanc 2002 when, looking deep into the thread-like strings of tiny bubbles that spiralled through the golden wine, he said how much he respected the work of barmen, 'but you know, *Kir Royal* is for me a crime. You cannot beat the enjoyment of the real stuff, it's just the very best'. He went on to explain that it was the seventeenth-century monk Dom Perignon who studied the champagne manufacturing process in detail, identified the importance of pruning and studying the local microclimates in relation to different grape varieties and individual growing characteristics.

'For him', Hubert said, 'the bubbles from the second fermentation were a problem. The bottles would explode, sometimes with the most devastating consequences if a chain reaction took place. Later, the scientists got a hold of it, refined the production techniques, made the bottles stronger, introduced better corks and from a problem came a rule. But it was you English from the very outset in the 1600s who delighted in the bubbles and more than likely first grasped how to make the second fermentation happen by adding extra sugar at a later stage. And you still represent the lion's share of our market, over 35 million bottles a year – and, year on year, we all find it harder and harder to meet the growing appetite for...*rosé*', he added, referring to the fact that the champagne industry is the only one in the world centred on a single patch of land 30 kilometres square. 'We all know each other, we all attended the Jesuit School in Reims and more often than not, we are relatives. My uncle ran Perrier-Jouët; it's very friendly.'

After lunch, I couldn't help notice that Epernay was different from everywhere else I had passed through; it was like an oil town in a state of permanent boom, forever rich thanks to its production of the ever-popular wine, with wide boulevards and handsome buildings that had a hint of the imperial about them; even the litter was grand – the ubiquitous beer can replaced by the champagne bottle.

In the evening, to complete the day's picture of alcoholic perfection and as if the Sparnaciens, as the residents of Epernay are known, wanted to prove that they can turn their hand to anything that involves yeast and a barrel, the market square was transformed into a village of tents, braziers and tables laid end to end like servants' quarters in the Field of Cloth of Gold. It felt as if all France, in varying shapes and sizes, had turned up to enjoy the local beer festival and a French-Irish tribute band. Ales of every colour and flavour known to man were available in this wonderful encampment and, after sampling a number of blondes, I eventually settled for the Duchess of Burgogne, a Flanders red that was bubbly, sweet to the tongue, made me feel good all over and helped me sing all five verses of The Pogues' *Dirty Old Town* in French; soon after I had to admit defeat.

1,019 miles to Rome.

8

Châlons-en-Champagne to Brienne-le-Château

'It is not for my crown I am fighting,
but to prove that Frenchmen
were not born to be ruled by Cossacks.'

Napoleon in 1814

FRANCE HAS THE LARGEST network of canals in Europe; nearly 5,500 miles of them to be precise, engineered to link the country in a web of waterways from end to end with Paris sitting spider-like at the centre. My friend, the journalist and walker Brian Mooney, is besotted with the things because of the distances you can cover in a short space of time when walking down them – understandable but, to my mind, canals are like eating cornflakes without milk: very dull and not much fun. Straighter than a Roman road, with trees planted on both banks for shade, they offer a tunnel-visioned vista that drives the walking man to insanity – even the water looks dead.

At the end of the first day on the Canal Latéral à la Marne, I arrived in Châlons-en-Champagne which is to be confused with Châlons-sur-Marne as that was the town's name from the Middle Ages until 1998. Indeed there is a lot to be confused about in Châlons; a pretty city, it is a quarter the size of nearby Reims. A sensitive bone of contention between the two is that Châlons, and not its much larger pedigreed neighbour, is the capital of the Marne Département because it remained loyal to the crown during the Wars of Religion.

And, for those of you in a rush after a long day stomping down a turgid dry cornflake of a canal, the Pilgrim Passport stamp is not to be found in the Cathedral of St Etienne, where logic would dictate, but further away in the Church of Notre Dame-en-Vaux. This important piece of information I learned to my cost as, late, I chased all the way around the former thinking it was the latter until I had to chase all the way around the latter in search of what should have been at the former. I eventually found a poor lady with her ink pad at the ready sitting bemused at the door where I had rushed in – she had been there all along, if I had turned left instead of right.

As a result, it was in a flustered state that I knocked on the door of the Cuvelettes' sixteenth-century house not a block away from the church that was now indelibly imprinted on my mind as the cathedral. The Cuvelettes routinely welcome pilgrims into their home as they pass through. I was greeted at the door by François, a towering white-haired former surgeon who would have been Abraham Lincoln's double had he lived beyond Wilkes Booth's bullet. I was offered a glass of barley water by Brigitte, his wife. She announced how much she loved our Queen and wished me a 'Happy Jubilee', before the couple declared that they had to join friends in '*Les Jards*' for an artistic festival being held in the town that night. I was welcome to come along once I had freshened up. They waved goodbye, slammed the door behind them and there I was, not five minutes arrived, a complete stranger in their home, entirely on my own.

Not, you understand, that I thought Brigitte's and François's action out of place; it was the unquestioning faith they placed in me that overwhelmed – a display of old-world kindness, generosity of spirit and heartfelt welcome that seems so alien in today's world.

I met up with them again in a circus top in the heart of *Les Grands Jardins*, on the banks of the river Marne. I couldn't help notice how the town seemed to resemble a second-hand clothes stall, the main square hung with old coats on hangers while ranks of folded shirts in parade ground formations blocked the streets, to the bewilderment of the local populace who seemed to accept this artistic disruption with good-humoured shrugs.

After dinner, we, along with a few thousand others, were herded Pied Piper-like towards the Hôtel de Ville which, now surrounded by a cohort of screaming and prancing cadavers whose intention was to terrify, entertain and confound in equal measures, had been as good as zombiefied – in keeping with the Western World's preoccupation with these mercifully fictional creations. The neatly folded shirts and old coats, after a degree of elaborate cavorting, ended up on a large bonfire while the cadavers took to nudity, which was not so pleasing given that the budget evidently didn't extend to 'model quality' casting. After skipping a few circuits around the fire, the naked zombies la-la-ed off through a now very confused crowd never to be seen again, leaving the assembled audience thoroughly puzzled. François commented that whatever it was, it had been '*une expérience unique*' and, baffled, we headed home for a drink.

*

Another day by the canal followed by a night with some monosyllabic nuns and I was poised on the edge of 'The Middle of Nowhere'. Pretty country, there is nothing in 'The Middle of Nowhere', not a face, café or shop for miles. There is even a sign as you walk into the village of Outines pointing back the way to '*Au Milieu de Nulle Part*'. I jest not.

*

From afar, the Château de Brienne dominates the skyline in an unflattering Colditzian way. This is odd because the 'Versailles of the Aube', as it is known, is very much the opposite when you get closer, which is still at a certain distance as the place is now a home for the mentally ill. This magnificent eighteenth-century building, of perfect proportion with a sweeping carriageway leading to a suitably grand main entrance, remained – short of 'certification' – frustratingly out of reach.

Since the tenth century, the château has been home to some of France's greatest families, all of whom held the title of Comte de Brienne at differing stages in history. One scion who provides a fascinating chapter in the town's illustrious history was Jean de Candia-Nevers, penniless second son of Erard II, the sixth Comte. Jean, who had originally been destined for the Church, opted instead for the more exciting life of a knight. After 20-odd years at court, he had risen to become one of King

Philip Augustus's premier barons and was much respected for his ability in chivalrous tournament.

In 1208, at the request of envoys from Outremer, as the Crusader States were known, the King appointed his trusted noble to assume and secure the throne of Jerusalem. The kingdom was now centred on Acre, the city itself having fallen to Saladin in 1187. The incumbent queen, Maria, was 17. Jean, however, could only accede to the title by marrying and so, at the age of 40, well into middle age by thirteenth-century standards, he took marital vows and was rewarded handsomely for his troubles by Pope and monarch alike, with a payment of 40,000 livres from each. Marriage was to prove a life-changing event for Jean.

Two years later his wife died, leaving him as regent for their infant daughter, Yolanda. For the remainder of Jean's life, it would appear that his situation would be dominated almost entirely with fighting wars and marriage – just the ticket for your later years.

In 1214, he married Stephanie, eldest daughter of King Levon I, ruler of Armenian Cilicia. Not long after, he found himself playing an unwitting lead role with King András II of Hungary, Duke Leopold VI of Austria and the 19-year-old King Hugh of Cyprus in the doomed Fifth Crusade to recapture Jerusalem, which, from the outset, was beset with problems. After eight years, no territorial gain and Jerusalem still firmly in the hands of the Ayyubids, the Crusade was concluded with an eight-year truce and the promise to return a piece of the True Cross which Sultan Al-Kamil, the Ayyubid leader, didn't in fact have.

During the conflict, Jean's second wife died. In the meantime, he gave his daughter Yolanda's hand in marriage to Frederick II, the Holy Roman Emperor. On the face of it, marrying into one of the most powerful monarchies in the known world would be considered a sound decision. Frederick, however, was an unsavoury character; a Muslim once observed that the Emperor would have gone dirt-cheap in the slave market. He seduced Yolanda's cousin while on honeymoon and, once he had acceded to the title of King of Jerusalem, tossed Jean aside.

After the Fifth Crusade and now without a job, Jean travelled Europe, marrying for a third time in 1224, this time to Berenguela, younger daughter of King Alfonso IX of Leon and Queen Berengaria I of Castile. In 1228, at the age of 58, and in return for his son-in-law Frederick's outrageous treatment, Jean led the papal troops that invaded the Emperor's Southern Italian possessions while the latter was in the Holy Land on the Sixth Crusade.

In his sixtieth year, Jean was invited by the Latin Empire of Constantinople to become Emperor-Regent on the proviso that his daughter Marie marry the then 12-year-old Baudouin de Courtenay in due course. Jean accepted but again his regency was to be no easy task; in 1235, the city was besieged for a summer by John III Doukas Vatatses, Emperor of Nicaea and Tsar Ivan Asen II of Bulgaria. The epitome of the knight errant, Jean died two years later at the age of 67, after what can only be described as a full life.

At his prime, my landlord at the Hôtel Austerlitz in Brienne would have been a good bet at a prizefight. He was a large, thickset man who filled the cramped space behind the bar with ease, and was neither given to much thought nor idle conversation. The hospitality trade, I quickly concluded, had probably not been the first choice on his career form – perhaps he was doing his friend a favour, standing in for the day. It was hard to tell but, one thing for sure, he certainly was not pleased to see me. I was a distraction from his book and, no matter how charming I tried to be, the look of disturbed evil on his face, like a guard dog woken from its sleep, told me he simply wasn't having it.

As he rose from his chair, the foyer momentarily darkened like a solar eclipse; the man was solid like a gaming machine with an unruly mop of grey hair and beady eyes. He wore a black apron that was covered in white fingermarks and an enormous pair of boots that wouldn't have looked out of place on Boris Karloff. As he walked, so he swayed from side to side in the shambolic manner of an orangutan deprived of trees. He motioned me to follow him upstairs to my room which, in darkness, feigned to be in a good state of repair.

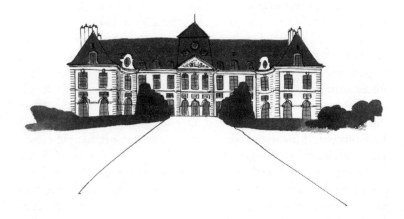

Château de Brienne
...This magnificent eighteenth century building, of
perfect proportion...

After he left, I drew the curtains wide, expecting a stellar vista of the château, but instead was greeted by a pair of grimy knees and a gnarled hand wielding a cement trowel. A jet of water danced across the pane. I shut the curtain and returned to the gloom; my bed for the night was cheap for good reason.

In early 1805, Napoleon stayed at the Château de Brienne for a night. He made tentative enquiries of Madame de Lomenie, its owner, about buying the place. 'It means so much to me', he said.

'It means everything to me', she replied and the matter was closed.

Brienne had left a lasting impression on the Emperor. It was home to one of the 12 regional military schools set up to prepare pupils for entry to L'Ecole Militaire in Paris, the French officer training establishment of the time. Napoleon, the son of an impoverished Corsican aristocrat, Carlo Buonaparte, was sent to the little school as a ten-year-old, under the patronage of the Comte de Marbeuf, military governor of Corsica and close friend of the future Emperor's mother.

The school buildings are no larger or more remarkable than any village school. That summer day, looking out across the car park that had once been the playground, it was hard to imagine that Napoleon's talent as a military commander was supposedly first noticed here when he rallied his fellow pupils during a snowball fight in the winter of 1784.

Brienne was also the scene of Napoleon's first battle on French soil when the Sixth Coalition advanced on Paris, led by Field Marshals von Blücher and Prince Karl Philipp zu Schwarzenberg, in January 1814. It was the prequel to what some say represent the Emperor's finest victories during the Six Days' Campaign that mid-February when Napoleon engaged the might of the Allied Armies, some 500,000 in all, with his 70,000 rump of inexperienced *Marie-Louises* – the nickname given to young French soldiery. It consisted of an exhausting game of tactical cat and mouse, Napoleon's strategy being one of rapid manoeuvre to meet each army head-on and defeat them piecemeal. Blücher was Napoleon's first target.

The Allies crossed the Rhine on 1 January. Napoleon entrusted his wife, the Empress Marie-Louise and their son Franz, King of Rome, into the hands of the National Guard on 25 January, and set out to join the remnants of his army that was still reeling from the reversals of the Russian and German campaigns of 1812–13. The Emperor's original plans were thwarted when the Allies captured his messenger but nonetheless, on 29 January, Blücher with only about 25,000 men to hand was forced to confront Napoleon's army of 30,000 at Brienne. After some particularly hard weather, the thaw had started and the going for artillery and the wagon trains carrying ammunition and supplies was at best difficult. The fighting, a series of frenzied skirmishes in which Marshal Grouchy engaged the Prusso-Russian Army while Marshals Ney and Victor secured the town and château, didn't really get under way until mid-afternoon.

This was a day when, on two occasions, if the dice of fate had rolled any other way, the course of history might have been very different indeed.

At one point, Napoleon's entourage inadvertently rode into a detachment of Cossacks, forcing him to draw his sword. The Emperor was only saved from a lance in the back by the timely discharge of General Gaspard Gourgaud's pistol. Then, come dusk, the situation grew confused. Von Blücher and von Gneisenau, the Field Marshal's deputy, felt confident of a French withdrawal. Preparations were made for the two Prussian commanders and their staff to dine in the château. I imagine them, tired and muddied from a long day in the saddle, sitting down with great anticipation to bowls of soup and plates of stew.

Just before, however, as luck would have it Napoleon came across an old school friend, a Monsieur Royer.

'Do you remember when we were children, how we would go down into the château's cellars without being seen?' the Emperor asked.

'Sire', Royer replied, 'give me some men and I will lead them there myself.'

As the Prussians had just sat down, so Royer led a column of soldiers into the building. How the ears of the old Field

Marshal, as he brought a long-awaited broth-filled spoon to his mouth, must have pricked at the unmistakable disturbance in distant corridors and down far-off passageways as the French tried to seize the advantage.

'*Schnell, schnell!*' must surely have been the cry when they realized what was afoot, supper rudely interrupted as the commanders were forced to flee the dining room or face imminent capture. In the ensuing mêlée, the old Field Marshal ran out to the front of the château to rejoin his men in the town, but got caught between the French. In the confusion, his aides, Captain von Heyden, who was badly wounded, and Captain the Count Hardenberg were captured, while Blücher and Gneisenau only just managed to escape thanks to the foresight of a dinner guest, a German named Dietschin, who had lived in the town for the past 20 years and hurried them to safety through a side gate.

While the French indeed gained the château, to some the victory was not nearly as decisive as Napoleon had hoped it might be. Blücher rejoined his troops and went on to defeat Bonaparte at the Battle of La Rothière three days later. However well the Emperor may have acquitted himself in the Six Days' Campaign, it was not enough to defeat the Allies. Twenty years of war had taken their toll on France and, contrary to Napoleon's express wishes, Paris surrendered on 31 March. On 6 April, the Emperor, exhausted and beaten, was forced to abdicate unconditionally, agreeing to his own exile under the Treaty of Fontainebleau.

In a charged speech made on 20 April to his general staff and the officers and men of his Old Guard, Napoleon placed his lips to the regimental colours and bade them an emotional farewell: 'Adieu my friends, would I could press you all to my heart.' And with that, he left France for Elba.

In less than a year Bonaparte would return to face Blücher and Wellington on the field of Waterloo. How different history might have been had either of the two commanders that fateful day in late January 1814 been captured or killed?

Even in death, however, Napoleon never forgot Brienne. He left the town a bequest of 100,000 gold francs, which is how the Hôtel de Ville came to be extravagantly adorned with imperial eagles, a gargantuan relief of the Emperor and the statue of the young Bonaparte in the courtyard. For a time, even the place was called Brienne-Napoléon.

I got back to the hotel for something to eat about 8 p.m. that evening. The Prize Fighter was sweeping up some builders' mess and gave me a begrudging 'oh, he wants his dinner now' look. I was motioned to sit at one of the many empty tables, each decorated with a glass of plastic flowers. The main course was served surprisingly delicately, given the Prize Fighter's hands were like bulldozer grabs. There was a strong smell of putty whenever he was about.

The menu offered one piece of '*fromage du jour*'. The Prize Fighter asked me which cheese I would like.

'Local please', I replied.

He reappeared with a piece of white cheese which, at whatever angle he held the plate, defied gravity's call.

'What cheese is that?' I asked.

'Local.'

'Which local cheese?'

'I dunno, local innit? You asked for local cheese, *this* is the local cheese.' He cut me another portion. 'Yer only meant to have the one slice ya know.'

940 miles to Rome.

9

Clairvaux to Langres

This is the weather the shepherd shuns
And so do I,
When beeches drip in browns and duns,
And thresh, and ply;
And hill-hid tides throb, throe on throe,
And meadow rivulets overflow,
And drops on gate-bars hang in a row,
And rooks in families homeward go ...

Thomas Hardy, *Weathers*, 1922

THAT MORNING, I WAS on my way from Bar-sur-Aube to the Abbey at Clairvaux, a complex of monastic grandeur that is set aside from the world amid thick forest in a valley all of its own. It was founded by Bernard de Clairvaux with land given by Hugh, Comte de Champagne, in 1115. A veteran of three crusades, Hugh joined the Knights Templar in 1124, four years after the Order was founded for the protection of pilgrims in the Holy Land.

Coming down out of the woods, I was confronted by a substantial tiled wall around which ran a large channelled and sluiced stream. Clairvaux, originally a Cistercian monastery, was once an enclosed order. The Cistercians, identifiable by their white robes, were established in the late eleventh century to follow the rule of St Benedict more closely. They were the agricultural and technical pioneers of the Middle Ages. In medieval times, Cistercians were considered highly proficient in the art of animal husbandry, metallurgy and hydraulic engineering. To this day, they remain great horticulturists and brewers.

Bernard, a Burgundian of noble birth, was one of the principal driving forces behind the Order, responsible for its rapid expansion, including the founding in England of Rievaulx Abbey in 1131 and subsequently Fountains Abbey in 1132. He was arguably one of the most influential churchmen of his time, involved in the establishment of the Knights Templar and the promotion across Europe of Pope Innocent II over the antipope, Anacletus II, following the schism caused by the former's irregular election. Finally, and to his eternal regret, at the behest of Pope Eugene III, he preached the Second Crusade.

On 31 March 1146, in a field just outside Vézelay, Bernard whipped the many thousands who had come to hear his sermon into a tumultuous frenzy over the fall of the County of Edessa to Imad ad-Din Zengi, the Atabeg of Mosul, Aleppo and Hama. Edessa was one of the three crusader states established after the First Crusade in northern Syria. The crowd replied to his sermon with cheers and shouts of '*Deus vult! Deus vult!*' or 'God wishes it! God wishes it!' 'Cursed be he who does not stain his sword with blood' was the great monk's response, whereupon the French King, Louis VII prostrated himself at his feet to receive in person material to make the cross for his robes. So great was the demand to receive cloth in the name of the cross that it is said Bernard even had to cut up his own habit.

The Second Crusade was an immense call to arms, and, like the First World War, had the nobility and masses alike clamouring to rally to the cause, which involved armies commanded not only by the King of France but also by Conrad III, the Holy Roman Emperor. This was the first crusade to be led by royalty and, beset by disagreements and differences of ambition and motive, ended ultimately in disaster and defeat, some even referring to it as 'the work of the devil'. Bernard, humiliated and ashamed, sent a formal written apology to Pope Eugene for his part in sowing the seeds of such catastrophe.

Passing right by Clairvaux's front door, I couldn't resist calling in. The monastery had grown immensely powerful by the end of the eighteenth century, owning 37,000 acres of forest, 10,000 acres of farmland as well as mines, forges and significant property in the surrounding towns. Not surprisingly, it was closed down in the French Revolution and sold off for the benefit of the State. Since 1808 it has been a prison but nevertheless, acknowledging its great importance, the authorities have now opened parts of it to the public.

As I walked into the newly restored Visitors' Centre, I met a girl on her way out, who looked at me quizzically. 'What do you want?'

Returning the look, I replied, not unreasonably, that I wanted to see the Abbey.

'You can't', she replied with some glee, 'we are closed for lunch. Come back at 2 o'clock.' Sometimes, it is easy to forget you are in France.

The village of Clairvaux, built on a crossroads and supporting, in the main, the prison warder population and the odd family visiting inmates, isn't the most inspiring of places these days. It has the deserted feel of a Wild West town that has seen better times. I lunched in the Hôtel de l'Abbaye, complete with wagon wheels at the front that merely underlined my Western convictions.

Bang on time, I presented myself back at the ticket office where the same girl now stood her ground behind an enormous counter.

'Yes, how can I help you?' Having only met her an hour earlier and wearing a broad-brimmed hat, carrying a rucksack and large stick as I was, I could hardly be accused of blending into the crowd, had there been one readily to hand.

'I'd like to see the Abbey please.'

'You are how many?'

I looked about me to see if anyone else, whom I hadn't noticed, perhaps had sneaked into the room. But there was no one.

'Just the one', I replied.

'*Non*', she beamed with a finality and degree of, dare I add, satisfaction, 'it is not possible.' She looked me up and down with disdain. 'There are not enough of you', she continued, 'maybe try again at 3.30.'

I politely explained, I really did, that as I had another six miles to walk that day, I didn't have the time to hang about on the off chance of a busload of Japanese tourists suddenly breezing up. She refused to be swayed.

So, the mysteries of St Bernard's magnificent Abbey with its pillared cloisters and elegant refectories remain to me forbidden, forsaken and closed-off. The main entrance, with a broken lamp that hung from its fitting limp with shame, was now no more than a rusting grey gate that buzzed in annoyance when opened. It was watched over by a decaying clock tower with spewed roof tiles around it and a pair of French and European flags that twisted themselves in embarrassment around tatty plastic flagpoles. I needn't have rushed my lunch.

Returning to my rucksack at the Hôtel de l'Abbaye, so began the first of a sequence of events over the coming weeks that initially I put down to coincidence and good fortune. However, as the incidents began to occur with greater frequency, so I became increasingly of the opinion that, even though I may have been physically on my own, I was certainly not travelling alone.

Billowing clouds that spread an eerie darkness across the sky had replaced the sun and a chill wind blew at my back as I returned to the Hôtel de l'Abbaye. No sooner had I reached the door than a squall tore down the main road chased by a volume of rain dispensed with a ferocity that I had not seen since travelling in Latin America. Both the road and the car park disappeared under water, the street lights came on and the hotel, a homage to neon lettering and pea lights, lit up like the Starship Enterprise. Soon it was impossible to see to the other side of the road. I watched as cars and lorries struggled in vain and then, coming to their senses, pulled off the road.

Just as the hotel lights flickered for the first time, a couple from Somerset ran in. 'The road has been closed up ahead; it's chaos out there. The Police have turned us back, is there any chance of a bed for the night?' It was evident that the weather was setting in. It started to hail. The lights flickered again.

'We have one room left', Madame replied. They took it. I then asked the same. 'Oh *désolé* M'sieur, but we are full', she replied.

'Not to worry', I replied, 'it's not that far to Ville-sous-la-Ferté, I have a reservation there in the Hôtel de l'Abbaye'.

'Non, M'sieur, this is l'Hôtel de l'Abbaye'.

'I know it is', I shouted above the din on the roof, 'but my reservation is in the next village.'

She demanded my name, ran a finger down her register and smiled, '*voilà*, you do not have to get wet' and, grabbing a key, took me to my room. By dinner, the storm had blown out.

There was not a cloud in the sky, the air fresh with a hint of wood smoke on the breeze.

*

The beech woods were already busy that early June morning. Foresters were readying themselves to cut and thin while in and about the tree line I could see the occasional hunched figure carrying a basket foraging in the undergrowth. But as I ventured ever deeper into the heart of the vast Forêt d'Arc-Châteauvillain so a profound sense of timeless mysticism came over me; far removed from man, it was as if I was being invited to enter a private and altogether different world from the everyday – as at one with nature as perhaps could ever be imagined.

Every now and again, I would stop, hunker down on my haunches, and rest on my stick. These were privileged moments when I would just watch and listen as the woods reverberated all around me in continuous melody; the wind caught in the trees, the sun danced on leaves and all about wood pigeon, jay and pheasant called.

And then, up the ride, something suddenly caught my eye. I stopped, swallowed, head half-cocked and mouth ajar, to sharpen my hearing and waited. There it was again. One, then two, then three, out they tumbled onto the track – fighting, biting, grabbing and screaming, it was hard to tell who was who, where was front, where was back as a brown ball of ragging fox cubs spilled out not 20 yards in front of me. Their joy was tangible as they played, oblivious to my presence, but somewhere nearby, perhaps in the bracken, their old vixen mother had one eye on them, I was quite sure.

In an instant, they stopped, alert – one more so than the others. For a moment, he sniffed the air, looked me straight in the eye, held my gaze for a second and, sensing all was well, turned on his heels and plunged sharp young teeth into his brothers and sisters who returned the gesture with added gusto. For a while they just lay in the sun, gently gnawing a leg or a dangling paw; to interrupt seemed criminal but Rome called and all that. I stood up, took a swig from my water bottle and the cubs scarpered.

It was not long after, however, that I became aware of the presence. I couldn't put my finger on it at first; nothing threatening, just a feeling, a hunch. But for sure, I was not alone. I marked him as he crossed the track not a hundred yards ahead, a dark silhouette that unmistakably ran across my path – this was no mere shadow. I marked the point and made a mental note that, when I reached the spot, I would look to my left and seek him out to ask what he was searching for.

And yet when I reached the place on the track, there was no one. Not a sign, not a whisper. Whoever or whatever it was, a woodwose, a sprite, dryad, maybe a faun or perhaps even Pan himself, had disappeared and was nowhere to be seen – yet it wanted me to know that it was there. Unequivocally. Why else would it have passed so blatantly in front of me? And its presence was all about. I could feel it. I stopped. Puzzled, I looked about. I had without any doubt seen someone cross up ahead. A shiver ran down my spine, the whole of my right side tingled, prickling the hair on my legs and arms, but I wasn't meant to linger, that much I also knew. It was not that I was unwelcome; whatever it was was neither sinister nor dangerous – far from it – but I was, quite definitely, to carry on my way. It was as if someone, or something, was watching over me.

*

I had come about 540 miles or so by the time I reached the hilltop town of Langres. Cresting the ridge is special, as the town sits on a fortified promontory that lords it a good 1,000 feet over the French countryside. The enormous crenellated bastions and walls give the place a great sense of foreboding; they accentuate the drama when taking in the panorama from the windswept ramparts. I couldn't help think of sentries standing guard on freezing battlements in midwinter, scanning the horizon in readiness for some potential foe bent on incursion.

At the heart of the fortifications lies the cathedral. A curious hybrid building, it has an eighteenth-century façade that masks a twelfth-century nave and choir. Tucked away in the corner of a tree-shaded square, you can never fully appreciate its size or readily notice that, in the Burgundian tradition, it has a tiled roof that shimmers like psychedelic snakeskin, a maze of greens, browns, mauves, yellows and reds laid in neat diamond-like patterns.

The cathedral is dedicated to St Mammes of Caesarea, a child-martyr, who in his day was something of a cult figure. He is honoured in Lebanon, Cyprus and Greece as Agios Mamas, Italy as San Mamete and Spain, San Mamés. Orthodox icons of Mammes depict the young saint riding an impressive-looking lion while holding a lamb across its withers. His legend is confusing, as some claim he was a hermit who lived in a cave on Cyprus, while the consensus would appear to believe that the boy lived in Caesarea, now Kayseri in modern-day Cappadocia in Turkey.

Mammes was born in captivity during the third century to Christians who were subsequently martyred for their faith. As a teenager, he too was tortured for his beliefs, first by the Governor of Caesarea and then by the Emperor, Marcus Aurelius, who threw him in jail where, legend has it, angels helped him to escape.

Captured on his return to Caesarea, the youth was thrown to the lions. Miraculously, he managed to tame the beasts and evidently was able to walk away from the ordeal, unharmed and with a lion in tow. On the assumption that this occurred in public at an amphitheatre, it must have been a dramatic spectacle indeed.

Refusing to relinquish his Christianity, it appears Mammes then presented himself to a senior ranking official, Alexander, bringing the lion with him. The boy was immediately put to death by a trident thrust to the stomach. He was only 15. History overlooks the fate of the lion.

The cathedral holds pieces of the saint's neck, arm and skull, acquired in the eighth, eleventh and thirteenth centuries, after the dastardly Fourth Crusade that laid waste to Constantinople. In the Middle Ages, claim to such acquisitions would have created quite a stir among the devout, such was the fervour to see genuine holy relics. The only problem is that Mammes, however, appears to have two heads – the other is the property of the Church of Santa Maria Magdalena in Saragossa, where he is the patron saint of hernia sufferers.

After nine days on the go, I arrived in Langres to rest. With a day in hand, the town offered a chance to pause before taking up the road to Besançon, the Jura Mountains and the Swiss border.

In the street later that afternoon, I met Uli, a walker in his 50s from Bochum in Germany, who was on his way to Dijon, although I never got to learn quite why Dijon in particular. His approach was practical as he sought 'the 2,000 calories his body needed' to replenish after the day's exertions. I, on the other hand, was in search of something a little more atmospheric: a nice restaurant, a succulent steak, a good bottle of wine, some cheese and a restoring glass of brandy – it was, after all, a rest day and a break from the privations of the road.

I was just wondering how to reconcile our differing needs when coincidence intervened once again. 'I don't bloody believe it! 'Arry Bucknall? Is that you?'

It was an unmistakable voice and moreover one I had not heard in a good 25 years. Jason Cooke and Garry Burns had both served as Guardsmen in my platoon when we were stationed in Hong Kong in the 1980s. They were unchanged and instantly recognizable, except maybe a little rounder in the waist and fuller in the face. There was a great sense of kinsmanship about the unexpected reunion. This time, however, we met as friends rather than the more formal relationship that had been required of old. With me on the way to Rome and with them riding motorbikes back to England, what, we marvelled, were the chances of our paths crossing in as random a place as Langres? The invisible codes of trust and loyalty that exist between soldiers, no matter the rank, were instantly rekindled. It was as if we had picked up where we left off all those years before.

Uli at this point politely muttered something about 2,000 calories and made his apologies. True to the lore of soldiery, we never managed to reach a restaurant that night.

Leaving Garry and Jason to autoroutes, ferries and motorways, the following morning I set out in search of some culture in the museum – an improving excursion to see an exhibition celebrating work that the talented Fauvist artist Raoul Dufy had painted in the fields around Langres over three summers in the 1930s. As I gazed at the boldly coloured pictures brimming with life and statement, I could not help musing how Jason and Garry would make it home to England in five hours – the same amount of time it had taken me to get this far in as many weeks. I suddenly felt very insignificant. In the grand scheme of things, Rome was still a very long way off indeed.

868 miles to Rome.

10

Champlitte to Besançon

Henceforth I ask not good-fortune, I myself am good-fortune,
Henceforth I whimper no more, postpone no more, need
nothing,
Done with indoor complaints, libraries, querulous criticisms,
Strong and content, I travel the open road.
Walt Whitman, *Song of the Open Road*, 1856

THE DAYS WOULD RARELY pass without someone or other waving, flashing their lights or sounding their horn as they drove by. I would return the gesture with a flourish of my stick high in the air, my spirits soaring in the brief moment of acknowledgement.

But one occasion stood out in particular, not long after I had made my way down from the battlements at Langres. It was pouring with rain. Crossing a junction, I grew suddenly aware of a beaten-up car approaching from behind on the wrong side of the road – it had once been shiny red but now the sheen had been replaced by a matt undercoat look that was more dusky orange in appearance. As I glanced over my shoulder, something convinced me the vehicle was in its death throes and I was about to be coerced into resuscitating it, an operation that would inevitably involve a deal of pushing.

I noticed the jalopy draw closer. The passenger door swung open, and before the heap had stuttered to a halt a young man jumped out and ran towards me.

Philippe was beautiful; dressed in a coat of flowing brown linen, he must have been all of 25. Dark-featured with piercing brown eyes, he had thick black hair that was drawn into a pigtail. To complete the romantic ideal, he sported a fashioned moustache and goatee that made him perfect for the pages of an Alexandre Dumas novel. In his outstretched hand, he held a packet of biscuits.

'*Ici, pour vous pèlerin...*' He insisted I accept the meagre offering, apologizing that it was all he had. Maria, his girlfriend, Thisbe to his Pyramus if ever, joined us and took his arm as if to underscore ownership. Philippe, it soon transpired, had walked to Santiago de Compostela three years earlier and together the couple urged me to jump in their car and take refuge from the weather at their home near Pressigny. 'It is not much; we have wine, we have food. You will have to sleep on the floor but it is warm and dry and it would be an honour to make you our guest.'

I consulted my map – Pressigny was way to the east and well off my track. I thought, looking again at the tiny packet of biscuits in my hand, which at any other time would have been of no consequence but at that moment meant so much. And then Philippe asked: 'Why are you going to Rome?'

The question hit me like a boxer's jab. For a split second, I faltered. Caught off guard, my response was murmured and without recourse to thought.

'I want to put some meaning back into my life.'

No sooner had I shut my mouth than, shocked by my own frank revelation, I knew I had to bring our meeting to a swift conclusion. Until then, my journey was still the romantic jape I had always conceived it to be. No longer. In that swift reply, it had, I realized, taken on a greater import than ever I had intended or could have imagined.

It was as if I now acknowledged that the sum of my time on earth so far was nothing more than a carefully constructed veneer, which, standing for little, risked at any moment crashing to the ground. In Philippe and Maria's company I felt vulnerable, laid bare. I now understood that somewhere I had sacrificed the greater values and long-term rewards of life for the hedonistic, tangible pleasures of the everyday – family and friends thrown aside in the selfish pursuit of the immediate. I felt a fool, shocked at my admission to a pair so young, so trusting and so possessed of moral value.

Panicked, I sought the comfort of the road; I needed to be alone where I could trouble no one – except myself.

Looking the couple in the eye, I abruptly terminated the conversation and thanked them for their kindness. We embraced fondly and I took my leave. I think they understood. Moments later, the little red car shook past with horn blaring and hands waving out of the window. I watched it round the corner, ran into a layby, threw my rucksack off and, seeking refuge behind a mound of gravel, buried my head in my hands. It was no longer just a walk. How naïve I had been ever to think such.

*

Stopping at a crossroads to check my map, I suddenly heard someone singing loudly, 'Bop-bop-bop, bop-bop-bop-PAAARP!'

Over the rise, there appeared a battered umbrella, whose forward spoke was broken such that, with a flap hanging down, seeing out must have been nigh on impossible. The umbrella was moving at some speed. The bop-bop-bopping continued until the silhouette of another pilgrim gradually appeared. With close-cropped grey hair and beard, he was lean and lithe, carrying an enormous rucksack with a silver rain cover on it, making the thing look more at home on the moon than in eastern France. In his hand was a stick, which was held horizontally amidships and swung back and forth as he went, giving him a distinct air of purpose, while about his neck hung a canvas hat on a loop of string. '*Hi ho! Vous allez où mon ami?*' the man cried in a foreign accent, his voice a deep bass.

Mario, who looked far younger than his 67 years, was from Bergamo in north-eastern Italy. I was the first pilgrim he had met since leaving Canterbury and, in the same breath, he told me that day was his youngest granddaughter's second birthday.

The retired geologist's manner of pilgrimage, having walked to most shrines in Europe and beyond, was far more demanding than my own method of peregrination. Walking by day, he would only seek a bed on arrival at his destination that night and, if that proved unsuccessful, he would ask in the street or carry on until such time as he found somewhere to sleep. In comparison to my more scheduled approach, his was a progress of 'maybes', never knowing more than one day ahead at best where he might finish – journey's end being his only constant. This time he would only be going as far as Vercelli. 'I have walked from there to Rome already, so no point going again.'

We crossed from Haute Marne into the Haute Saône; the wheat in the fields turned from green to a gentle yellow, the buildings grew yet again more solid with firewood piled high outside them in readiness for winter, and the church steeples changed from drab slate to ornate 'dôme comtois' bell shapes with pretty patterns in the tiling. There was a distinct feeling that we were beginning a steady climb; the plains of the last ten days were behind us.

The grey cold of day seemed inconsequential while walking with Mario; behind the rather gruff exterior, he was a gentle and caring man who found beauty everywhere he looked regardless of whether it was people, the countryside, local architecture or, his favourite, churches and chapels. Everything about his person had a story to tell, which he would always begin in the same endearing manner. 'My stick, yes, well, oh by the way, my stick I cut down in a wood outside Bolsena while walking to Rome for the first time. It has been everywhere with me since, Santiago, Jerusalem, across France. Very useful you know for fighting off dogs, especially in Turkey and Syria – they train the dogs to attack you there, you know; also for hanging up washing and holding up electric fences. This is my very dear old friend', he added, stroking it with affection like a much-loved cat.

Puzzled, I asked him what was the significance of walking across France. 'Well, by the way, very early one morning I was walking from Lourdes to Rome, I think for the second time – to Rome that is – and I was in the middle of a large forest. There was a thick fog, it was cold and I became lost and ... frightened. All of a sudden, there was someone beside me ... breathing ... his feet, you know ...' He glanced across, suspecting, I suppose, that I might not believe him. Spotting my interest, he carried on: '... but there was no one there. I was alone and yet, I wasn't alone; I no longer felt frightened. There was definitely someone with me, you know, how do you say it?' He looked at me, stumbling for the word.

'Guardian angel?'

'Exactly.'

'And, by the way, he is always there. That's why you see me ask everyone all the time, because my guardian angel always provides – when I don't know where I am, how to get somewhere or need a place to sleep, he always puts someone out for me. So, as St Michael is in charge of the Angels, I walked from San Michele near my home town to Mont St Michel in France to give thanks to him for that morning in the wood.'

A shiver ran down my spine; my mind raced back to the shadow that crossed my path in the forest after Châteauvillain a few days earlier. Was it possible that St Spyridon of Corfu, who I am convinced has guarded over me ever since I nearly lost my life on a cliff in the Greek Islands, was with me on this journey too? I was beginning to wonder.

'Another dead French town', Mario commented as we arrived in Champlitte and he headed off to find a bed, 'what is it with this country? Where is everyone? Uh-oh...three people, here comes a crowd!' We agreed to meet for dinner at 7 p.m.

In the restaurant that evening, Mario was disconcerted. He had lost his hat. 'I bought it when I arrived in Jerusalem', he added. Without hesitation, I offered him mine; I couldn't bear the thought of my friend for the day – matters not that I would probably never see him again – walking in the sun without protection for his head. I had two, after all, and the broad-brimmed one was too big for me but, spookily, fitted Mario as if it had been made for him.

We talked of the next day; Mario was off to Gy, 'probably', which was about as firm as he made plans. I, on the other hand, needed to get new boots; mine had given up the fight and, unlike St Aderald, the tenth-century Archdeacon of Troyes, I didn't fancy crossing the Alps barefoot or even on soles of foam, which is what I had been walking on for the last few days. We parted warmly and, as I went to leave, Mario said: 'Oh, by the way, when you cross the river Po, say hello to Danilo the Ferryman for me. He is a very good person, just tell him Mario the Bergamesco is your friend and you will get along fine!'

As I walked back to my lodgings, I couldn't help wondering if Mario's guardian angel had not had a hand in the day so that I would be there to replace his hat; and, perhaps, I thought, my guardian angel had found Mario as a companion for me too. I was the better for his company.

*

'Do you know what Clemenceau called English?' the old hunchback man in a suit said, as he squinted up at me over his glasses. With the headache I had that morning I was neither in the mood for petty games nor the bickering rivalries of nations. I could hardly stand, let alone see. It was my own fault; crossing the mighty Saône a couple of days earlier, seeing a road sign to Lausanne, the dark undeniable smudge of the Jura Mountains rising up before me and then reaching Besançon, which was teeming with life, I had arrived the afternoon before full of anticipation.

To my joy, as I jostled and barged my rucksacked way through the crowds of shoppers, I had found an Irish pub.

The trouble about the good black stuff – some clever ingredient in Arthur Guinness's secret mixture, no doubt – is that you can never have just the one pint. True to form and being weak of character in this respect, I did not partake of 'just the one'. At some point during the evening my diary entry became increasingly confused and my memory hazy. I recalled the shock of stumbling into the lavatory and being presented with nothing other than a deep hole with two bricks to stand on. When the chain was pulled, it washed my boots at the same time. After that the night was one big blank, save a sore throat, an inexplicable bruise on my forearm and an empty wallet.

I leered back at the old man in response to the Clemenceau quip; in the circumstances, it was the best I could offer to indicate that I didn't know the answer. 'French, badly pronounced', he gleamed at me in small victory. Everybody else in the cramped room, mostly Japanese, collapsed in hysterics. I leered again.

We were in the clock room of Saint-Jean Cathedral and the aged Clock Keeper was getting flustered as, like an ineffective prep school master, he tried to restore order to the unruly mass of oriental amateur photographers assembled around him. He had less than ten minutes to explain the complex machinery in front of us before the hour, when the majority of its 30,000 working parts would spring to life and unleash a short sprint of mechanical mayhem as they readied bells for tolling across the city.

Astronomical clocks are nothing new. The Ancient Greeks had in all probability been using them long before the

Antikythera Mechanism, which was dated to 100–150BC. The Arabs navigated by astrolabe, and elaborate timepieces such as the Prague Orloj or the Wells Cathedral Clock have been in common existence since the fourteenth century to inform the townsfolk of the time by both bell and clock face mounted high on a tower for all to see. Astronomical clocks also showed the phases of the moon, day, date and even planetary activity.

The curious fact about Besançon's clock, however, is that it was commissioned in the mid-nineteenth century long after the instruments were obsolete. Furthermore, its many fascinating dials, which I was struggling to make head or tail of, are not mounted high on some pedestal for everyone to observe but hidden away in an obscure back room at the top of some nondescript stairs – almost as if Cardinal Mathieu, when he commissioned Auguste Vérité to create the apparatus, wanted it all to himself.

Nonetheless, the clock is a magnificent masterpiece. It is mounted on a cast iron frame that looks like an oversize gilded and pillared dresser, 18-feet high with 60 beautifully enamelled and golden dials variously lodged about it. The highest is a clock, the lowest an orrery, while the rest in between and on the sides include church and civic calendars, the year, month, day, hour, minute and second, planets according to date and season, the sign of the Zodiac and the equation of time which is, as we all know, the difference between apparent solar time and mean solar time. As if that were not enough, the hour in the 'great cities of the world' was also displayed, with the notable exception of London, plus the eclipses of sun and moon in the year and leap years and leap centuries, the latter only moving for the first time in AD2000 and which won't move again until AD2400. You may now appreciate why trying to get to grips with the clock first thing in the morning after a difficult night was not perhaps the wisest activity to embark upon.

The Keeper, who had just about explained all this in the short time given, drew his explanation to a theatrical close just as clutch plates clunked into life, cables wound, fly wheels whirred, pulleys whizzed, two flags fluttered and cogs ratcheted away while two apostles struck the hour, assisted by the Archangels Michael and Gabriel and the three virtues,

Faith, Hope and Charity. It being before midday, the resurrection wasn't played out, as it is every 12 noon, nor did we see Christ returned to his tomb at 3 p.m. To complete this magical masterpiece of engineering bewilderment, the Virgin Mary, as Queen of the World complete with sceptre, presided at the very top.

The Japanese, confronted by this frenzied mechanical circus let loose, couldn't contain themselves. Their joy was palpable as tiny ships bobbed up and down on metal wavelets and various members of the Heavenly Host ducked and weaved in front of their eyes. Their cameras flashed away, while I tried to find a chair and look as discerning as possible given that I now felt very delicate indeed.

Besançon overlooks a meander of the sweeping Doubs river. Mont St Etienne, standing guard over the approaches, is its dramatic and commanding sentinel.

Charles V, Holy Roman Emperor in the sixteenth century, dubbed the once-autonomous Archbishopric and Imperial Free City 'the shield of his vast empire' as it butted up against France. The ruler, who had inherited the Habsburg Empire, the Burgundian Netherlands and the Crowns of Castile and Aragon, was not only *de facto* the first King of Spain but also held authority over vast tracts of Europe, the Americas and Asia – or, to put it more simply, the larger part of the known world at the time. His titles from Empires to Kingdoms, Dukedoms and Earldoms, including my favourite, Lord of the Islands and Main Ocean Sea, were of such multitude that they ran to ten lines when printed on paper. He was an immensely powerful man who spent much of his life fighting the French in one way or another. It is believed he was instrumental in blocking Henry VIII's attempts to seek a divorce from Catherine of Aragon who was his aunt; Pope Clement VII, following the sack of Rome in 1527, was the Emperor's prisoner.

In old age, Charles abdicated, passing the Habsburg Empire to his brother, Ferdinand, and the Spanish territories to his son, Philip – of Armada fame. Besançon remained under Spain until 1678 when Louis XIV finally wrested the city from the clutches of the Habsburgs to whom it had effectively belonged for over 650 years.

The commander responsible for this success was Sébastien de Vauban, Marshal of France, a military engineer, expert in the art of defensive construction and offensive destruction. He personally led over 45 sieges. A master of fortified design, at the age of 34 he was put in charge of France's defences, travelling the length and breadth of the country. He drew its territorial limits and set about strengthening the fortifications, no matter whether they be on sea or land. It was said at the time: 'A city fortified by Vauban is an impregnable city; a city besieged by Vauban is a conquered city.'

In wig, silver cuirasses, white silken sash about his waist, full-length blue frock coat with gold lace facings and deep scarlet cuffs, spurred and booted with a sword at his side and marshal's baton in his hand, Vauban was impressive to behold. His lasting legacy bears testament to him, running to 160 fortresses across France, of which 12 are World Heritage Sites.

The Marshal's great skill was to incorporate the ground in his design, using it to further defensive advantage. Since the fifteenth century, artillery had evolved such that high walls were as good as useless. So he developed the concept of multiple bastions. These were low, densely packed walled constructions of pentagonal shape that mutually supported one another – each design individually tailored to complement the lie of the land. From the Ile de Ré in the west, St Vaast in the north, Briançon in the Alps and Villefranche in the Pyrenees, Vauban constructed great star-shaped fortresses of enormous strength and military might but, of them all, Besançon was his finest.

In 1678, he wrote to Louvois, the Secretary of State for War: '... make of Besançon ever after one of the finest strongholds in Europe, on which the King may depend, more than any other in his kingdom'. The cost of construction was so great that at one point the minister asked if the citadel was being built of gold. Every worker in the city was requisitioned for the task as parapeted, curtained and covered walls were built to a thickness of up to 20 feet, networks of underground passageways were excavated, yawning ditches were dug and towering ramparts, casemates and demi-lunes thrown up to enable artillery fire from multiple levels. As late as 1814, the Austrians failed to breach the defences.

The Citadel is a very different place now that Europe is at peace. I toiled my way up the hill passing under the Front St Etienne to parkland where families picnicked on the grass. Crossing the bridge over the moat at the Front Royal, I noticed movement in the undergrowth in the depths beneath. Was it a dog? Or perhaps a man? Holding my hand up against the sun, I squinted to see better. It was a family of baboons.

As I progressed further into the Citadel itself so I became aware of tigers, kangaroos, monkeys and goats all about the place. All too quickly, however, it also became apparent that dark secrets, which pointed to a not-so-glorious past, lay within this oasis of calm far from the city below. Just past the well, four stakes stood dignified and alone on a gravelled square, a *Tricolor* hung from a flagpole like a sentry with head bowed in mourning.

On that spot, between 1941 and 1944, 84 men of the French Resistance, along with 16 of their Dutch, Italian, Swiss, Luxemburg, Spanish and Polish comrades, were shot by Nazi firing squads in the fight for freedom. Besançon had been part of Nazi Occupied France in the Second World War.

Further on, a stick-like blackened statue held out its arms in plea, the names 'Auschwitz, Stutthof, Mauthausen, Flossenburg, Ravensbruck, Struthof, Buchenwald, Sachsenhausen, Neuengamme, Gross-Rosen, Dachau and Bergen-Belsen' nailed in bronze lettering on the stone wall behind – a stark memorial to the 76,000 French Jews and other 'undesirables' who never returned from the concentration camps to which the Nazis and Vichy authorities forcibly deported them.

789 miles to Rome.

11

Ornans and the Loue Valley to the Swiss border

Then travelled onward and down behind
The pine-clad heights of Jura, lighting up
The woodman's casement, and perchance his axe
Borne homeward through the forest in his hand;
And on the edge of some o'erhanging cliff,
That dungeon-fortress never to be named,
Where, like a lion taken in the toils,
Toussaint breathed out his brave and generous spirit.
                    Samuel Rogers, *The Lake of Geneva*, 1823

NO SOONER HAD I crossed the ridge into La Vèze, after a steep haul into the hills the far side of Besançon, than the cows wore bells about their necks, hanging from sturdy embossed collars. Their gentle tune was now the music of my day. It was a joyful sound that made the spirit soar like the Jura Mountains around me as I walked down lanes flanked by verdant pastures that brimmed with summer flowers, past barns stacked high with straw bales and through woods of cooling fir. This ancient and impressive countryside was the new backcloth to my journey as nature fused landscape and river in a seamless union, the Loue speeding its way over rock and pool while naked phalanxes of pine-topped limestone hovered precipitously above.

'*Bonjour!*' I shouted as the girl careered past me ever so slightly out of control.

'*Vous allez où?!*' I cried after her.

'I do not speak French', she barked back, at which she slewed to a halt at the side of the road. I ran over. Kneeling down by her wheelchair, I asked if she too was off to Rome. 'Yes, but not tonight', she replied, and thus I met Sylviane, a 30 something paraplegic from Linz in Austria who had lost the use of her legs falling down some stairs many years earlier. This was her first time on the Via Francigena, but, she was quick to add, she had already been to Santiago four times.

I looked admiringly at the rig that transformed her chair into a tricycle; festooned with paniers and grab-bags, it had that utilitarian feel of a military scout-car about it, the contraption driven uphill by a front wheel chain powered by handles and controlled downhill by braking with gloves.

'I have got through two pairs of mitts already', she remarked.

We sat together on the roadside, me feeding her wild strawberries picked from the verge as we took a break, laughing and joking in the sun. Sylviane's was a different journey once again; car atlases were the cornerstone of her adventure, a thin luminous line drawn in felt tip marking the way.

Our time together was a moment stolen from the road, a chance to savour that magical kinship that exists between pilgrims when they meet, forging in a short matter of minutes an intense allegiance never to be broken. These occasions, so filled with joy, almost seemed to celebrate the unifying bonds of hardship shared and isolation endured, the two pillars that most distinguish pilgrimage as an undertaking so wholly different from the everyday.

Like me, Sylviane was dropping down into the town of Ornans for the night, where nuns would look after her. Such is the kindness of people on the route that despite the Herculean challenge she would face in the weeks ahead, there would be plenty of volunteers on hand to ensure her continued progression. Of that, I was confident; and yet, despite this, I worried about her in the days to come. The Alps would ask a question of Sylviane.

'How will you manage in the mountains?' I asked.

'It's the same for you as it is for me, you know. And don't forget, you have to walk!' she chided.

Sylviane, who never stopped smiling, planned to reach St Peter's by early August, after which, she declared, she thought she might take a train north and pick up the trail to Compostela once again. For me, I responded, it was an aeroplane to Athens and a slow boat to the Cyclades.

'Is it downhill all the way to Ornans?' she asked, her map void of detail.

I replied that it was and, looking back at me with a broad grin, she turned her wheel into the road. As she did, I told her she needed a flag so lorries could see the wheelchair properly.

'God is my flag', she said, pointing to a crucifix that swung from her handlebars, and smiled again. I watched as she picked up speed until, rounding the bend in the road, she was gone. I never saw her again.

Ornans is a delight, full of tumbling geraniums, pansies, daisies and ducks. In fact, there are ducks everywhere – waddling down the streets, sunning on the walls, promenading around the squares and on the march down the riverbanks. Clinging to the sides of the river Loue, the town was duck heaven.

For a moment, however, we will swap the peace of the countryside for Paris where the mood is tense and charged with anger. It is the afternoon of 15 May 1871. We are among a large crowd being sucked, like debris in a vortex, inexorably towards the Place Vendôme. Vengeance hangs putrid on the air. We are caught unwittingly in one of the most notable incidents in the short-lived history of the Paris Commune, the elected council that broke away from the French government when the latter fled for safety to Bordeaux as the Prussian Army advanced ever further into France. The barricades were going up round Paris once again.

The Garde Nationale, who deserted *en masse* in favour of the movement, marshal the swirling throng to the edges of the square, the middle roped off. The people around us, jostling and chattering excitedly, are staring and pointing up at the great Vendôme Column, fashioned from cannon captured in December 1805 at the Battle of Austerlitz, Napoleon's finest victory.

That column, a metaphor for French might and military prowess, was now demonized as 'a symbol of brute force and false glory'. The myth shattered by the fiasco of the Franco-Prussian War whose nadir, the humiliation at Sedan, saw the capture of Emperor Napoleon III himself.

Gustave Courbet, the artist and leader of the Realist movement, suggested the creation be dismantled and moved to the Hôtel des Invalides, Paris's military heart. The Commune, however, disregarded his suggestion, voting instead some months later to tear down the column and be rid of it all together.

Imagine the sound, like a football stadium in full chant, when the tumult erupts into a spontaneous rendition of *La Marseillaise*. As the rousing chorus of '*Aux armes citoyens*' roars around the buildings, so the signal is given for the capstans to turn. Ropes and guys take up slack and tighten, the structure's brass plates begin to groan and buckle, rivets pop and the monument begins to totter and crumble until, with a loud crash, it smashes to the ground in clouds of ricocheting rubble and dust. The singing is abruptly replaced by a deafening cheer as the head of Napoleon's statue bounces over the paving stones like an apple tossed from a bough. The red flag is swiftly planted on the empty pedestal.

In but a matter of days, the Commune would be overthrown by the Versaillaise, as the government was known, in an horrific orgy of carnage and violence that culminated in *La Semaine Sanglante*, the Bloody Week, when the Seine ran red with blood as tens of thousands were killed and executed, many identified from photographs taken that fateful spring day. Equal numbers were jailed or deported. Courbet, who was elected to the Commune after the event and did not participate in the vote to destroy the column, was fined 500 francs and spent six months in prison for 'his part'.

The artist, one of the greatest of his time, came from Ornans. His childhood home is now a museum, the building enshrined in a large steel and glass casing that is reminiscent of a giant kitchen garden cloche.

I took to Courbet. A revolutionary to the core, he was the power behind the Realist movement. His work had a profound influence on the Impressionists. Enamoured of controversy and debate, an evening with the artist by your side would surely be a most lively affair. His enormous tableaux are full of detail and emotion and, like Rembrandt's work, social statements of their time.

My favourite painting of his, however, is the intimate *Pirate Prisoner of the Bey of Algiers*, a small work that depicts an old buccaneer in captivity, his face thick with beard, half-naked and filthy. He is lost to thought as he ponders his destiny and, imbued with a raw muscular quality, the once-proud mariner is now broken in his confinement. The picture reminded me of a detail in Delacroix's 1824 *Massacre at Chios*, that commanding picture which played so pivotal a role in garnering international support for the cause of Greek independence decades earlier.

It would take just two years before the authorities elected to rebuild the Vendôme Column and, in May 1877, the 323,091 francs and 68 centimes bill for its restoration was laid firmly at the feet of Courbet. The painter, forewarned, had fled over the Swiss border four years earlier. In his absence, it was decreed that he could repay 10,000 francs every year until his 91st birthday. He died the day before the first payment was due.

Leaving the museum, I noticed there was some sort of commotion in the town as I crossed back over the bridge. A small crowd had assembled around the War Memorial. There was, however, a sense of occasion and import about the gathering, as I spotted the unmistakable glint of gold fringing on military colours bobbing about and the silver helmets of the Sapeurs Pompiers. A car drew up carrying the local police officer in full uniform, followed by a van of Gendarmes in képi and tunic, while veterans from across the years looked on in assortments of Sunday best, all sporting their medals.

The Mayor, sashed in the colours of his country, called everyone to order as the National Anthem was played. The speakers crackled and the unmistakable voice of Charles de Gaulle, statesmanlike, measured and calm, rang out across the little square. In silence we listened as he declared in robust tones that, '*Quoi qu'il arrive, la flamme de la résistance française ne doit pas s'éteindre et ne s'éteindra pas*' (Whatever happens, the flame of the French Resistance must not and will not go out). It was the anniversary of *L'Appel du 18 Juin*, marking that fateful day in 1940 when Britain and France stood alone against Nazi Germany, one of the darkest hours of our shared history; two days earlier, France had been forced to capitulate against overwhelming odds. On de Gaulle's arrival in London, Churchill laid the resources of the BBC at the leader's disposal to broadcast a call to arms to the Free French and so begin the long struggle for freedom. How paradoxical that across the Channel it was Waterloo Day.

*

It was raining heavily when I left Mouthier, perhaps, with the benefit of hindsight, not the wisest moment to set out. I dropped down into the valley to begin the climb to the source of the River Loue. Amid the greenery of the forest, the moss-draped boulders and ubiquitous waterfalls, it was like being back in the jungles of Borneo as I felt my way along sinewy paths that clung precariously to the mountainside. Stern-faced chamois looked down from the heights.

Crrrack! Something high above broke free. I could tell by the urgent and unforgiving nature of its descent that it was not small. I froze. Like being caught in artillery fire, it was impossible to tell where the rockfall that was bursting its way downhill at increasing speed would come to rest. Instinct kicked in. I ducked under a dripping overhang. *Thud – fly – thud – fly* – until suddenly a boulder the size of a small fridge pirouetted through the air with surprising grace right before my eyes and struck the trunk of a tree with some force, before lodging itself like a demented beetle in the ground not three feet away from me with a spectacular *thlumph.* Its resting place was almost the exact point that I would have been standing.

In Pontarlier, with its impressive sandstone arch mounted with clock and bell like the formal gateway to the mountains, my German hotelier demanded cash up front. 'People come and go so easily here', he smiled as he folded the cash neatly into his pocket. With a darkened disco at one end and some particularly dubious types staring me out from the bar at the other end, I felt that if I gave the correct knowing look, I could have probably rented my room by the hour.

That evening, I ate a celebratory last dinner in France, consisting of a large plate of *cassoulet* followed by an even larger bowl of *îles flottantes,* which is essentially caramelized shaving foam swimming in custard. Loaded with sugar, the dish is a sin but quite delicious and, for me, about as near heaven on Earth as can be imagined.

My overriding memory of the town, however, was that it had an excellent bookshop where I discovered the work of Pierre

Loti, the French Naval officer and writer. Born in 1850, he managed to visit and write about almost everywhere of interest in the entire world, with the exception of the polar ice caps. His output was enviable, penning over 40 books between 1879 and his death in 1923, including the wonderfully titled *L'Inde (sans les Anglais)*.

The following morning, full of breakfast, the route out of Pontarlier up through the forest to Fort Mahler was severe. It would, I was assured, be well worth the effort as the view of the imposing Fort de Joux, 'that dungeon fortress never to be named', was supposed to be spectacular. Since the eleventh century, Joux, which was modernized by Vauban in 1690, has stood guard over the Cluse de Pontarlier, a formidable gorge on the approach to Switzerland. In its heyday, the fort served as both prison and fortress.

One of its most notable inmates was General François-Dominique Toussaint Louverture, a remarkable man of African descent who led the largest slave revolt in history. He was born in 1743 in the French colony of St Domingue on the island of Hispaniola, now Haiti.

Known as the 'Jewel of the Antilles', by the late eighteenth century St Domingue supplied over 40 per cent of Europe's sugar and nearly two-thirds of its coffee. Managed by a white population of 32,000, the workforce numbered almost a million – a breathtaking figure that accounted for well over a quarter of the Atlantic Slave Trade. The colony represented France's third largest source of income.

Freed by his master at the age of 33, in liberty Toussaint soon grew to be a wealthy man. He played a leading role in the slave revolts of the 1790s, both on and off the field, until 1794 when slavery was abolished by the revolutionary government in Paris. The resourceful Toussaint then set about re-establishing the economy, which included the delicate task of persuading former slaves to return to their plantations as employees. But, at the same time, he also began to run into conflict with Napoleon.

In 1801, the General was expressly forbidden to capture Santo Domingo. Disregarding the instruction, he took the Spanish colony with ease – a move which gave him control over the entire island of Hispaniola. It was an act of defiance that no doubt would have rankled with the Emperor in distant

Fort de Joux
...with its impressive array of walls, keeps and turrets...

France. Toussaint then appointed his own assembly, fearful that slavery might be reintroduced as it had been elsewhere. A constitution was quickly agreed, confirming continued emancipation and also giving the General near-absolute power with neither provision for French representation nor preferential trade treaties. Napoleon dispatched a sizeable force with orders to take over the island and deport all black officers.

The fighting that followed was bloody and inconclusive. The French, decimated by disease, resorted to trickery, treachery and atrocities to gain the upper hand. Toussaint, now nearly 60, agreed a peace, but his presence was still privately considered a threat to French rule. He was duped into attending a meeting. But, on his arrival, the General was arrested, placed on board ship and deported to France. He died in 1803, the ignominious death of a prisoner from complications suffered in the dreadful conditions of Joux.

That same year, Napoleon reintroduced slavery to St Domingue. It would not be abolished in France again until 1849. The French, however, were driven from Hispaniola in 1804 and, ever since, the Haitians have lived in liberty. So perhaps Toussaint's death had not been entirely in vain – which was more than could be said for my slog up to Fort Mahler. Joux, with its impressive array of walls, keeps and turrets that should have been stretched the length of the cliff's edge on the far side of the valley below me, was nowhere to be seen. The place was in thick fog.

I had been on the road for just over six weeks and walked about 680 miles by now and, as I made my way past lines of resting chairlifts and ski hire shops abandoned for the summer, I couldn't help reflecting that a significant landmark in the journey was about to pass. I would miss France with its magnificent countryside and wondrous history, where the ever-welcoming people had an unfailing old-world gentility to them, but another chapter had to open if I was to reach Rome.

By my reckoning, which is often questionable, there was a good fingernail's width of wood to go on the map before I reached the border. Indeed, had I obeyed the yellow route marker that beckoned me into the trees, I would have missed it altogether. Instinct told me otherwise. I followed the road and as it rounded the bend so a nondescript flat roof appeared, above which flew the Swiss flag.

723 miles to Rome.

Part 3

Switzerland

Thursday 8 November. *My ill humour continued. I was angry at myself. I saw my weakness. In such cases one must be open. I said to Jacob, 'I should not like to go to Switzerland in this humour'. 'Ah, Sir', said he, 'when you see the peasants with their great breeches and long beards, the humour will pass off quickly enough'.*

James Boswell, *On the Grand Tour*, 1764

12

Sainte-Croix to Lausanne and Geneva

Within the Switzer's varied land,
When Summer chases high the snow,
You'll meet with many a youthful band
Of strangers wandering to and fro:
Through hamlet, town, and healing bath,
They haste and rest as chance may call,
No day without its mountain path,
No path without its waterfall.
    Richard Monckton Milnes, *Switzerland and Italy*, 1838

TWO LARGE LADIES LOOKED up from hoeing their garden as I pushed on the door to the Customs Post, which screamed and shook in protest as if reluctant to let me in. Maybe for good reason – the place was deserted. I left, dismayed. No stamp for my Passport.

'Excuse me! Excuse me, M'sieur!' the startled young man in shorts and t-shirt shouted after me, not ten yards further down the road. By the dishevelled look on the face of Swiss authority, he had just woken from his 'duties'. 'What do you want?'

'What I *want*, M'sieur, is to come into Switzerland', I said, 'but as you can see, I am now already *in* Switzerland. What I was *after*, was a stamp in my Passport...'

'Oh, *désolé*', he said, suddenly sheepish, 'we don't have one any more, I am afraid. We...er...lost it'. Crestfallen, he waved a hand in farewell.

I jumped over a fence and walked through the fields to the village of L'Auberson, followed by a long trickle of inquisitive cows. In Sainte-Croix, an ugly town of near-Soviet charm, I had little option but to buy a map for 27 Swiss Francs. I found myself reeling at the cost like I had been punched in the guts, never mind that it was printed on special waterproof paper. An hour earlier, I could have mapped most of France for the same price.

*

The descent to the plain, on Midsummer's Day, from the heights of Sainte-Croix through the Gorges de Covatanne was steep. However, before I helter-skeltered into the forest, I marvelled at the view of Switzerland, which stretched like sweeping parkland to the distant skyline where its progress was abruptly halted by a barrack of white cloud. But as I took in the landscape, so the nebulous shapes began to form and gradually I realized that in actual fact the clouds were my first glimpse of the snow-clad peaks of the Alps, somewhere beyond which lay Rome.

I headed down the dark and slippery path into the spectacular ravine; it reminded me of Samaria on Crete. A river rushed noisily at its base, crows cackled overhead and a cold wind pierced the valley; even in the sunlight, the place felt sinister as if touched by the hand of Carabosse herself.

At the bottom of the escarpment, the Jura now behind me, the only place I could find a cup of coffee was, incongruously, in a Chinese restaurant. As I left it, a sudden wave of loneliness washed over me, perhaps brought on by the eeriness of the descent but more probably because I hadn't spoken meaning-fully to anyone for the best part of a week. I wrote that I was 'desperate for company and good conversation – not in two days' hence or with some passing stranger for a minute...but right now'.

No sooner had I put my notebook back in my pocket and paused to check my map than, looking over my shoulder, a young man suddenly approached out of the gorge, wearing a rucksack front *and* back. He called to me in a heavy Spanish accent: 'Jou a *peregrino*? Where are jou going?'

The answer to my prayers came in the form of Domingo, a short, hirsute freelance journalist from Pamplona, who just happened to be walking to Rome too. He oozed garlic and, from the moment we met, he never once stopped talking.

In time-honoured tradition, we exchanged the usual pilgrim gossip: who had met whom, where each had stayed and the various paths taken. And, as we swapped tales, so the familiar pattern of 'same route, different journey' emerged, just as with everyone else I had met. We soon concluded that, while we were the youngest on the Via by a good 15 to 20 years, we were way the slowest.

'No one said this was a race', Domingo said, dazzling me with his mirror sunglasses, 'I mean it's not like you walk to Rome every day; it's important to enjoy too, you know.' He planned to arrive in Rome on 15 August in eight weeks' time.

'And do you know another reason why I am taking my time? I tell you. In September, I will turn 40. I am not necessarily religious but I have just come back from the Dominican Republic and there is no work in Spain – at all. I want time to reflect, to think about the future, life with my girlfriend and the next step. I mean, do you think you will go back to England a different man?'

I thought for a bit, then replied that I doubted it was possible to return from a journey with so much time for contemplation and not be affected in some way or another. But 'different' implied an almost grail-like quest for some divine yet ever-elusive transformation, the answers to which can never be found in the perpetual agonizings of the mind. I was uneasy with that. I didn't feel I was so inherently broken in the first place that I was in need of repair. And if I were, a pilgrimage, where strength, determination and resolution of purpose are the order of day, would be the very last place I would seek refuge.

'OK, same hardware, new software.'

'Yes, a bit like restoring factory settings on the laptop.'

'But Harry', his tone changing, 'things can never be the same, you know that. Otherwise, what will be the point of all this effort?'

Down the road and out onto the rolling Swiss plain we walked, the sky a cloudless blue, the wheat in the fields all around us shimmying in the breeze. And as we went, so we talked and we talked and we talked. First about literature, travel mainly, Kerouac, Chatwin, Twain and Laurie Lee, until we got onto the subject of music.

'I sing when I get bored', he said.

'You should see me dance', I replied. 'Man, the woods are fantastic for it.'

But Domingo looked shocked when I let slip that I had Black Sabbath on my iPod.

'Just because we're on a pilgrimage doesn't mean it has to be all hair shirts and misery, you know. They had plenty of fun in the Middle Ages – troubadours, mead, wine every night.'

'Really?' he raised his eyebrows and changed the subject. 'The way here is marked beautifully, no?'

By now, we were virtually, but not quite, arm in arm – both more than a little happy to be in each other's company like Estragon and Vladimir in Beckett's *Waiting for Godot*, 'holding the terrible silence at bay'.

We stopped at a junction and sat down on a triangle of grass; there were butterflies everywhere.

Domingo grabbed a handful of lavender. 'Smell this', he said, 'mmm...wonderful!' and then from nowhere remarked, 'did you notice how in France only the old people had cars?'

'Or how here in Switzerland all the fences are electrified?' I replied. 'What is that on your wrist?' I asked, noticing a coral bracelet.

'It is a kiss from my six-year-old niece, to keep me safe. She told me I had to wear it.'

'Oh, you mean like this one', I said as I dug into my rucksack and produced a *misbaha*, a string of 33 blue prayer beads, not dissimilar to the rosary, that are passed through the fingers to the Islamic mantra that 'God is great'. My friend Sonja, in Muscat, had insisted one dinner that I take it. Her words still rang in my ears like a benediction: 'It has looked after me all these years; it will do the same for you too, Harry.'

Domingo held them with reverence in his hands; of little material value, to me they were of immense personal worth. I looked on as he caressed and turned the beads, which glinted as the sun caught the silver. I found myself watching him with great affection like being reunited with a long-lost brother, for we communed on such a level that it felt as if we had known one another for a great deal longer than the matter of minutes we in fact had. Indeed, so bizarre was our manner of meeting that I began to wonder if perhaps, in a previous life – if such existed – we hadn't been the greatest of friends, brothers in arms, joined in battle or perhaps in chivalrous pursuit of that ever-elusive grail. Once again, there was an undeniable spiritual element to the encounter; it was a moment, a day, that I wished would never end.

'Nothing has changed', I said, as Domingo handed the beads back to me. 'People have journeyed with charms and talismans since the dawn of time.' I thought of Mario with his beloved stick and that hat he lost in Champlitte.

'We travel with people's prayers, that's what these are; symbols of hope. It's not just for ourselves that we do this pilgrimage, it's for many others – we carry so much good will with us, you know', Domingo said.

'So why Rome? You live on the Camino.'

He furrowed his brow. 'I watch every day literally thousands of people pass through to Compostela. It is for me a tourist trail; sure it's a great adventure, a real party for some, especially now, with this crisis in Spain, a lot see it as a cheap holiday. It has become something very un-special, people drunk, stealing things. You know, if you want, there are even guys who will carry your backpack the whole way for you. It's a joke. I wanted something different, something a little bit special. I like it that very few walk the Via.'

We both looked at our watches, we had been talking for three hours. The day was getting on. We had reached the fork in the road; Domingo had to turn left for Yverdon on the shores of Lac Neuchâtel where Archbishop Sigeric had stopped overnight on his way back to Canterbury 1,000 years earlier. I, less pragmatic, especially as the town represented a bit of a deviation and an added day, needed to turn right. We embraced and parted reluctantly, our individual paths calling to us.

I had nowhere to stay after the 18-mile hike it took to reach Orbe. The charming town with its medieval tower and fountain was draped in a thick perfume of coffee. Nescafé, it transpired, is made there and conveyed across Europe by the train-load from a large and workmanlike goods yard on the outskirts, which I discovered when the Town Hall sent me to lodgings in

The Alps
...The snow-clad peaks of the Alps, beyond which lay Rome...

Chavornay – a good deal further than the 'ten minutes' they assured me the 'quick hop' would take.

'Yoo hoo! This way! Over here!' Madame Daisy Nicolet, my splendid hostess for the night, shouted at me quite unabashed with arms outstretched from her bedroom window. Past chickens, a goat, a pile of firewood, a bath overflowing with lavender, under lines of washing, some sunflowers and an unruly bush thing, I was ushered into her house by a statue of Donald Duck, complete with hat off. It was a homely place cluttered with a considerable collection of teddies, bells, clogs, wellington boots and a fine selection of feline postcards. The place, like everything in Daisy's life, steeped with love and a welcoming fragrance that indicated excessive use of fabric conditioner.

Daisy was a wonderful woman, a mellowed Mrs Slocombe type who sported massive hair piled on high that would have been the envy of an eighteenth-century perruquier. She was in an advanced state of excitement – it was her daughter's wedding the next day. There was little that wasn't enthused about as I was regaled with the various wonders of 'Cam-den' Town where she and her husband had stayed for the Diamond Jubilee. I don't think there was a bad bone in her body and I doubted very much if frowning was in either her know-how or capability.

'The Town 'All posted a notice saying there was this Via Franky, oh, that Via Franji, I can't remember the name but, you know, the pilgrim route to Rome passing right by and would we all like to volunteer to have pilgrims to stay. I said to my husband well, now our girl has left home, that bottom room is empty, so why not? I love helping people out. We had two Italians here a few weeks back and they slept in the same bed. No matter, they weren't bothered, we weren't bothered, they were that tired out. Left at 4 a.m. the next morning, they did, the poor things.'

Then I too confessed that in order to reach Lausanne before the heat of the afternoon set in, I would have to do the same. Daisy looked momentarily thoughtful, smiled again and announced it wouldn't be a problem. Despite putting bread, jam and coffee out for my breakfast before turning in, she couldn't resist getting up to give me a farewell hug, pressing a scribbled note into my hand that reminded me to watch out for perilous tree roots on the mountain paths between Martigny and Orsières.

But Lausanne wasn't my final stop that day. For there I would break my journey and jump on a train to my real destination, Geneva, where I had been summoned to a party. The chance to break free momentarily from the Via Francigena was one I seized on but, despite my excitement at the prospect of the night ahead, I was also aware that I had grown strangely apprehensive, even wary, of cities. In these great fora of sophistication, I felt visible, clumsy and strangely vulnerable – places to be avoided in preference to the quiet life of field and village where I could pass by, an unnoticed part of the scenery.

Coming out of the woods, there were, I noticed, seagulls overhead and, as I reached the crest, so the lazing expanse of Lake Geneva appeared in the distance. I laughed for joy, giving this refreshing change to my view furtive glances, like a child with a new toy, until once again the path drew me back into the tree line. Under foot there was a strong smell of bitumen. Looking down, I noticed that the tarmac was melting.

I walked into Lausanne on a Saturday afternoon, through neat little streets of neat little houses with neat little gardens and neat little cars parked outside. Everywhere people were relaxing; swimming in pools, cooking on the barbeque, sleeping on benches or sunbathing on roof terraces – the lake dotted with sails and the brushstroke wakes of speedboats.

In the heat, I sweated up and down Lausanne's numerous hills to reach its great Gothic cathedral of Notre-Dame. Built in the late twelfth and thirteenth centuries, the many-spired Notre-Dame was originally a Catholic cathedral, until the Protestant Reformation swept through parts of Switzerland in the sixteenth century. Now it belongs to the Swiss Reformed Church.

By the time I put my weight against its substantial door after eight hours on the road, I was defeated. I walked straight in, sat down heavily on a chair in the Pilgrim Chapel, caught my breath, drank some water and said a prayer. I paused and looked up. Almost everywhere I gazed, the place was richly decorated in elaborate beautifully coloured patterns. Gilt leaves and branches reached across vaulted ceilings, bold stripes, twists and swirls picked out pillars and columns while stars, crests and figures that were rich in detail filled the upper reaches on backcloths of reds, blues and greens. Nowhere else did I encounter such luxurious embellishments. They added a whole new level of experience to being in a church, making the place feel warm and inviting, in total contrast to the cold, unwelcoming whitewashed interiors of churches almost anywhere else in northern Europe. The decorations had been restored to their full glory in the early twentieth century, having been covered over for nearly 500 years. I took one last look at them over my shoulder as I opened the door back out into the sunshine and headed down the hill to the ferry head at Ouchy, where I would pick up my trail once again in a couple of days.

The larger-than-life figure of Richard Foden greeted me at the front door of his house on the outskirts of Geneva in his usual boom that, tinged with a hint of gravel, commands attention as if someone had just fired a howitzer right by your ear. In another age, he would, I fancy, have been a privateer under Letters of Marque from the Admiralty, roving the high seas on his ship, engaging in the King's work when it suited and dabbling in roguish pursuit when more often than not it didn't. A man's man, I hadn't even the chance to step inside before I was presented with a large glass of wine.

I was led into the garden, the place embowered by flowers, where we sat under a large awning by the pool. On the table, I noticed a copy of *The Spectator* which lay mischievously open at a page announcing *The Daily Telegraph Walking Diet*. While we chatted, Richard started to chain-smoke furiously, on which I eventually had to remark.

'Ah, well, you took your boots off. Would you mind...?' he winced, indicating with shoos of the hand the direction to the shower. 'Oh, and you are going to remove that abomination of a thing from your face before tonight, aren't you?' he cried after me.

I was proud of my beard – the Grizzly Adams look suited me, I thought, and although I held out at first, after detailed inspection and some reflection in the mirror, I saw the merit of returning to the smooth-faced me; the shave felt so civilizing.

The guests at the festivities round Gillie and Vincent Wuidart's pool that evening looked inaccessibly perfect in every way. The grounds, picked out in pea lights, glittered like the heavens had been invited down from the night sky to join the festivities. Everybody seemed to be involved with money in one way or another, but it was those who had just gained Swiss nationality who strutted about with an added confidence as if they had just won the Euro Millions. The champagne flowed, the music played, Toupie the terrier barked, there was much dancing and, come the early hours, inevitable and unplanned swimming. The party was good, indeed one of the best – the proof of which was our hostess's arrival the following morning with her foot in plaster and one arm in a sling. But despite being in the company of good friends, I couldn't help feeling that I was but an observer to all the shenanigans. I felt apart and wholly removed from the frippery and frivolity. However much I sought inclusion, the inescapable fact is that I was in an altogether different place both mentally and spiritually from those around me – the rolling stone passing through.

Dinner the next evening was in the glamorous surrounds of Dominic and Isabelle Park's well-appointed residence near Nyon – she, of infinite beauty, was once a top London vet while he, loaded with an inquisitive enthusiasm for discovery, was a former cognac distiller now bent on nomadic exploration. It was an eclectic bunch that they assembled in the dining room, a Habsburg Archduchess, a clutch of polished bankers, a Greek-American real estate developer, Henry, their ramrod-straight son bent on a career in the Foot Guards, and me. From the feckless but joyous babble around the pool the night before, the conversation was grave and the mood sombre as talk lingered on the problems of Greece, whether it would burst the Euro and the potential for uprising and revolt in the beleaguered state. 'The conditions are perfect for war', someone muttered not so *sotto voce*.

When I told one of the girls that in less than five days I would reach the Grand St Bernard Pass she threw her hands up in disbelief: 'But my darling, you will surely die of the cold up there?!' At which, I daintily removed the cashmere shawl from around her shoulders and said: 'No my dear, because with this I shall stay warm...'

678 miles to Rome.

13

Villeneuve, the Alps and the Grand Saint Bernard Pass

Shall I find comfort, travel-sore and weak?
Of labour you shall find the sum.
Will there be beds for me and all who seek?
Yea, beds for all who come.

Christina Rossetti, *Uphill*, 1861

LEFT ON THE JETTY at Villeneuve with a couple of bemused swans looking up at me expectantly for bread, I watched as the gilded stern of *La Suisse* steamed away across Lake Geneva. I didn't realize then that having completed 755 miles since leaving London, I was now over halfway to Rome; that was a landmark I had prepared for in a few nights' time when I reached the Grand St Bernard Pass.

It was raining by the time I arrived in Aigle. I knocked on the door of the Priest's Residence and was greeted by the Curé, a short man in his 60s who, despite my best efforts, was not much of a conversationalist. The smell of stew simmering on the stove seeped out from behind his diminutive frame.

Rather than invite me in, as was the norm in France, I was ushered immediately across a yard to a derelict shack. Paint peeling off its woodwork, its windows held together with tape; the door opened stiffly with the aid of a kick to reveal a room that looked as if it had been recently vacated by the Secret Police. The walls, lined in thick horsehair blankets, would have drowned the loudest of screams, the shutters were closed and the frames hung with limp muslin. All that was missing in this vision of hospitality was a vase of dead roses. A table, two armchairs and a sofa in violent orange filled the room and,

Crossing Lake Geneva
...I watched as the gilded stern of *La Suisse* steamed away...

from the look of the stains, the carpet had been the scene of a recent and major vehicular overhaul.

The elderly cleric pointed to a mattress behind the sofa and, shrugging apologetically, said: 'We're not very well equipped for this, I am afraid.' But it was perfectly adequate and, more importantly, free. I would make do, I thought, spotting a blanket on top of a cupboard that, from the look of the holes in it, was home to many a moth.

'Is there a chance of a shower?' I asked. It was as if Oliver had asked for 'more'.

'A shower?!' the man virtually died on the spot. 'Well, there', he pointed to an outhouse, 'is your toilet, you can wash there but...a shower...' He looked stumped as I gently nudged him with my eyes back towards his large, empty and warm house where the stew bubbled enticingly on the hob.

Reluctantly, I was led upstairs to a spare bedroom with an enormous freshly made double bed that looked so inviting.

'Would you like a towel?'

I declined, more on principle than anything else, even though my own miniscule travel towel was about as pleasurable as being wiped down with blotting paper. Leaving, I gave the bed one last loving look, savoured the delicious bouquet of stew that hung on the staircase and stepped back out into the rain for the supermarket, where I bought a pint of milk and a packet of 'gummy bears' for my supper.

Returning to the hovel, a lone strip-light illuminated my home for the night. I laid the foetid mattress on the floor and covered myself for warmth in the holey blanket. I was just beginning to doze off when I noticed the first itch on my leg, which I rubbed nonchalantly with the back of my hand. Within a minute my whole being felt like it was alive with fleas as I began to scratch furiously. Sleep was hopeless. I ventured across the yard to the dripping lavatory, with its solitary lightbulb that hung from the ceiling like a hangman's noose. There were three sheets of loo paper in the box. '*Aigle welcomes Pilgrims*', I thought to myself.

In the morning, I walked up the course of the mighty River Rhône; it was a good deal cooler there than the heat of the Via. There was not a cloud in the sky. Way overhead, almost in emphasis, a lone airliner scored a trail of brilliant white across the blue.

It was against this dazzling backdrop that I reached St Maurice. The scenery changed dramatically. Like Ibsen's Peer Gynt in the Hall of the Mountain King, I was caught centre stage in a giant coliseum packed with ridges and peaks that crowded the horizon everywhere I cared to look. Grizzled rock faces, full of pathos and drama, stared out at implausible angles, trees clung impossibly to cliff edges, gullies choked with scree and the land, irreparably creased and buckled over millions of years, stared in wondrous grimace all around me – the Alps!

The first image I recall as I opened the door to Ronnie and Carole Thomson's chalet, high above Martigny, was that of a blizzard. Carole clucked over towards me, pushing away their two scrapping border terriers, Bobo and Dougal. 'Oh Harry, forgive the mess; it's Dougal. He's just discovered that you can eat bean bags. You'd never guess I've been on the hoover all day but the wretched things just keep popping up everywhere. I'm ever so sorry...' But I didn't mind; for me, it just said 'home' and, to boot, there was yet another strong smell of stew wafting up from the kitchen.

Ronnie, with the chiselled good looks of Buzz Lightyear, was all firm handshakes and broad grins. A former Scotland rugby international in the 1960s, on hanging up his boots he had turned his hand to international business and was now, latterly, the Laird of a hectare of vine that clung precariously to the mountainside. It was impossible not to like the couple, who were infectious in their welcome, as they fussed over me like one of their own.

The view from the vineyard side of the chalet, looking directly down the mountain, was spectacular, like being in the gondola of an airship. Ronnie's office, a spacious corner room, was presidential in size, with papers spread out on tables and walls covered with memorabilia and photographs. He was in his element here in the mountains; it was as if they had been made for him. Before long, the maps were out and spreading hands were poring over the contours, feeling every inch of the terrain that he knew in intimate detail. 'My advice, Harry, is get as high and as far as you can tomorrow. It'll make the final reach up to the Grand St Bernard the day after all the easier', he said.

It was one of those remarks that makes you both love and respect the mountains; even at the tender height of 2,500 feet, there was still that need to be prepared, which adds a certain edge to the everyday and always sends a frisson of excitement down my back.

'Amazing to think that Hannibal passed through here...' I remarked, looking out of the enormous window down the valley as it reached into the distance.

'Yes, except that he didn't come this way', Ronnie's eyes delighting as he put me right. He went on to explain that the General's much-lauded achievement, at the start of the Second Punic War between Carthage and Rome in 218BC, while loaded with surprise was in many ways a disaster in comparison to others who went before and after.

A mercenary army of Gauls had passed through a couple of years earlier, in springtime, without incident and Hasdrubal, the General's brother, likewise ten years later. No, he affirmed, it was late autumn, even early winter, when Hannibal led his army all the way from the Iberian peninsula, over the Alps and into Italy. Martigny and the Grand St Bernard would have been too high – accepting that in those days the snow line was higher. Most probably, based on criteria in the reported accounts, which were written some years later by the Greek and Roman historians Polybius and Livy, Hannibal made for the Col du Montgenevre from Briançon, arriving in what is now Italy at the town of Susa. Other schools of thought indicate that the Col de Clapier or, less likely because of its height and difficult going, the Col de la Traversette may have been used.

Ronnie spoke with passion of the General's daring and determination, yet with dismay that, in driving his plan through, by the time Hannibal's force reached Italy it was much depleted through a combination of the need to garrison, desertion, capture, attacks, appalling weather or the harsh mountain terrain. Starting with a force of 80,000, he arrived in Italy with a mere 20,000 infantry and 6,000 cavalry; of 37 war elephants, only 20 survived, led by the indomitable Syrus, an Indian elephant complete with a prosthetic tusk fashioned of metal and silver. 'But', he added, 'the interesting thing is no one really *ever* knew the route Hannibal took, except that one day in midwinter he arrived among the Cisalpine Gauls of northern Italy and took Scipio and his Roman army completely by surprise at the Battle of the Ticinus. To the Romans, he was the original bogey man; the very mention of his name struck the fear of God – sorry gods – into them.'

Carole called us to the table; just as we were tucking in, I noticed a small Madonna on a ribbon around her neck.

'It's for luck', she said, her guard dropping. 'My...my sister sent it to me' – she paused again – 'the cancer has come back, you see.'

However upbeat she tried to sound, it did not manage to conceal the shadow that the news had visited upon the couple, 'Oh, but I'll be okay. Beaten it once before and I've just started the radiotherapy again. I am sure in a few weeks again all will be fine, won't it Ronnie?' He looked across, and gently took her hand in his.

In a bid to lighten the mood, I dashed upstairs and returned moments later with a pocket-sized icon of St Spyridon, on a square of wood no larger than an outstretched thumb. Carole stroked the diminutive carving as she turned it over in her hand.

She placed the amulet down in front of her and gazed at it.

I recounted the episode on that Paxos cliff a few years earlier, when falling off, for some inexplicable reason, I had invoked the saint's name and remarkably escaped almost certain death.

'Oh, that's beautiful', she sighed.

Dinner over, the couple, determined not to be won over to maudlin, dragged me out to the wooden cabin in the vineyard, where we embarked on the altogether happier quest of sampling as much of last year's production as possible in the short space of time before the dropping temperature forced us back inside.

Breakfast the next morning was hearty. Carole piled first bacon then sausages then eggs and finally a large dollop of beans on to my overburdened plate. 'You've got a big day ahead', she said, despite my protestations. After last night, it was business as usual for the couple. I gathered my kit and, readying for the off, threw my rucksack onto my shoulders.

'Now, have you got everything?' I nodded. 'You sure?' Carole repeatedly asked like I was being packed off to school.

'Yes', I pleaded in reply while Ronnie's repeated mantra of 'don't worry the poor boy' echoed in support. How I hated those goodbyes.

I waved and, setting off down the hill, smiled to myself. Of course I had left something behind. On the bedside table, with a page from my notebook in explanation, St Spyridon was waiting for Carole. The moment I fetched the icon down to dinner the night before, I knew that I had been meant to bring him especially for her.

Taking Ronnie's advice, I immediately climbed high up into the valley, contouring the steep slopes by following *les bisses*, ancient water-channels that had been dug into the hillsides centuries ago to irrigate the pastures. Hundreds of feet below, like a scene from a miniature train set, an endless stream of juggernauts and lorries climbed up the big road that winds all the way to the Grand St Bernard Tunnel and Italy. For a moment I watched the ungainly beasts, their noisome grind so at odds with the tranquillity that was all about me before I headed on to Bourg St Pierre.

In the meadows, gangs of men raked hay, the fall of the mountain too severe for machines. Like sepia-tinted images from yesteryear, at teatime the ladies of the family joined them, spreading rugs at the field's edge, laying out picnics with enormous plates of sandwiches, cakes and flagons of lemonade.

At such height, even in the trees, the blasts of heat that coursed up the valley felt at times as if the doors of Hades itself had been flung open. I thanked my lucky stars that I wasn't following the lorry-choked road far below, cooling myself whenever possible in the plentiful streams that flowed in abundance everywhere.

All the same, by the time I reached Bourg St Pierre, I was wrung out, so much so that I had neither the energy nor the will to seek a bed in the true pilgrim manner. I knocked on the door of the first Bed and Breakfast I came to. I was not a very elegant sight.

After dinner – a piece of steak the size of a table which disappeared almost in one mouthful – I walked back through the darkened village, woodsmoke hanging on the darkness and in that moment, out in the fields, there was suddenly a sense of soldiery all around me. I inhaled the rich scent of ancient campfires as Frenchmen, Gauls, Romans and Franks huddled in groups outside their bivouacs and horse lines. The night felt alive to ancient tongues and foreign dialects as the men chatted, gambled and mumbled in hushed tones. These were the souls of the many invaders who had ranked through the village as it played unwitting host to a multitude of passing armies over the millennia.

The next morning was cold and, in the mist, again I walked among ghosts as the French Armée de Réserve slogged its way alongside me up the mountain. For over a week, 6,000 men a day passed through Bourg St Pierre with engineers constantly surveying and improving the route. Waggoners goaded on horse teams hauling artillery pieces cased in tree trunks, while cavalry, infantry and baggage trains all made a struggled progression in the wearing and bitter conditions of that May in 1800.

Amid the now-silent cacophony of troops on the march, up ahead I could just make out a small party moving independently of the column, a lone figure at its centre being led on a shaggy mule; swathed in blankets against the snow, he was wearing that unmistakable grey greatcoat pulled tight about him and a black bicorn hat on his head. Such was the secrecy of the crossing, the beleaguered guide, Pierre Nicholas Dorsaz, toiling alongside, never realized the identity of his charge. At 30 years old, and recently installed as First Consul of France, this was none other than Napoleon himself – the architect of possibly one of the most successful enterprises in military history. His was a seemingly impossible task that would herald the defeat of the Austrian Army at Marengo four weeks later on 14 June, and see the return of French domination over northern Italy.

On one occasion, Pierre Nicholas, who walked on the precipitous outer edge of the track, saved the mule and Bonaparte from near death when the beast slipped on the ice. Napoleon subsequently rewarded Dorsaz for 'devotion to his task', with enough money to buy a farm, a field and a cow. The touching afternote, for Dorsaz, was that he could then marry his sweetheart.

For the monks in the Hospice du Grand-St-Bernard up on the Pass, however, the passage of Napoleon's Army was a costly affair. Every man, it was agreed, was to be given food and wine to eat on arrival, before making the descent into Italy. The final tally, when the last soldier filed past, came to 21,724 bottles of wine along with 1½ tonnes of cheese and 800 kilos of meat. The total cost was 40,000 francs. In 1850, the French government paid Fr 18,500 toward the Hospice's outstanding debt and in 1984, President Mitterand made a further token gesture while on a visit, but the lion's share remains unsettled to this day.

Leaving the tree line, as bushy tailed marmots scampered for cover and the lorries were swallowed into the hillside by the gaping mouth of the road tunnel, I entered an upland world of butterflies, orchids and hardy banks of purple-headed mountain azalea. I watched a herd of black and mahogany brown Herens cattle in impressive jousting tournaments. Powerful muscular beasts, they locked horns noisily with wild snorts and grunts, kicking up flurries of dust that momentarily engulfed their opponent as they charged headlong at one another. It was an exhilarating sight, like they were in rehearsal for the cow fights that are so popular throughout the region.

Fording streams, crossing bogs and walking at times along the old mountain road that works its way to the summit, I was passed by a couple of open-top Ferraris, the odd tour bus and a steady stream of panting cyclists. I thought of Sylviane, the girl I met outside Ornans in her wheelchair, and wondered how she had fared on this difficult stretch of the Via.

On and on the track continued, sometimes paved with ancient worn stone, the grass increasingly giving way to shale and rock until finally succumbing to knee-deep snow that marked the entrance of the gully that leads up to the Hospice du Grand-St-Bernard. As I waded my way up the last few hundred metres, I noticed a large group of bearded, black-leather-jacketed men, all in sunglasses, lined up at the head of my little valley. I could see what was about to happen, but however much I whispered under my breath, 'please no, I've got to walk there in a minute', the Hells Angels, oblivious to me, proceeded to relieve themselves to a man, quite unabashed and in unison. I can only assume that they must have drunk an awful lot before they set out.

The tight little community at the St Bernard Pass, engorged with day-trippers, was a busy place that lunchtime. I passed the twin blocks of the Hospice, souvenir shops and restaurants until I reached a spot overlooking the ebony waters of the lake, where a large blue and white sign read 'GRAND SAINT BERNARD PASS, 2473 m, 8114 ft'. A blackbird flitted past just as a pair of large St Bernard dogs were being led out by a kennelman. I had reached the highest point on the Via Francigena; it was St Peter's and St Paul's Day.

Released from the euphoria of the climb, I slumped down on a bench in a quiet corner away from the crowds and called home. After some moments, my mother picked up the phone, hesitantly.

'Hello.'

'Ma, it's me, I've made it, I am at 8,000 feet on the Grand St Bernard Pass.'

In the background, there was an indecipherable yet distinct noise.

'Oh...erm, how wonderful darling...yes, umm, well done.' The mystery noise persisted. 'Are you by any chance watching the television? Federer is about to beat Benneteau, it's most exciting – you really shouldn't miss it ...' I looked around me; up here in the Alps, no one was taking the slightest interest in the fortunes of Switzerland's most famous sportsman. Wimbledon was a very distant prospect indeed.

It is believed that people have been crossing the Alps at this point since the Bronze Age. The present hospice, which dates back to the sixteenth century, was founded in the mid-tenth century by St Bernard of Menthon or Mont Joux, as it is sometimes known, a reference to the Pass's earlier name derived from Mons Jovis, the Mountain of Jupiter. There was a temple to the god nearby and traces of buildings that date back to Emperor Claudius's time have also been found.

St Bernard was a French noble by birth, who devoted himself to Christ from an early age – even, it is alleged, jumping 40 feet from his bedroom window in the Château de Menthon to escape an arranged marriage. He established an order, the Congrégation du Saint Bernard in the Hospice, to offer care, shelter and protection to travellers and pilgrims on their way to Rome from the weather and the many bandits in the area.

Outside, the buildings are drab and featureless, as you might expect given the Pass spends much of the year shrouded in snow, but within lies an ancient maze of flagstoned passages and corridors smoothed by the footsteps of time. They led to a warren of kitchens, refectories, floor after floor of sleeping quarters, a much-gilded chapel and an intimate crypt. Immaculately clean and, like most monastic buildings, smelling ever so slightly of Brasso and incense.

There are only three members of the order in the Hospice today. However, assisted by an army of volunteers and local workers, the place is no less busy. I met Brother Frédéric, a canon who had been resident for the last 14 years, in the Pilgrims' Refectory. A compact room with pokey windows that looked out over the Alps, it was filled end to end with long tables. The kindly Frédéric quickly sensed I was in need of something to drink, which arrived in the shape of two large steaming metal jugs, one of milk and one of tea, which he then proceeded to pour together from height and with some ceremony into a big mug. Four frothed cups in quick succession and the jugs were emptied. I was shown up to the sleeping quarters, which turned out to be a dark, panelled dormitory crammed full of wooden bunk beds. It reminded me of my barrack room as a recruit in military training. It even smelt the same.

Not long after, there was a knock on the door, which flung wide open and Marco, an Italian from Rome in his late 30s, apologetically bundled in. He looked exhausted.

On a short walking break to Orsières, Marco had spent the last two days climbing up from Aosta. It had been hard going. Previously, he had shared a room with Mario, whom I had met on the road to Champlitte, in the Capuchin Monastery at Châtillon. I asked after my hat. 'That was your hat?' he replied. 'In my opinion, it is too good for a pilgrim hat!'

Moments later and the relative quiet was shattered once more by the arrival of Luca from Turin, again via Aosta. A towering figure, he appeared in the doorway with a rucksack like a strap-on double-decker bus, so large that he was forced to enter sideways. This enormous container, like Mary Poppins's carpetbag, held most conveniences known to man, from gas stoves to plates, tents and seemingly an outfit for every eventuality. Unpacking its contents made a noise like a brass band falling over. The confined space quickly took on the smell of a dirty laundry basket while much of the room disappeared under a thick carpet of camping paraphernalia and assorted accoutrements.

But there was a melancholy to Luca; something didn't seem quite right. As his story gradually unfolded, it became apparent that, unable to find work in Italy, he had embarked upon an adventure with no definable objective that was in effect an escape from life. He might, he said, go to Lausanne, and yet he could well go on to Canterbury, if the mood took him; but then, as he couldn't be sure of anything, he would see where the wind blew, so where and when he might end up was anybody's guess. Luca was friendly and warm-hearted. I couldn't help feeling for him as he set off on his journey into the unknown alone. Perhaps, I hoped, by striking out in such a bold manner he might stumble across the happiness he was searching for.

By late afternoon, with the tourists gone, the Pass became a relaxing and gentle spot. We were 77 for supper that evening, the Brothers were overjoyed – the place was so busy they were reminded of wintertime when the Hospice is awash with skiers. The numbers were swelled by the arrival of a choir of all ages from Le Puy. One of the ladies, hearing about me, sidled up and announced that, as a pilgrim to Compostela, she 'carried the shell', to which I replied (not that I am big on one-upmanship) that, as a pilgrim to Rome, I carried 'the key', and then added, for good measure, that I would be absolved of all sin on arrival at St Peter's.

The kitchen served a simple meal of alphabet soup, risotto and fruit salad. The wine flowed, friendships were made and there followed much noise and laughter as you might expect in a room so full. However, when pudding finished, someone in a far corner called silence, a tuning fork was sounded and, as if that was all that was needed, the whole room immediately burst into song. At first the singing was solemn as Rachmaninoff's *Vespers* filled the room in deep sonorous tones, followed by Bortniansky's *Cor Jesu melle dulcis* and the Jewish hymn, *Yigdal*. It was magnificent. But then a bottle of home-made *Eau de Vie* was passed around with dramatic and almost immediate effect, as the singing became glee-like and animated in contrast to the rigid choral discipline earlier. We sang, we clapped, we cheered and we drummed on the tables in time to tunes like *The Song from the Moulin Rouge* until time was called after a riotous rendition of Piaf's *Milord*, complete with encores. It was exhausting. We parted with fond handshakes, much smiling, good wishes for the road ahead and our respective beds.

Back in the dormitory, Luca and Mario tried to give me a crash course in Italian. My rudimentary knowledge was confined mostly to hazy memories of schoolboy Latin. It was, however, futile as, after all the fun and games of the day, the need to sleep quickly took over.

In the early hours of the following morning, we said farewell on the steps of the Hospice and parted, the best of friends. Marco and Luca turned right for Orsières, while I turned left for Italy, Aosta and Rome. It was snowing.

588 miles to Rome.

Part 4

Italy

Italy is an unhealthful country and grows harmful food.
St Alcuin of York, AD798

14

Aosta to Santhia

*The atmosphere of the border – it is like starting over again;
there is something about it like a good confession: poised for
a few happy moments between sin and sin.*
Graham Greene, *The Border*, 1938

LIKE ANY STONE THAT has tumbled from a great height, I rolled
into Aosta at some speed. My first impression was one of
noise, like I had landed feet first in the middle of an enormous
cocktail party; everybody shouting, everyone laughing and the
whole place running on chaos. There were flowers everywhere,
brightly coloured washing hung over balconies, bedding aired
from windows, dark glasses were mandatory and all the men
drove with one arm out of the car window. Italy, I thought to
myself, is going to be fun.

As if to emphasize this feeling of infinite jolliment, when I
strode up to Aosta Cathedral to get my Passport stamped, I
walked straight in on the closing stages of a marriage ceremony.
This included confetti, cheering, clapping, a glass of champagne, a
lot of kisses and, of course, inclusion in the wedding photograph.

Cesare Gerbelle and Carmela Camodeca's chic and airy
apartment had expansive views over the city and across the
valley that you could never tire of. The couple work in property
and academia. The gorgeous Carmela, possessed of the most
exquisite auburn hair, had thoughtfully laid histories and literature out for me on my bed in welcome. Having run most of
the way down from the St Bernard Pass, however, I was, to put
it mildly, subdued – especially given that in a matter of hours, I
knew I would have to be up again and on my way.

At dinner, I chided myself for not having the time to stay
and enjoy this fascinating city that was named after that
most inspirational of Emperors, Augustus. Carmela, however,
reminded me that I was a pilgrim and that Rome should be the

unerring focus of my journey rather than sightseeing along the way. All the same, I felt, despite her words, that in some way I was letting myself down, gripped as I was by a self-imposed momentum to keep heading south.

In the morning, as I made my way towards the Augustus Arch down the Via Sant' Anselmo, I noticed a plaque the size of a tombstone high on the side of a building, announcing the birthplace of St Anselm. I guess the clue was in the street name but at 5 a.m. I am not routinely tuned into matters historical.

I thought back to Canterbury and the altar, which Canon Clare had been at such pains to show me before I set out for the coast. Standing in the side chapel where the saint is buried, this substantial gift from the citizens of Aosta, made by the sculptor Stephen Cox, consists of two large green slabs of local marble, from the ends of which a jagged vein of white trickles down to a centre point as if in outline of the Alpine summits that converge on the city, tucked at the head of its valley, far below. The simple piece, so cleverly worked, makes for a powerful statement against the cathedral's Caen stonework, echoing the great man's life.

Anselm was a deeply spiritual man and a learned Christian philosopher who spent much of his life as a monk in the Monastère du Bec in Normandy. In 1093, at the age of 60, he was understandably reluctant to become Archbishop of Canterbury, not only because of his advancing years but also because King William Rufus, who appointed him, was more than difficult to reason with as he vied for primacy over the Church. Like many other monarchs across Europe at the time, William was continually frustrated by the interventions of the Pope in England's affairs.

But, in a time before democracy and freedom of speech, the Church represented a significant check and balance on absolute rule by the Crown. The principled Anselm fought valiantly to maintain this important status quo by persuading William Rufus to recognize Pope Urban II, refusing to support the King's suppression of the Welsh or acquiesce in the monarch's refusal to agree to Church reform. The latter led to the Archbishop's first period of exile.

Anselm, threatened with the prospect of total submission to the monarch and the withdrawal of his right to appeal to Rome, left England and was received with high honour at Capua in southern Italy by the Pontiff, who was in attendance at the joint Catholic and Saracen siege to restore Prince Richard to his rightful seat. He became a popular figure among the Muslim soldiery, who were impressed by his holy demeanour. After the siege, he took up residence in Lyon.

Rufus, meanwhile, was killed hunting in the New Forest, with his younger brother Henry and other nobles at his side. His death was dressed up as an accident but could be construed as a simple and successful assassination, especially given that the monarch's body was abandoned where it fell and Henry hightailed it for London to be crowned King three days later.

After three years in exile, Anselm was invited back. Henry I, the new monarch, now needed the Archbishop's support to strengthen his claim to a throne that would be contested by his eldest brother, Robert of Normandy, on return from the Crusades. Anselm obliged, but demanded the restoration of Archbishopric lands which William Rufus had seized. He refused to pay homage to Henry, a layman, who considered it his right to appoint and invest clergy, like his brother before him. When Pope Paschal II upheld Anselm's appeal to Rome over this and excommunicated the bishops appointed by the King, the Archbishop returned to France for a further four years.

Eventually Henry agreed to the return of many powers and property to the Church, but it was not until the King personally visited Anselm in Bec that the Archbishop came back to Canterbury, following the Concordat of London in 1107 confirming the agreements reached. Anselm died two years later at the age of 76, having spent nearly half his tenure at Canterbury in exile, battling with the Crown.

Not long out of the city, the cows lost their bells, the first fig trees came into view and that music of summer, the cicada's washboard rasp, started up. It was to become a permanent fixture that would, from that day on, accompany me all the way to Rome. But, in comparison to pristine Switzerland, the Italian villages were run-down and derelict, the land parched, policed by oversized dogs and strewn with irrigation systems that seemed to delight in soaking me yet did little to alleviate the oppressive humidity that lingered in the narrow airless confines of the Aosta valley.

In Nus, I stopped to see the house where Pontius Pilate is believed to have broken his journey en route to exile in Gaul, before I reached Châtillon, whose streets were choked with stalls selling cheeses, breads, honeys, jams and cured meats. It was market day and I was welcomed to the Capuchin monastery by a friar, Luca, who warned me not to leave my boots outside in case they weren't there come morning.

In the simple room, I slept fitfully, my legs still smarting from the rapid 6,000-foot descent a few days earlier. Outside, the valley became engorged with rain as thunder and lightning took charge and the storm at last broke.

The bell for Matins was still sounding as I ventured into the wet early morning to continue southward. Climbing high into the hills I happened upon a wondrous land with vineyards all around and every peak and summit that poked through the mist below me was crowned with a castle. The gale that raged overhead, however, was so overpowering that at times I had little option but to seek shelter variously in a deserted house, under a spreading tree, a cliff, and finally the questionable sanity of the lee of an enormous lone rock. The last left me fearful of being discovered centuries later pitta-bread-like following its collapse under the sudden deluge that surrounded both it and me without warning.

After the angered waters of the Dora Balthea, whose course I had been following since Aosta, had charged through a spectacular gorge, the signs for the Via Francigena led me into the heart of the old town at Bard, which looked to be a short cut across a meander in the mighty river's course. It led, for some distance, to an abrupt cul-de-sac where a large red and white barrier proclaimed no further access. Wet and tired, I was darned if I was about to turn back.

This was my first encounter in Italy with what would become the phenomenon of many *Viae Francigenae*. The skill, which I was not always adept at, was to identify the direct route. Pilgrims, after the first few hundred miles, tend not to be so interested in the scenic detour – the constant, and usually confusing, daily suggestion of which would from now on become a feature of the route for the weeks to come.

I hadn't had the opportunity, since arriving in Italy, to buy any maps. Navigation was easy at this stage, a simple case of following the river. This was a mercy, given that my burdensome guidebook, with its indecipherable diagrammatic schemes that were short on detail yet long on notes and inaccuracies, was by now a redundant and weighty irrelevance. I chucked it, with some glee, off a bridge.

No sooner I had done so than I wished I hadn't. Lost in that 'I know roughly where I am' sort of way, I found myself persisting down an enchanting road, which – starved of traffic in any form – nature was busy reclaiming until tarmac yielded to bramble and the way was lost to impenetrable thicket for ever. Thus I ended up, in the dark, walking down the main railway track to Donnas, which, in the scheme of things, is probably 'not something to try at home'. Or abroad, come to think of it.

The bridge at Pont St Martin, at the end of the line, is quite wonderful. Yet another remarkable monument to the enduring qualities of Roman architecture, it is instantly reminiscent of the celebrated sixteenth-century Stari Most, the bridge built by the Ottomans at Mostar across the River Neretva in Bosnia and Herzegovina, except that the bridge at Pont St Martin was completed about 1,700 years earlier. Even in the pelting rain, I was fixated. Built in substantial alternating layers of slab stone, this perfect arch stretches 107 feet to the far bank of the Dora Balthea that roars below. Walking back to my room after dinner, over the grass-entwined cobbles burnished smooth by the years, I couldn't help but ponder the many who must have crossed before me: churchmen, soldiers, saints, rulers, merchants, pilgrims and even Archbishop Sigeric himself – all had taken advantage of this vital crossing over the great span of time.

The farther I walked out of the valley, so its precipitous sides began to fall away and the sky, once again a pastel blue following the previous day's tempest, poured in. The view ahead convinced me, had I not known to the contrary, that just over the rise, the sea would open up as a vast expanse before my very eyes. It was cruel; I couldn't have been further from the coast and yet, that morning, I yearned to be at the water's edge, such had been the closeness of my surroundings in the past few days.

'Good mor-r-ning, I am Pilgrim Harry from England, desirous of house me three Juglio, yes?' In this rather unsatisfactory manner, I managed to secure a room for the night at the Canoe Club in Ivrea. After years of inattention during Latin periods and watching adverts featuring a large man proposing just one ice-cream cone from a gondola, my Italian was coming along just nicely.

I arrived, cursing, after an unexpected detour around a lake, courtesy of Italian signage. It had added a good three hours to my day and underscored the urgent need to find a map if I was to reach Rome before Christmas. Ivrea is a pretty town, with a hilltop castle that looks out over a higgledy-piggledy scene of pantiled roofs tumbling down to the banks of the river, which, no longer constrained by the valley, had broadened out to progress at a more sedate, but no less powerful, pace.

The Canoe Club, overseen by a caretaker with a mouthful of shattered teeth, was a busy place, preparing for some international championships at the weekend. Youth in all its beauty seemed to be draped everywhere – canoodling on benches, reading under trees or preparing to ride down the exhilarating slalom course. I watched as a member of the British team shot the rapids; paddling in vain, she disappeared at some speed into the distance, crying out 'too much water!'

The day had been tainted throughout by the determined presence of a dreadful smell. The odious bouquet seemed to hover momentarily about my right ear and then, just as I would turn my head to investigate, mysteriously disappear and, not five minutes later, return with renewed vigour. For some time, I assumed the odour was emanating from the orchards I was walking through; however, leaving them behind, I realized that the stench had to be somewhere about me. There followed a number of futile roadside halts and much sniffing of kit, all of which proved inconclusive, until, after greater detective work, I traced the elusive redolence to the top of my bergen which, rushing to shelter from one of the previous day's downpours, I recalled sitting on – at the same time inadvertently grinding it into a dead rat's rotting carcass, bits of which were now infused

The Aosta Valley
...Every peak and summit...crowned with a castle...

with the fabric of my backpack. The rucksack was added to the evening wash.

Ivrea was the first major town I had been able to take stock in since leaving Geneva. There, in a large modern bookshop, I was able to buy the much-needed maps that would guide me on the remainder of the Via Francigena to Rome. Each leg was printed as a strip, showing only a narrow band of terrain either side of the direction of travel, and bore a remarkable resemblance to the maps I had pored over in the British Library before I left. Prepared and illustrated by Matthew Paris, the thirteenth-century Benedictine monk and chronicler, in his *Chronica Majora*, they depicted the pilgrim route from London to Jerusalem almost identically. In my haste, though, I left the legend in the shop, which would mean that having to guess what I was looking at every day would add a certain edge and element of surprise to navigation from hereon.

I also bought an Italian phrasebook, a delightful little publication that I believed would open the doors to the intricacies of my host nation's language, thus avoiding more stumbling performances. The nice lady behind the till, noticing I was a pilgrim, thrust a tiny silver Madonna into my palm, to join the already jingling collection of ID discs, a crucifix, an imprint of a foot and a rosary that hung around my neck in case of real emergency. 'You can call it Maria d'Ivrea', she smiled. I never used the book, but Maria still hangs on my chain.

Wandering the town, I watched as families chatted to one another from balconies across the street. In a piazza I sat at a table, ordered a drink and enjoyed a cigarette, while overhead the swifts screamed through the cloudless sky. Life was all about me but, like a Hadean spirit, I passed unnoticed among the people of Ivrea. I hadn't had a meaningful conversation in over three days. What John Fowles described as the 'monotony of solitude', at once both beautiful and horrifying, had returned – this time, though, no Domingo to my rescue. Looking at my phone, I noticed a text. It was Alain, my fellow pilgrim from Canterbury, telling me he had to return home '*pour raisons familiales*' – a reminder that the Via Francigena was a long road indeed.

As I put out my cigarette, the grand marble pediment over a large nondescript door caught my eye. Pushing on it revealed within a church of golden wonderment whose columns and *trompe l'oeil* Corinthian pilasters flanked frescoes, while grandiose oil paintings encased in elaborate gilt frames were looked on by adoring marble *putti* (chubby winged male children), and in the blue skies that filled the dome above circled a Heavenly Host of angels.

The baroque excess didn't feel kitsch or vulgar at all. Indeed, in comparison to the many other churches I was to visit in due course, quite the opposite; it was beautiful – perhaps the pots of flowering plants that were placed here and there added a touch of humility.

I sat in the pew, staring ahead. Motionless. Thoughtless. Then, an old lady came in and knelt behind me, muttering her catechism in a husky voice. There was a gentle therapeutic rhythm to her praying and, as I listened, so a great sense of calm embraced me. I waited until she finished and, as she got up to go, so I followed her outside, determined to engage.

'*Scusi signora, qual è il nome di questa chiesa?*' What is the name of this church, I asked. Quite where this sudden burst of Italian came from, I am at a loss to explain; rarely, if at all, did I repeat such a command of the language again.

The old lady looked suddenly coy and, pulling a smile, confessed she wasn't sure – 'there are so many churches', she said, shrugging her shoulders, 'it could be San Savino or...' She stopped and asked a passing lady with a Jack Russell in tow, who also looked a little bewildered. After an earnest exchange they agreed, with much laughter, that it must be San Ulderico.

The interesting thing, however, is that Saint Ulric, as we know him, was German. Born in the late ninth century, he was Bishop of Augsburg, near Munich – a position he held for nearly 50 years. The local legend is that the church was built on the site where he carried out a miracle in 971. In one of the wonders he performed, it is alleged that he turned meat on a Thursday into fish on a Friday. In 993, he was the first saint to be canonized by a Pope. The earth from his grave was believed to be quite the thing for repelling rats.

After, I decided to stop for a drink on my way back to the Canoe Club. The girl behind the bar asked me where I was going next.

Santhia, I replied.

'*Zanzare!*' She exclaimed. Mosquitoes.

There was a strong scent of straw on the early morning air as the dew burnt off the fields, and I bid a final farewell to the mountain kingdom; the harvest had just begun and acres of sunflowers now added roadside colour to the Via.

My water consumption rocketed – four to six litres in the parching conditions was the norm just to keep going. By 1 p.m. the temperature was so crushing that there was little alternative but to seek the shade. Italy was in the grip of a record heatwave.

Everywhere I looked, there seemed to be cyclists. Covered in body-hugging lycra, sporting aggressive ant-eyed sunglasses and oversize helmets, I would watch as these lone figures powered their way towards me from afar on sleek racing machines and then stand in amazement as they passed by at considerable speed. Time after time, without fail, it was always an old man in the seat, panting, gasping, sweating in the heat, as if in futile pursuit of tender years that were lost forever.

At Lake Viveron, I stopped for a large bowl of ice cream and a cappuccino. The youth who served me looking as if he had stepped straight out of an Abercrombie & Fitch advert. But all around me, dripping in the latest designer this or that, quaffed and manicured, were pensioners. I walked down to the shore where boats rode gently at their moorings, but again, whether in deckchairs, laid out on towels, paddling or waterskiing on the plate-glass water, there were old people everywhere.

As I passed bars and cafés, so all I would see were groups of elderly men. Anywhere I looked, there was hardly a young person to be seen. Thanks to the steadily rising cost of living, the birth rate in Italy has plummeted; the country now has the highest percentage of old people in Europe. In ten years, it is estimated that nearly 18 million Italians will be over 65, while only 7 million will be under the age of 20. Fifty years earlier, it was the reverse.

Santhia is basically a long street; at the end lies a sprawling railway station, on the far side of which stretch the rice paddies. It's a homely place, as you might expect of a town where people still drink coffee at 7.45 p.m. There not being much to do that night – I was alone in the pilgrim hostel – I studied the visitor book entries of those who had passed through before me.

It turned out that I was the 78th pilgrim to stay in the hostel that year. The majority were Italians, 20 were French and the rest a hotch-potch of Europeans, plus three Australians, a couple of Americans and a Cuban. The oldest was 77, the youngest 21, and the average age was 55; 49 were walking to Rome, of whom six were then on their way to Jerusalem. Only ten had started from Canterbury and, as I suspected, not only did I appear to be the only Englishman on the route at that time, but I was also walking in my own little bubble – the nearest group of pilgrims was two days ahead and LN, my friend from Reims, was one of them. I texted her.

I was 87 miles into Italy when I found myself on the edge of the rice plains of Vercelli, the largest rice-producing area in Europe. Paddy fields stretched as far as the eye could see, water coursing down the broad irrigation ditches that run everywhere through the featureless landscape beyond Santhia. And where there wasn't rice, there was maize – thick forests of the stuff towering seven or eight feet high. The brilliant green fields were a haven for egrets, cranes and herons, which I would watch as they picked their way daintily through the inundated crops or sat hunched on banks as if deep in thought.

Walking down the road, I was passed by two cyclists, Helmut and Franz, who had set out for Rome from Stuttgart. As custom, we exchanged pilgrim gossip – the three of us happy to take a momentary break from the tedium of the flatlands around us.

'Have you seen anything of Sylviane?' I asked.

'The girl in the wheelchair from Linz?'

I nodded.

'No, but we saw her name in the book at Cavaglia, where we stayed last night.'

So, the remarkable lady had made it across the Alps. I was overjoyed and for that news alone I could have danced a jig there and then.

491 miles to Rome.

15

Vercelli to Pavia

Wee be souldiers three,
Pardona moy je vous an pree...
Attributed to Thomas Ravenscroft, *Deuteromelia:*
or *The Second Part of Musick's Melodie,* 1609

As soon as I set foot into the rice paddies the far side of
Vercelli that July morning, I was besieged by mosquitoes. All
precautions taken were completely useless. In fact, such was
their attraction to me that it was impossible to stop even for a
moment.

It was peaceful as I walked in the soothing dawn light, the
land unfettered by the day, save the odd pheasant going about
the undergrowth or the bumptious interruptions of a bullfrog.
As morning gently broke, so I would come across farmers
flooding field and path in unruly surges of muddied water that
were pumped by noisy tractors from the dykes that crisscrossed
the plain. They created small inland seas, crossed on tiptoe or
in large sploshing strides until the sanctuary of an embanked
track could be found.

In late May 1859, Palestro was host to dramatic scenes from
the Second Italian War of Independence, the short-lived but
intense conflict that would see the defeat of the mighty Austrian
Army, thus removing a major obstacle that lay in the way of
Il Risorgimento, as the struggle for unification was known.
The cause, with King Victor Emmanuel II of Sardinia at its
head, dominated the political agenda of the kingdoms, duchies
and states that made up the Italian peninsula for much of the
nineteenth century.

Here, after two days of fighting, the Austrians suffered one
of a series of defeats at the hands of a Franco-Piedmontese
coalition. The battle was part of a grander scheme to tie down
the Austrian military while French troops redeployed, by train,

144

to advance on Milan where the Austrians were weakest. It was one of the first occasions that railways were used to gain strategic advantage in war.

One of the most decisive moments, towards the end of the battle, was the charge by the 3e Régiment de Zouaves into the Austrian flank. This daring action forced a battalion of Austrian infantry to falter and led to the capture of a brigade's-worth of artillery. Victor Emmanuel was personally involved in the incident and the following day the regiment made him an honorary corporal in recognition. The greater allied scheme was successful.

Events at Palestro, however, were a mere curtain-raiser for the fiercely fought final encounter at Solferino three weeks later. Along with Garibaldi's successes at Varese and Como, that costly victory, which involved 300,000 combatants and only ended after nine hours' fighting with over 5,500 dead, 23,500 wounded and 11,500 either missing or captured, brought the ten-week war to an end. Austria sued for peace with Napoleon III. The armistice, signed at Villafranca, ultimately forfeited Lombardy to Sardinia. It was a significant gain – a turning point that gave the unification movement considerable added momentum.

Within a year, many of the northern states were annexed to Sardinia. It would not be until 1861, however, that the Kingdom of Italy was proclaimed and a further nine years before the map began to look anything like the Italy we know today.

As I walked up to Palestro's solitary café, I saw a great bear of a man sitting outside. His face was weathered like old brown boots and he wore a full white beard with brilliant teeth to match – unmistakably a pilgrim.

'Ho *Pelegrino*!' I greeted my fellow traveller before establishing that German was easier, despite the fact that Andreas, who since 18 had lived in Dortmund, was originally from Gdansk in Poland. Apart from the colour of his hair, there was little to suggest that the enormous Pole had just turned 60. He, like me, was also on his way to Mortara that day. But, as I went to sit down, so he stood up and with a smile and a wave, left. It was only as he turned that I noticed the scallop shell, the symbol of the Santiago pilgrimage, and a photo of Pope John Paul II attached to his rucksack.

Bored with the interminable paddy, which was a section of the journey that simply had to be 'got through', I stopped again a few miles further on in Robbio. While making a phone call, I noticed Andreas pass by. I motioned him to join me. Call ended, we elected to defeat the *ennui* and heat by continuing our onward journey together, which resulted in a non-stop conversation over the ensuing hours in his fluent and my not-so-fluent German.

Andreas was a good man with great religious conviction. But it only took one look at him, as he towered over me, to realize that walking at his pace was going to be quite a test.

He was quick to relate that the hordes he had encountered walking the Camino had left him empty, unfulfilled and searching for a greater spiritual experience. Since leaving Canterbury, his experience had been far more accentuated than anything he had enjoyed while crossing Spain. Then, just as I was about to ask, he added, '*und, Harry, die Engeln wachen über mich...*'

My jaw dropped. But he was adamant, and not in some fanciful dreamt-up way either, that there had been too many coincidences. From people popping last-minute heads out of windows offering beds for the night to finding water or just being shown the way by strangers appearing from nowhere – even our meeting, he argued, was the work of angels. It was hard to disagree.

I found myself, however, in a constant trot to keep up with the Falstaffian figure who, despite the soaring temperature, only ever drank *bier*; he rarely touched water. This gave him a certain medieval aura as the practice harked back to a time when water was so consistently foul that ale was the only safe alternative.

And, when not talking, we whistled, hummed and sang. Our first song was 'Hitler has only got one ball', sung to the tune of 'Colonel Bogey', which translates remarkably easily into German. I learnt some new vocabulary in the process, resulting in a momentary halt until we regained our composure, much to the astonishment of bewildered passing Italian motorists.

An hour or so later, I spied a lone umbrella on the roadside with someone sitting in the shade under it – '*erdbeeren?*', I gesticulated at Andreas.

The Pole glanced at me in disbelief, '*Nein, Harry...*' The look said it all. As we closed, so it was obvious. There were no crates of strawberries for sale, just a pretty girl in an over-tight dress who, sitting on a deckchair minutes earlier, was now emerging, 30 euros the richer, from a thick curtain of mosquito-infested maize, followed not long after by an old man wobbling about on a bicycle with a grin that was way too big for his face.

Mortara, with some grandiose buildings at its centre that hint at a prosperous past, was a compact little town fraying at the edges in customary Italian style. The pilgrim hostel of L'Abbazia di Sant'Albino was a church with a sixteenth-century red-brick campanile and neoclassical frontage set among some cream buildings that had clearly once been part of something far larger. It was in a secluded spot at the edge of the rice fields, surrounded by poplar trees. The intermittent call of duck and children at play in the garden gave the place a tranquil feel – the very same, I suspect, that pilgrims on their way to Rome had experienced for centuries.

Banging on the barn-like doors, we were greeted by Franca, the cheerful lady who ran the place, and her husband Gigi. They ushered us into a large modern and utilitarian hall that would not only be our refectory for the evening but also our dormitory for the night. We were the only guests that day. Padre Nunzio was sent for – a smiling old boy who, as a young priest 38 years earlier, had officiated at the couple's wedding. He checked our Passports with some small ceremony before stamping them with the insignia of the Abbazia in a beautiful shade of green.

There was nothing presumptuous about Andreas as we talked over a supper of veal Milanese. Devoted to his family, he was solid and reliable, like ancient oak. Of late, he had clearly been thinking a great deal, as we chatted up a storm on the mores of life. Andreas affirmed that 'without belief, your family, a business, a goal, I don't know, something...you are nothing'. He hissed the '*s*' in '*nichts*' as if for emphasis.

'A life without purpose', he continued, glass in hand, 'is not worth living. People have to regain their values – pilgrimage is good for this reason because we forget. We forget that it is important to pause, and re-learn, not remember, Harry, but re-learn', he emphasized in his deep voice. 'To be happy, to be truly happy, we must strive for life.'

After eating we went to sit in the garden, passing a large mural high up on the wall. It was of two knights – one lying mortally wounded on the ground while the other was riding to his aid just as horseman and steed were fatally struck through the neck and chest by an arrow. The words *'Morte di Amico e Amelio – Paladini di Carlo Magno'* were written below.

Andreas and I looked up at it. For a moment, perhaps out of respect at the clear message the picture sent out, we fell silent.

Just then, Franca popped her head around the door.

'*Was ist das?*' the Pole asked, pointing at the mural.

In a mixture of Italian and faltering English she explained the story of the painting, which I, in turn, had to repeat to Andreas in my simplistic German.

'Well, in the early times this place was called *Pulchra Silva*, the Beautiful Wood, and on 12 October 773 it was the scene of a terrible battle between the Emperor Carlo' – Charlemagne, I explained to Andreas – 'and Desiderio, the King of the Longobards. As a matter of fact, so many people died in the battle that they changed the town name afterwards to Mortara, which is from the Latin, *Ara Mortis* – the Altar of Death.'

Franca looked at my Polish friend, who gave a grim frown and nodded his head in understanding. 'Anyway, during the fighting here, two of Carlo's most trusted knights, Amis de Beyre and Amile d'Auvergne, were killed. He had 12 knights in all. They were called the Paladins, as famous in those times as your English King Arturo and 'is Lancelot. But, this pair, they were special. They had never been parted since the day they first met as teenagers. And always they fight side by side. They even swore an oath of, er...how do I say it, 'Arry, 'elp me?'

'Loyalty?'

'Yes, precisely, an oath of loyalty to each other. They were the very best of friends', she added, looking up once again at the picture.

'So, after the battle was finished, that night, Carlo said that one of them should be buried in the Church of Sant'Eusebio and the other in San Pietro. The next morning, 'owever, true to their oath, both bodies were found together in Sant'Eusebio.

And nobody know how they got there. Carlo, he said they should remain together.'

Franca then looked over at me. 'Some say your Sant'Alcuin, 'Arry, who was Carlo's priest, suggested that they build the Abbazia here on the site of the old Sant'Eusebio. But for me, I like to think that one of the reasons that this is such a happy place is because here it's all about a celebration of friendship. That is why it was so popular with pilgrims on the way to Rome in the Middle Ages – they came to pay tribute to the famous *Paladini...*'

Tip-toeing about before dawn, we prepared to leave for Pavia, creeping into the intimate chapel to dwell a moment in its darkened shadows. In the silence, I thought about the two Paladins and the desperate fight that had befallen this place so many years ago. We prayed, looked at the names carved by our forebears over the centuries and ventured out into the early light.

After the initial bravado of the day, the whistling and the singing gradually died away. First, my feet blistered, and then, once my ankle turned, it became apparent that keeping up with Andreas would be nigh on impossible. I was reduced to a pitiful hobble languishing in his ever-lengthening wake.

And then the sun rose in the cloudless sky and its unforgiving rays began to drain us as vampire-like it fed on our will to live. We walked into a Lucifer's Paradise that blurred the vision and frayed the temper. My head bent forward as if in plea for the executioner's axe, progress in the imprisoning heat was often reduced to little better than a stumble. Hands and joints swelled while flies cloyed at nose, mouth and eyes that were already raw from the acid trickle of sweat. The little spit that could be mustered was dry, tart and stuck to our tongues, which, no matter how much water we drank, were never sated. The only option was to doggedly push on. My mind poisoned with anything but devotion, I journeyed with the Devil that day, a voice constantly whispering in my head, 'this is folly...all folly'.

We staggered the last of the 22 miles it took to reach Pavia like survivors coming out of the desert. My feet were in desperate need of attention, as if I had spent eight hours walking on broken glass. Come day's end, I sank into a major decline.

Abbazia di Sant'Albino, Mortara
...all about a celebration of friendship.

No sooner had I arrived in the comparative luxury of the *Ostello di Santa Maria* in Betlem than I wanted to leave it. Sensing my state, the kind-hearted Andreas reminded me that our situation, two-thirds of the way to Rome, was like hitting the 'wall' in a marathon.

'In these times, Harry', he said, stirring a pan of noodles in the kitchen, 'you must remember, it's not the strength in your muscles but the strength in your mind that counts.' He touched his temple. He was right. Nothing other than sheer bloody-minded determination was going to get us to Rome, as the day itself had proven.

I tended my feet and, leaving Andreas to his cooking, took my stick and limped over the Ponte Coperto in search of piazzi, bars, people and life; in short, anywhere and anything that had absolutely nothing to do with the walk whatsoever.

Pavia was abuzz that evening. Sitting outside, a few *Aperols*, most of a bottle of wine and a large plate of *vongole* later, life began to look up again.

I was just enjoying a contemplative cigarette when I noticed a young guy dining at a table nearby. His eyebrows furrowed to take a closer look and eventually he got up and came over.

'Excuse me, but don't I know you from London?'

And indeed he did, but when you find people the best part of a thousand miles out of context, it takes a few moments for the brain to recalibrate.

'Marco?' I said, 'what are you doing here?'

'It's my home town, I am here with my family for a few weeks…'

We agreed to meet for coffee the following morning.

In the cramped street, the sandstone façade of the Basilica di San Michele Maggiore seemed to hang over me like pipes in an organ loft. Marco, my self-appointed guide for the day, met me outside the carved doors sporting a ridiculously large pair of dark glasses. Like a well-rehearsed tour bus guide with a bundle of cue cards and hardly a word in greeting, so he began. 'Welcome to Pavia, laid out in the classical Roman design that we call "*cardo e decumano*" – that is to say the "*cardo maximus*", the main street which runs north to south, where all the shops are', he winked and gave a big grin, 'and the *"decumanus maximus"*, which is the road that runs east to west and is the second street. And behind you', pointing to San Michele like an air steward indicating the aircraft exits, 'is, for us locals, the real church of Pavia.' He ushered me inside. It was refreshingly cool.

'It was here that Charlemagne and Frederick Barbarossa, the red beard, received the iron crown of *Lombardia* at their coronations as the Kings of Italy. You know, they say it is made from a nail of Jesus's cross?'

'Really?'

'*Si, certo*. But, that Barbarossa, you know, 'e never really tamed us Longobards. He laid siege to Milan twice and got swept away crossing a river in the Crusades', he said with a degree of triumph, as if that was just reward for daring to lay a finger on one of the fashion capitals of the modern world.

'See how the stone keeps the hairs fresh?'

'Air', I said.

'*Si*, the hair', he replied. 'My sister was married here last week. *I* was the best man...imagine...me...*all* in *Prada*.' He glanced back over his shoulder and gave a look so glamorous he could almost have been centre-frame in the *Breakfast at Tiffany's* poster. Under exquisitely blue and gold frescoed ceilings, Marco led me to an icon of San Michele standing over a dragon. 'See here', for a moment he became uncharacteristically pensive, 'how the archangel he protects us', pointing to the image, 'from the dragons; the bad things of life.'

We drove in his little car to the Duomo, Pavia's cathedral, the dome of which had dominated my horizon for much of the previous day. It was a strange sensation as we sped through the streets. I found myself continually doing time and distance calculations in my head, constantly looking at the speedometer in wonderment at how quickly we managed to get everywhere.

Enshrined in scaffolding, the Duomo was very shut. The chance to gaze upon the relic of the single thorn that had been taken from the Crown of Thorns at the Crucifixion was denied me. All the same, I couldn't help remarking on a giant statue of a Roman dignitary on his horse that stood outside. Some wag had painted the stallion's balls gold.

The Castello Visconteo is now home to pigeons and swallows. Once it had belonged to the great Visconti family who ruled Milan and Pavia for over 200 years. In its rather sorrowful state, it was hard to imagine carriages clattering back and forth over the bridge that spanned the now-dry moat. We stared through massive iron grilles at an overgrown courtyard where some staging had been left half-dismantled.

'You know the director, Luchino Visconti, the one who made *Death in Venice*?'

I nodded.

'Well this is the house of his family – one of the houses', he laughed. 'In the grounds, which were once very big, the French Army was smashed to pieces at the Battle of Pavia by Carlo Five, the Holy Roman Emperor in 1525.'

'You mean Charles Quint', I interrupted, referring to the ruler's French name whose trail I had come across weeks earlier in Besançon.

'I dunno, I am not bloody French.' Without batting an eyelid, he continued. 'Anyway, as I was saying, Carlo, he put an end to the French here in Italy, thanks God – we like to do that from time to time. After the Second World War we put the stupid King and all his House of Savoy on a plane too and waved bye-bye to the lot of them.' But then as we looked into the yard, he added: 'Sad, so much life and now all the castello is used for is the odd concert. But, we had the *Jump Up* festival here a few days back...ten thousand people... imagine...'

Before going into the Basilica of San Pietro in Ciel d'Oro, we paused to watch a large monk feast, with some delight, on an equally super-sized ice cream. Entering, the far end of the church was dominated by a shining white magnificence that, on its plinth, almost seemed to touch the golden-mosaicked ceiling that represented the *Ciel d'Oro*.

'This is the tomb of Sant'Agostino, one of the most important saints in all the Church', said Marco, 'because in the fourth century he renewed Christianity. Even Pope Benedict, he say how influential a person he was.'

Such was the aura radiated by the great monument that it was with some trepidation that I approached it. The reliefs around the fourteenth-century tomb, complete with Gothic gabling, depicted scenes from the saint's life in what is now Algeria. In its raised state, to stare out of unabashed curiosity seemed mawkish. As if to underline this, a priest nearby spoke in hushed animated tones to an old lady who was clearly in some anguish.

'All that Carrara marble, think how much it cost', said Marco.

By now, I too was in need of a large ice cream. Marco, however, couldn't resist showing me a magnificent statue of Giuseppe Garibaldi, one of the founding fathers of the Italian State. Defiant, it stood on top of a large erupted rockery with a demonstrative and pertly chested nymph skipping with gay abandon down its side. At the base, a muscular lion in marble chewed nonchalantly on a bundle of fasces. To me, it said much about the great man's attitude to authority.

'Did you know his name was Marie?' Marco said. 'He was a sea captain who actually came from Nice, which is why he wouldn't speak to Cavour, Victor Emmanuel's prime minister, 'cos he gave the town to the French in the deal to help beat the Austrians.' I thought back to Palestro. 'But Garibaldi, what a man! He was all about independence – here and in South America.' He looked across at me. 'He knew what he wanted and he never rested until he got one Italy.' Then, looking fondly at the lion, he said: 'I like him. He's so expressive and powerful. Sums up Garibaldi, I think.'

Jock Davis, shaven-headed, dressed from head to toe in black, looked every inch the neo-fascist – except that at some point in the intervening months since I had last seen him, he seemed to have swallowed a large beach ball. Stood ramrod to attention outside Pavia Station, like the Guardsman he once was, it would only have taken a quick cry of 'fix bayonets' and I suspect most of the crowd would have been dispatched with the most horrifying efficiency. As we turned into the entrance, I hung my head out of the car window and shouted to him.

'Oh thank the Lord, 'Arry', he said in broad Halifax as he ran over, took one look at Marco with his oversized dark glasses and, turning to me, said, 'where the bloody 'ell 'ave you been fella?!'

I tried to explain about the statue of Garibaldi and his cavorting nymph, but it was lost in a giant bear hug which as good as suffocated me, followed by a hip flask that was instantly thrust in my hand. "Ere ya go, boss, drink that.'

'Boss', a term of endearment in military circles that makes me smart even to this day, felt all the more incongruous now we were in Pavia and on a pilgrimage. Three days earlier, Jock had texted me from Surrey. I could tell that life was none too good at home and it took little encouragement to get him to northern Italy for a much-needed break. Now in the Police, he had, for most of my time through the thick and thin of the British Army, been right by my side. Possibly the only three-fingered bagpipe player in the world (don't mend your car with the engine running), Jock is one of the very few people I know who can stop an enemy anti-aircraft gun firing by driving into it or make a Land Rover do a full 360-degree pirouette and, on both occasions, without meaning to. To this day, true to the code, never mind the fact that he can rarely if ever keep his mouth shut, he remains one of my closest friends whom I love like a brother.

On his way back home, Marco dropped us off at the *Ostello*. Don Lamberto, Santa Maria's bald, middle-aged priest, was standing on the steps calling out to parishioners in the street. In an open-neck shirt, he looked very jolly in comparison to the gruff front he had put on at mass the night before when I had mistakenly elevated him to the rank of Monsignor – a promotion which, he said, was most undeserved yet very welcome all the same.

The first challenge that presented me on return, however, was that Jock spoke no German, Andreas no English and neither of them knew a single word of Italian. I needn't have worried. A few minutes left alone in the kitchen, which we had effectively requisitioned, and the pair had somehow worked out a means of communication, largely based on Jock's residual knowledge of war comics. They quickly became friends, one of Jock's many qualities, such that I returned to hoots of 'Herr Major!' which, no matter how hard I tried to distance myself, stuck for the rest of the week.

The second, and greater, hurdle was the logistics involved in crossing the river Po in two days' time. After some frustrating telephone conversations, my Italian, which had fared so well until then, finally failed me. Michele, who ran the *Ostello*, came to my aid. Some more calls and he explained the convoluted arrangements, marginally less complicated than escaping a Prisoner of War camp, that would be required to meet the great Danilo Parisi, '*Il Grande Ammiraglio del Fiume Po*'.

'Tomorrow night', Michele began, intently, 'you will spend in Santa Cristina with Don Antonio, then at 8 a.m. the following morning, you telephone to Danilo to say you are coming. He will meet you in Corte Sant'Andrea at noon to take you across the river. When you get to the other side, at his *locanda*, the *Caupona Sigerico*, he will give you something to eat and', raising an eyebrow, 'if his wife, she likes you…then maybe you can stay the night but if she don't like then he will tell you to go further on to Calendasco.'

Back in the kitchen, I briefed the troops on the important stage in the journey that we were about to embark on. At the end of which I announced, 'and then, folks, it's only four weeks to Rome!' At which point, the room burst into song and marching around the table, for some inexplicable reason carrying broomsticks like rifles on parade, we sang at the top of our voices, '*I love to go a wandering, along the mountain track, and as I go, I love to sing, my knapsack on my back! Val-deri, val-dera, val-deri, val-dera-ha-ha-ha-ha-ha. Val-deri, val-dera, my knapsack on my back!*' Don Lamberto popped his head around the door in disbelief.

433 miles to Rome.

16

Belgioioso to Piacenza

...I want you to understand that,
in the Little World between the river and the mountains,
many things can happen that cannot happen anywhere else.
Giovanni Guareschi, *The Little World of*
Don Camillo, 1948

WHEN YOU ARE THREE burly blokes with staves and rucksacks it is hard to go unnoticed. Every time we stopped anywhere, we quickly became objects of much interest. The enthusiastic Italians couldn't resist finding out, with much ooh-ing and aah-ing, where we were from, where we had come from and where we were going. Given my pidgin Italian, this line of questioning would often result in some confusion, which, once corrected, would lead to restaurants and cafés in stitches of laughter and much cheering and clapping.

Stopping for breakfast in Belgioioso that morning, we were cornered in an eatery by a handful of old boys who had been watching our every movement in great detail. The questioning soon began but it was Emilio, speaking in a hoarse whisper as if he had just been kicked somewhere unfortunate, who, pointing at my foot, expressed concern that I was limping.

'No *problema*', I replied.

'Yeah, *no* chuffin' *problema*', Jock added not so *sotto voce*, 'just the Major can't bloody well walk.'

Emilio ordered us three grappa then disappeared. I looked up, questioning, but his comrades bade us stay with reassuring tuts and calming gestures of hand. And then another three grappa arrived. As the pleasant miasma worked its charm, so Andreas started to beam and Jock chuckle. Fortunately, before we got too settled in – remember it was only just after breakfast time for most people – Emilio emerged from a side street with a little box done up in tissue and ribbon. Presenting it with great dignity, he patted me on the back said, '*Buon viaggio pellegrino!*' and, with the whole bar joining in with cries of '*A Roma! A Roma!*' we were as good as sent on our way.

The box was so beautifully wrapped that it seemed a crime to open it, but such was the clamour from the other two as soon as we were out of sight that I had little alternative. Inside was a bottle of herb-infused foot powder, the scent of rosemary enveloping us as I lifted the lid. It was a kind, heartfelt gesture.

Santa Cristina was once the site of a large pilgrim hospital in the Middle Ages. We were met by a young boy who led us to the *Parrochia,* a noise-filled hall where Don Antonio, a red-faced priest with fathomless patience, was embroiled in youth school. It was a splendid place, with all the order of a washing machine on final spin. There were children everywhere – in the yard, in the dining room, in the kitchen, in the front and out the back playing every game conceivable from tag to hide-and-seek, football, table tennis, darts and pool. The noise was so great that their enjoyment was almost tangible.

This uproarious tableau was supervised by Piera, an elderly lady who presided over the rambunctious mob from behind the bar like an aged parrot on its perch. Every now and then, she would make ear-piercing demands for order at the very top of her voice. These sudden outbursts, together with the children's screams and shouts and indecipherable broadcasts over the tannoy, kept the three of us on permanent edge. It was all most unnerving.

After a lunch of cold pork sandwiches washed down with plenty of red frizzante wine, we felt more relaxed. Don Antonio showed us to our accommodation upstairs – a chaotic schoolroom of a place, stacked with chairs, bedsteads, mattresses and trestle tables.

We agreed, after the long morning's walk from Pavia, it was time for a siesta. Fortunately, there were no bunk beds. I was reminded that the last time I had shared a room with Jock was in Bosnia when, one evening, we had got stuck behind Muslim lines and had to spend the night in their rear area. I had been in protracted negotiations with the local commander and returned, exhausted, to find Jock already hunkered down fast asleep – my sleeping bag thoughtfully laid out on the top bunk of the neighbouring bed. Wearily, I climbed up. The consequences of reaching my destination were immediate, loud and disastrous. All but two of the slats had been removed.

Lying in his sleeping bag, Jock rolled his eyes as I anointed myself from head to toe with mosquito repellent.

'I don't get bit me', he asserted with some confidence and then, referring to the continued racket downstairs, added, 'noisy bastards', shoved a pair of earplugs in, rolled over to face the wall and farted loudly.

Needless to say, when Jock awoke later in the afternoon, he had a head that looked like it had been in a pressure cooker for too long. He became a rapid convert to the merits of the application of mosquito repellant.

We toiled down the embanked road through maize and rice paddies to the riverside hamlet of Corte Sant'Andrea. In the oppressive heat, I had little energy to respond to Jock's constant stream of queries, the most memorable of which was the repeated question as to just why did poplar trees grow in lines.

Nearing the outskirts of the village, I watched a short roly-poly man in white shorts and a red sweatshirt climb up on to the track. The moment I set eyes on him, I knew that this was none other than *Il Grande Ammiraglio del Fiume Po*, the famed Danilo Parisi of whom I had heard so much.

The very instant he took my hand in both of his and looked me in the eye, I could tell that the self-appointed Ferryman of the River Po was a special, selfless man of enormous heart; one of the Via Francigena's, if not life's, great characters to whom material wealth mattered not one jot. For Danilo, the experience, not only for him but more importantly for others, along life's great way counted for all.

Amid much welcome, we were ushered down the embankment to the shading eaves of a lean-to at the back of a *locanda* that was hung with washing at one end and strings of drying vegetables at the other. Here Renato, the local '*cheffy*' of Police, as Danilo referred to him, had laid out large bottles of lemon barley water as if in sacred preparation for *Transitum Padi*, the crossing of the river Po – or, to use its Latin name, the Padus. Our Passports were franked with a large blue stamp, the Po running across its centre with two keys above and a tiny rowing boat beneath.

Danilo then asked where we had all come from.

'Canterbury', said Andreas.

'*Londra*', I added, after which the old ferryman burst into raucous laughter as pointing to the somewhat spherical Jock he remarked, '*you* have *not* come from *Londra*!'

We were led down to Danilo's motorboat, the *Sigerico*, moored at the bottom of a steep iron jetty. Kit stowed, with Andreas and Jock in the stern and me sitting up for'ard, we pushed off from the jetty with a loud cheer and at last bade farewell to the rice paddies of Lombardy. Danilo steadily pulled back the throttle and powered the craft out past looming white sandbanks into the lazing tree-lined Po. The bow lifted and, cutting a swathe of wash, we carved our way in a diagonal direction the mile or so downstream to the far bank. It was liberating to travel at such speed.

As we crossed this impressive watery expanse, which runs from the Alps to the Adriatic, I couldn't help pondering the countless Ligurians, Etruscans, Celts, Veneti, Umbri and Romans – to name but a few of the ancient tribes and peoples – who had lived off Italy's longest river and its 141 tributaries since the earliest of times.

Landing on the southern bank at the appropriately named *Guado di Sigerico*, Sigeric's Joy, it felt as if another of the journey's great burdens had been lifted. We climbed up the bank and walked through vines and shrubbery until we reached a column that was set with the figure of a pilgrim carved in stone. At its base was an aged brick with a footprint clearly marked on it.

'This marks where they believe Sigerico landed', Danilo said. 'Of course no one really knows precisely where; some people say he travelled with over a hundred people in attendance, he was that important – and look', he said pointing to the brick, 'here is *il piede di Sigerico*.'

I raised an eyebrow.

'Okay! *Di Napoleone*...?'

Another eyebrow.

'Okay, okay...'

Despite being half-hidden amid trees, it was impossible to miss Danilo's *locanda*. It was a substantial geranium-festooned affair with a pantiled roof that proliferated with chimneys. The outside walls were plastered with signs and hoardings like a railway station, announcing '*Caupona Sigerico*', Sigeric's Inn, '*Hospitum Peregrinorum*' and a large brass plaque which stated it was 588 kilometres, or 365 miles, to Rome. It was a veritable shrine in celebration of the ancient Archbishop's journey back to Canterbury.

For the last 15 years, ever since Don Antonio, our kindly priest from the night before, had called on 12 September 1998 asking if he could help a Dutchman cross the river, Danilo had dedicated his life to the welfare and transport of pilgrims across the Po.

Inside, the *Caupona* was baronial, with a cavernous banqueting hall complete with refectory tables, bare brick walls hung with medieval pictures and tapestries of hunting scenes and all manner of fossils and memorabilia. At night, the room was lit by large iron chandeliers which hung high up in the rafters. On one table, there even lay an outsize bone that looked as if it was made of concrete. Danilo insisted it was part of a mammoth. It was a magical place.

At the far end was a large fireplace, the preferred domain of Lika the dog, who found the ash and chimney draft cooling in the heat. Elsewhere in the house was a terrier, Missy, for whom escape was her sole preoccupation, while somewhere under the table lurched the aged Bilbo.

Taking the great room in, I was reminded of Mario, whom I had walked with to Champlitte, and the school trips he spoke of to this real-life never-never land that Danilo had created from nothing. It didn't matter if the provenance of the stories were every now and again a little stretched; here there felt a unique and long handed-down connection with time of which we were, at that moment, very much a part. I could think of no better place nor more fascinating a person than our host to inspire a child's imagination to wonderment at the greater world around.

Danilo, transformed from ship's captain to Maître D' by the simple addition of a large apron, reappeared with a bottle of chilled red wine, colanders of peppers, onions, tomatoes and lettuce and chopping boards of salami, cured meat and slabs of Parmigiano cheese. The second bottle of wine came with the steak, at which point we were having the usual catch-up about who had been through recently. I asked after Sylviane in the wheelchair.

'Ah, the lady from Austria?'

'Yes.'

'Renato he called me about her. It would not have been a problem, but the people in Orio Litta insisted she go by car across the bridge and took her to Piacenza. They said it would have been too difficult for her but I said, if she can cross the Alps, the river was easy money.'

Just at that moment I received a text from LN, whom I had stayed with the night before Reims. I didn't have time to fully digest the message in which she told me she had been diagnosed with tendonitis and had to rest for five days, ending with a rather despondent *'quoi faire?'* Its arrival coincided with the very pleasant sensation of a dog's nose against my calf.

'Ow! You FUCKER!' I cried, as teeth sank into me without warning. I nearly threw the table over, such was my shock.

Danilo collapsed in hysterics – as did everyone else.

'Bilbo? Is that Bilbo?!'

I really didn't care who it was, save that something in the dark depths beneath had developed an unhealthy and sudden appetite for my leg.

'Don't worry about him', Danilo said, 'he's got no teeth anyway. Imagine how it is for me, uh? He sleep on my side of the bed and every night, without fail, when I get up to take a piss, he bite my feet!'

Celebration at another hurdle passed was very much the order of the day. Not long after, with the arrival of the third – or maybe it was the fourth – bottle of wine, events grew a little hazy. It was a *Vita Bella* moment as Jock took to playing the spoons and, with Andreas on percussion using salad tongs and an upturned saucepan, it wasn't long before we were singing *That's Amore* a little more than *fortissimo*.

It was well into the third verse or, more accurately, the first verse third time around, that Danilo with a panic-stricken look on his face raced into the room, urging us to quieten down. 'It's my wife', he pleaded.

After a siesta, the *pelligrini pericolosi* – as we were now known – were summoned to an intimate walled garden where a cat dozed on a marble bench. Taking up most of the table before him was a large book bound in sumptuous red leather with the words *Liber Perigrinorum*, 'The Book of Pilgrims', embossed on the front. It recorded everyone who had passed through since that first pilgrim 14 years earlier. Danilo ran his hand over the many entries with an almost Bible-like respect; the pages were so heavy that, when turned, they made a gratifying noise like the opening of a treasure chest. Including us, Danilo had taken five pilgrims in his boat that day; last year, he told me, 350 had made the crossing – some going all the way to Rome, others making their way down the Via Francigena, one section at a time every year.

With much ceremony, he took our Passports and producing a larger-than-life stamp, about the circumference of a pint glass, made his mark in bright red ink on each of the documents. Danilo's was the largest of all the crests we would collect on the journey.

There were murmurs from within, to which Danilo, jumping up and running inside, responded with the urgency of a fireman on call-out. He returned to declare that we were welcome to stay the night, in an outhouse, and enquired what we would like for supper. We had passed muster.

Dinner was restrained, given that Bilbo spent the entire meal with his head in my lap.

Arriving in Piacenza, we bid farewell to Andreas. Having walked together for five days, the time had come to go our separate ways. Little needed to be said – we both knew it would not be long before we would catch up again on the road ahead.

Now was the time, I explained over lunch in the Piazza Duomo, to embark on a little culture which, in the improving spirit of the Grand Tour, I added, was a noble thing to do. Jock, however, seemed none too sure until, looking up, he spied a sinister-looking cage mounted high up on the side of the cathedral bell tower.

The cage, which was quite roomy, unlike the more figure-hugging British gibbets used to hang out the remains of murderers and other such undesirables, was installed at the behest of Ludovico the Moor, *Il Moro*, the nickname of the fifteenth-century Duke of Milan who famously commissioned Leonardo Da Vinci to paint *The Last Supper*. It would be wrong, though, to give *Il Moro* credit for inventing the beastly contraption. Long before, the campanile in Venice's Piazza San Marco had wooden cages where unruly priests, adulterers and other such problem cases were hung out to calm down – sometimes for up to a year, fed on bread and water alone. *In extremis, pour encourager les autres* criminals were simply left to starve. Later, in 1536, the bodies of three radical Anabaptists were left to rot in cages hung from the steeple of St Lambert's Church following the overthrow of the Münster Rebellion in northern Germany.

Such public punishment must have added a whole new dimension to the notion that obeying the law was a good idea. For a moment Jock considered this and then, sipping on his beer, commented that, given recent goings-on in religious circles, there was a very good case for reintroducing the things.

We reached the Palazzo Farnese, an ungainly half-finished barrack block built in the sixteenth century, via a circuitous route that involved a deal of refreshment along the way. We worked our way through room after flamboyantly stuccoed room of magnificent portraiture that extolled the virtues of the Farnese dynasty, which had spawned the Dukes of Parma, Castro, Piacenza and numerous church dignitaries. But it was in the depths of the building – almost hidden in obscurity – that we discovered the *Fegato di Piacenza*, otherwise known as the Etruscan Liver. It is a curiosity that for me ranks alongside the Bronze Age Phaistos Disk, which was unearthed on Crete in 1908.

The Fegato is a bronze cast of a sheep's liver that was found by a farmer ploughing a field on the outskirts of the city in the late nineteenth century. It is similar in shape and size to an avocado pear cut in half with the stone fashioned into three protrusions in the shape of a fig, mountain peak and tombstone. The upper surface of the dark green metal is scored with crude etchings and divisions that experts believe represent the different parts of the sky and the deities therein, except that in those early days they bore names like Satres for Saturn, the god of agriculture, Fuflus for Bacchus and Tin for Jupiter, ruler of the gods. There are five names or words whose meaning has been lost to time altogether.

This curious piece had Jock and me entranced as we craned necks, crooked heads and knelt down to peer intently at the piece, such was our desire to try to understand what this deeply attractive object could be. What we would have given to hold the Fegato as, it is believed, an Etruscan '*haruspex*' would have done. A haruspex was a soothsayer who specialized in haruspicy, or the art of prophesying the future through examination of sacrificed animals, especially chickens and sheep.

While the Fegato is not unique, unlike the Phaistos Disk, it is no less beguiling. Similar items have been found among Hittite ruins in Anatolia and Babylonian settlements along the Tigris and Euphrates, which flow through Mesopotamia where it is thought the practice originated. After much staring, Jock suddenly began to glaze over and we quickly agreed that there had been enough Grand Touring for one afternoon; with considerable relief, we headed out into the sunshine once again.

That evening, the time came for Jock to head home. I walked with him to the station.

'I tell you one good thing about this place, 'Arry.'

'What's that Jockie?'

'No bloody mozzies an' all!'

As we reached the entrance, my friend dug in his pocket and producing a package, said: ''Ere, I brought you this, H. It's for yer rucksack, so folk'll know who you are and no mistaking.'

I opened it to reveal a large eight-pointed Star of the Garter in silver with blue and red enamelled detailing, the regimental insignia of the Coldstream Guards.

I fixed Jock in the eye. How, I thought, he looked refreshed and invigorated again, ready to take on the trials that no doubt would face him back home. 'You will be all right, won't you?'

'I'll be all right boss, don't you worry.'

I smiled and, touching him on the shoulder, watched as he turned on his heel and marched off into the crowd.

395 miles to Rome.

17

Fidenza to Marinella di Sarzanna

I spent a long time over the maps. They covered all the country between the mountain and the crinale, the main ridge of the Apennines...the general effect was as if a band of centipedes with inky feet had spent a day scuttling over a sheet of paper.
Eric Newby, *Love and War in the Apennines*, 1971

ANGELS, I AM NOW convinced, inhabit people temporarily, such that a person can then do a good deed for another at precisely the moment required. When that is done, the angel flits off somewhere else. Why else would they have wings? Occasionally, however, in order to achieve whatever they deem needs to be done in a timely manner, angels will occupy the most unlikely of beings, and, I suspect, derive a degree of mischievous pleasure in the process.

After Fidenza I turned due south to climb into the Apennine Mountains and was immediately delivered into a sublime world of steep valleys, hilltop villages and tumbledown farmhouses – a land filled with oak, fir and cypress that reverberated to the cicada's *zed zed* lullaby and the gentle call of wood pigeon.

Costa Mezzana was not a pretty village. It was ungainly and too close to Fidenza for that, but all the same it had a certain charm, full of life and that happy noise of children playing which could be heard everywhere. Nevertheless, perched on top of its ridgeline with valleys falling away either side, it was removed from the suffocating heat of the plain, which had dogged me ever since leaving the Aosta valley.

No sooner had I arrived than I was hailed in the street by a wizened old walnut, Luciana. Not one for small talk, she took me to her now-defunct shop, stamped my Passport and led me back outside.

'There's the trattoria, yum yum, and...', she pointed across the way and, as we climbed the steps to the *ostello* entrance, so she prodded me with the key, 'up on the first floor you will find a bed. Your name is on the door. Don't make a mess. *Arrivederci, Arrigo*!'

Just as Luciana administered the *ostello*, so Franco, who wore a uniform of white vest and blue shorts with immaculately parted grey hair, ran the place – with a rod of iron. I knew his type well. I had suffered under similar martinets as a recruit in the Army. There was a notice for just about everything, posted everywhere on scraps of cardboard in indecipherable Italian.

Franco lived somewhere in the building; his patrolling approach could be heard staircases away by the threatening jangle of his badge of office, an oversized bunch of keys that hung from his belt. Outside was his steed, a moped with a crucifix stuck to the speedometer. He never smiled.

The trattoria, *Lo Scoiattolo*, was run by a genial fellow called Oliver who, after some explanation and a degree of demon-stration where the words fell short, prepared me a sumptuous plate of scrambled eggs on toast. A group of cyclists from Germany marched in and brusquely occupied a corner. With lean faces and aggressive ant-like glasses they seemed alien and cold, their feline suits in marked contrast to the shabby figure I cut. We exchanged pleasantries. They would reach Rome in six days, they said – unlike me who, after ten weeks and just over 1,000 miles, was faced with the prospect of another three or four weeks on the road.

But there was more to Oliver than met the eye. He was strangely adamant that he too should stamp my Passport and, despite the fact that I was fast running out of space, I handed the document over, which was returned with a glass of grappa. In the top right-hand corner of the franking was a shield of white with a red cross on it: the unmistakable mark of the Knights Templar.

'*Templari?*' I asked.

He nodded. 'The Order originally established in the twelfth century to protect pilgrims on their way to the Holy Land.

There will be no charge for your supper. You dine as my guest, *Pellegrino*.'

Back in the hallway of the *ostello*, before I went up to bed, I stopped to examine a large and rather attractive map of the Eastern Mediterranean that was framed on the wall; the land in plain white, cities dots in black and the sea a pastel blue. The Via was marked from the Grand St Bernard in its usual bold manner but something intuitively drew me to study it with a greater intent than other maps of late. Maybe it was the momentary chance to dream of lands beyond Rome as my eyes traced a course across the sea, my mind filling with the sights, sounds and spice-laden smells of far-off souks and bazaars. But perhaps though, and more importantly, that conversation with Oliver had awakened something in my subconscious.

Enrica Adorni was waiting for me on a bench outside the church in Sivizzano, her seven-year-old granddaughter, Marlene, playing at her feet. She led me up the path to a pair of tall iron gates that opened onto a cobbled cloister whose courtyard overflowed with geraniums. Built in the eleventh century, the building had once been a monastery and, ever since its foundation, had ministered to the needs of travellers and pilgrims. It was a quiet spot, except on the hour when the peace was shattered by the striking of the church clock, which presided over the tranquil scene with all the clamour and crash of Big Ben. 'Don't worry, he stop at 10 until 6 in the morning', Enrica said, looking up, 'but we used to it, living here since 40 years.'

I was led through arches into a long whitewashed room with low barrel-vaulted ceilings. It had walls of rough-hewn stone as thick as a crusader castle, making the quarters cool, if not cold, within. At one end were benches and tables; at the other, camp beds. Two were laid out.

'We have a Swiss pilgrim coming too', Enrica added. She never seemed to stop smiling despite the fact she must have been exhausted, having just returned from a full day's work cleaning for a family in Parma. She now had to look after Marlene and cook supper for her husband, Pietro, whom I could hear clattering about from time to time in the upper galleries.

Not long after I had cleaned myself up, he came down the stone staircase to see what today's new arrival was all about. A retired car worker, Pietro's knowledge was seemingly limitless. Indeed to sit with him was a delight, such was the breadth of his conversation. While Marlene played around the pillars and columns, we sat on a bench smoking. Pietro educated me in his mild-mannered avuncular way on the exacting standards required of Parmigiano cheese production in the region, which explained the ubiquity of freshly mown alfalfa everywhere I had walked that day.

Curious, I asked him where he had learnt such faultless English. 'Well you see, my father had been a Prisoner of War near Birmingham in the Second World War; he returned from Britain with a huge admiration and respect for the English. I was so impressed by this that I decided to teach myself your language. So, I started to read books…', at which he trailed off into a dreamy world inhabited by the likes of Walter Scott, Fielding, Dickens, D. H. Lawrence and Shakespeare. In fact every time I mentioned an author's name, Pietro would reel off intricate details of most, if not all, of their works.

'Talking of prisoners of war', he suddenly cut in, 'have you heard of Eric Newby?'

'You knew him?' I asked, such was the manner that he posed the question.

'Oh no', he smiled, 'but you know his book, *Love and War in the Apennines*, about his escape from the Italian POW camp helped by a girl called Wanda who later became his wife?' I nodded. 'Well, it all took place in the hills round about here', he said, pointing beyond the gates with his cigarette.

I could have sat all night with Pietro. He was a special person, softly spoken, humble in outlook yet grand in spirit; however, the clock striking eight interrupted. 'If you want to get something to eat, the *trattoria* in the *piazza* will only be open for another hour.'

The *piazza* in Sivizzano was a compact affair, more a large flagstoned yard than the classical Italian town square that springs to mind. As I approached the *trattoria* door, it was impossible to miss a wiry bohemian figure stretched out full length on a chair at one of the two outside tables. He was a cross between a singer from a 1970s heavy metal band and a scarecrow, with bouffant hair in some disarray that was held in a state of permanent uproar by a grimy hairband. Unshaven, dripping with sweat and smoking a roll-up cigarette, he had all about him the paraphernalia of a vagrant: the table laden with beer bottles, old socks and an ashtray piled high with dog ends, while all around – and therefore most of the square – was a trailing debris of soiled clothing that had spilt from his rucksack, which lay in a deflated heap at his pasty white feet. He blew out a long plume of smoke.

'Restaurant is clos-ed', he rasped in a chiselled German accent with some glee, 'clos-ed ten minutes ago', and then smiled to reveal a perfect set of tobacco-stained teeth as if he had just chewed a large bag of liquorice.

Reto, a teacher from Switzerland, had started out from Pavia four days earlier. For him, walking to Rome was a cheap adventure to fill the school holidays.

'You going to Rome too?' I asked.

'Maybe, depends.'

'The *ostello* tonight?'

'Dunno, I'll see…You done the Camino?'

'No', I replied.

'Twice', he frowned at me, nodding his head patronizingly.

Another long plume of smoke. 'You know, the second time, five *hundert* kilometres from Santiago I popped my shoulder out. Anyway, I ended up in hospital and there I saw this old lady with a shopping basket on wheels. I said to myself, Reto, this is what you need and so I checked out of the ward, found one in a shop, put my pack in the back and towed it behind me all the way to Compo-stela.'

I feigned my best look of utter English disdain.

'So', gathering up his dispersed affairs like a mother clearing up after a child, 'where is this Ho-stello then?'

It was cold as I walked up the valley into the Apennines the next morning. In the distance below me, I could hear the Sivizzano clock strike six. I wound my way up the old mountain road through Bardone, where friendly dogs ran out of kennels and stretched at me in greeting, to Terenzo, all the while the sun warming at my back. There I took the path that climbed into the woods which led to a crest that revealed a landscape of epic proportion, a secret world of sprawling forests, verdant meadows and pretty churches laid out in a vast panorama as if exclusively for me.

I emerged from the treeline at Cassio, and stopped to savour the view at a café with a cup of coffee, a glass or two of honey grappa and a large ice cream. It was a beautiful day, warm but not bothersome. I was supremely happy.

My reverie was broken by a noise that I can only describe as like a singing drunk let loose. The melody, that is what I shall loosely call it, a mix between dirge and rugby chant that veered wildly in and out of tune with all the control of a pilot wrestling a crippled Lancaster bomber coming in to land drew closer and louder. I cringed, prayed that maybe this wasn't for true until reality hit. Reto slapped me on the back and sat down next to me.

I looked at my map. The next *willage*, Berceto, was a good distance away. I ordered another grappa, this time a large one.

It grew oppressively hot on the path down the hill but Reto's constant 'white noise' chit-chat helped pass the time when he wasn't talking to butterflies or starting every other sentence with 'on the Camino...'

Berceto is notable for a well of fresh sparkling water, which is great to drink but makes water bottles explode. Apart from that, it is a cheerless place; neither of us heard the noise of slamming doors as we entered the town, but they did. While the heat of the day did its work, we weathered the sun over a long lunch in the town *piazza* served by a waitress who made it more than clear that she would rather have been at home.

Come the sixth or seventh re-telling of the shopping basket story, I could contain my silence no longer.

'Do you know something?' I said.

'Yes, of course, I know a lot of things, what would you like to know?'

'I don't want to know anything!' I snapped. 'Every other freaking sentence you utter starts with "When I was in bloody Spain"...!'

Silence.

I was worried I might have overstepped the mark.

'So', he said, 'when I was in France, on the Camino...'

After coffee, we embarked on separate and extended forays for a bed but, no matter how many places we tried, I could not help but agree with Reto when he announced over a final can of beer that 'Berceto is clos-ed'.

We had no option but to push on up into the mountains, to the Cisa Pass, where the maps indicated there was an *ostello*, except that, as no one answered the phone, we were none too sure it was open.

We arrived in perfect time for cocktails. The *Ostello della Cisa*, plonked in the middle of the mountains at the 58-kilometre mark on the SS62, was a square brute of a building daubed in ochre, originally intended to house the gangs that built the old highway that led over the Apennines to the coast. It had two large barn-like doors which, as we walked into the place, we noted with some relief were wide open. A lanky youth looked enquiringly up from a deckchair in the garden, while out of the kitchen door burst Katerina, a wonderful soul with something of the earth mother about her. She had a hint of party in the eye and, when not scooping up her son, Pietro, ran the place. We immediately ordered two large beers.

The youth, disturbed by our boisterous arrival, flopped in to see what all the commotion was about. Apart from arms and a nose savaged by sunburn, Fabio was white as a veal steak and, despite his 25 years, was as new to and unversed in life as a little fawn. He had read about 'this Via Francigena' and decided to leave Venice where he worked in a shop and take himself off on a five-day walking holiday in the Apennines. On learning this, Reto gave me one of those looks which at first said, 'is this guy for real?', and then quickly mutated more into 'welcome to the school of life, two rogues at your service, Sir'.

He announced, through a cloud of smoke, that we had to go to the 'terr-ass' to see the sunset and headed off, slopping his beer as he went like Theseus's trail to the Minotaur. Fabio trotted along behind like an innocent kitten waiting for his first lesson in morality from an alley cat.

The mountain ridges ensured we never did see the sunset, but it didn't matter much because, in the quiet of the evening, Reto took the opportunity to eulogize once again about the Camino and his old lady's shopping basket while Katerina served us up bowls of steaming *fagioli* soup, plates of salami, *formaggio*, eggs and boiled potatoes. The effete Fabio just nodded throughout and took it all in; sensibly he opted to drink only two glasses to our two bottles of wine, never mind the goading, as he announced he planned to leave at 4 a.m. the following morning to take the path through the mountains to Pontremoli.

'Mountains?! Oh, we're in the mountains are we?! I'll tell you about mountains...' but before Reto had the chance to eulogize further, Fabio interrupted, 'not on the Camino by any chance?'

My Swiss friend, suddenly silenced, lit a cigarette.

Fabio, it appeared, had printed off every document about the Via Francigena other than a map. They were bound in endless plastic covers, which were secured by an enormous elastic

The Apennine Foothills
...A secret world of sprawling forests, verdant meadows and pretty churches...

band. I sniffed drama ahead and urged him to stick to the road where he would see just as many trees as he would on the path except that if something went wrong, it might just be that little bit easier to get help. He was adamant that, on the strength of one day's experience, he would be fine. All the same, I gave him my number and ensured that at the very least he took more water than the tiny container he thought sufficient. Katerina produced two litre bottles, which he baulked at more because of the added weight they represented than the amount of liquid I expected him to drink.

'Oi!' I shouted at the sorry sight that shuffled past oblivious to my presence as I sat outside a roadside café enjoying a morning coffee. Wearing sandals, with his boots swinging wildly off a rucksack that was festooned with discarded clothing like a rabble army in retreat, I beckoned Fabio over and went to fetch him a much-needed cup of tea. The boy was in disarray; with his route cards lost, feet blistered, limbs aching and kit poorly fitted, in this current miserable state, his holiday was as good as over. There followed a short sharp lesson in caring for self and equipment followed by dispensing a degree of patching up and a good breakfast. Footwear and spirit restored, we carried on together down from the Cisa Pass through thick forest filled with deafening birdsong that was interrupted now and again by the ghostly bark of distant deer. Every so often, the trees would part, affording us exquisite glimpses of the magnificent green-swathed ridges and strident valleys that marched in parallel with us.

After the somewhat blunt humour of my Swiss friend, the gentle-natured Venetian was pleasant company. Easy to talk to, there was an innocent charm and soothing nature about him.

We stopped in Montelungo for a break. The village was a quiet place in a minding-its-own-business sort of way, or it was until the unmistakable scent of cigarette smoke wafted down the hillside and the most appalling rendition of Whitesnake's *Here I Go Again* shattered the calm of the day. Reto swung into view, just at the point he was telling the world – or the Apennine bit of it anyway – that he *'was born to walk alone...'*

'Oh God', I cried, 'your alarm clock works...'

'Mountain men don't need alarm clocks...', at which he threw his rucksack on the ground, sat down next to me and proceeded to eat my cake.

'What kind of felons precisely does your school turn out?' Fabio asked.

'They all love me', Reto replied, chewing noisily, 'especially the women – as you can imay-gine', he winked. Fabio blanched.

The walled city of Pontremoli, literally 'Quaking Bridge', lies at the convergence of the Magra and Verde rivers. It is dominated by a bell tower, *Il Campanone*, that was originally built in 1322 by Castruccio Castracani, a leading member of the House of Antelminelli, Ghibellines who had wrested control of the city from the Malaspina family three years earlier. The structure, rebuilt in the sixteenth century, formed the central part of a 'peace line' designed to keep some semblance of order by separating the pro-Papist Guelphs from the Ghibellines who supported the Holy Roman Empire.

Since the Antelminelli days, Pontremoli has had a busy time. It was owned by John the Blind, King of Bohemia, the Lords of Verona, the Viscontis of Milan, the Fieschis of Genoa, the French, the Spanish, the Dukes of Milan and the Grand Duchy of Tuscany until finally becoming part of Italy during *Il Risorgimento* in the nineteenth century.

Eventually, we arrived at the town gates, a medieval arch. At the side was a plaque in Latin. I asked Reto to tell us what it said – not an outlandish request, seeing that he was a schoolmaster. For a moment he thought and then, 'well, mmm... my goodness, it's from the Mayor and it says...' lowering his voice to a deep bass and drawing himself to full height, 'On this special day, the Eighteenth of July Two Thousand and Twelve AD, the streets of Pontremoli await the three intrepid pilgrims from the Passo della Cisa. The moment you proceed under this arch the red carpet has been freshly swept and the city band will strike up. At the end of the street, the bar is at your disposal with freshly chilled champagne on tap and twelve reclined naked girls at your disposal concealed under a carapace of freshly picked grapes. Gentleman Waymen of the Via Francigena, *prego*, your city awaits!'

'A-mazing', a passing man said and walked off.

Inside, it was market day. An opportunity to play to a new audience was too great an opportunity for Reto to miss as garments were lifted from dress rails and he danced and jigged his way down the street, pursued by anxious market traders. In a fruit stall, he began to get on a little too well with the Moroccan proprietor until he started to make lewd suggestions with a watermelon. The outcome would have been interesting given the prizefighter proportions of the man. Fabio and I came to the rescue before there was trouble. Lunch, it was agreed, was the better part of valour.

Over a large salad eaten under the shade of many umbrellas, while it was the end of Fabio's day, Reto and I agreed that we would carry on to Villafranca after 4 p.m. It was a good way to beat the heat and yet still cover the ground, at which the Swiss man added, 'but there is a train direct, so maybe we take that instead. It will be so much time saving...'

Three hours later, and after a respectable 22 miles walked since 6 a.m., we took up residence in the Station Bar at Villafranca, which we would use as a base from which to find lodgings for the night. It didn't take long to work out, however, that the Station Bar was not the every day drinking hostelry we had believed it to be. After two men got into a fight over cards, we began to look around and soon realized that the rest of the occupants all looked like they had escaped from the set of *One Flew Over the Cuckoo's Nest*. Again, there was that now-familiar feeling of doors slamming all around us; Villafranca was very shut. Well, to us anyway.

'Have you noticed something?' I bawled.

'I know, it's embarrassing, all the girls smile at me...'

'Seventy-three blasted days I've been on the road and not a problem, then, two nights with YOU', jabbing my finger across the table, 'and everywhere we go the whole boiling place is sodding well closed. And...Pontremoli looked so nice too!'

Reto looked at me, smiled and blew out an enormous smoke ring. 'Maybe I took my shoes off too early...'

There was no option but to push on to Aulla.

We dug about for the number of the Abbazia di San Caprasio.

Reto was the first to call. His Italian was marginally better than mine.

'No room at the inn', he said, after hanging up – or, more to the point, the inn keepers would be tucked up in bed by the time we ever reached the town.

'Why am I not surprised?' I laughed.

A helpless *Godot* feeling began to creep over me; perhaps we were doomed to just wander the night aimlessly, most of which, whatever the outcome, we were going to walk through anyway. I wasn't particularly bothered either, which was strange.

'Give me that phone', I barked. In my execrable Italian, I pleaded with the ladies at the far end, saying something along the lines that we were two weary pilgrims on our way to Rome, that we had walked all the way from London and, more importantly, since before sunrise this morning we had traipsed some distance over the Cisa Pass from Berceto. I might have stretched the truth a little, but I put that down to my vocabulary not suffering intimate points of detail.

'Over the Cisa Pass?'

'*Si*, above the Cisa Passes', I replied.

A grunt...then a muffled conversation...'Okay Signor, but no later than 11 o'clock please.'

There followed profuse gratitudes, whereafter I hung up.

'I was right, it is YOU', I growled victoriously at my Swiss friend, at which we fell about in uncontrolled laughter.

But my friend I could see was suddenly none too happy. In the hour or so since we had stopped and in the short space of time I had been on the phone, fatigue had caught up with him and, having been on the road but a few days, complaining muscles had begun to stiffen up.

'I have to eat something...'

'But we have to be there by 11...'

'Just half an hour, they will wait for us. We are pilgrims...they always do. They *like to*...' I wished I too had Reto's gutsy self-confidence, which so often nearly verged on Teuton arrogance. So, after a pizza-based piece of nastiness which summed up Villafranca, reinvigorated like he had a new battery, Reto and I set out on our fourteenth hour on the road.

We were walking through some roadworks when somewhere

to my left, up in the trees, I could hear the faint plaintive cries of a cat in distress. It was nearing dusk.

'Can you hear that?'

'Hear what?' Reto replied. I threw my rucksack into the verge and ran up a little track. Twelve feet up in the branches of a leggy sapling I could see a tiny black and white kitten, its wide eyes staring at me. Every now and again it gave a weak mew that revealed a mouthful of healthy sharp white teeth. Instinct took over, but how, I pondered, was I going to get to it? The answer, of course, was simple – climb the bank, shin up the tree, wriggle along the branch and back down again with rescued feline. I could see the headlines in the local paper already as some poor old lady was reunited with her pet kitty by a passing pilgrim and an Englishman to boot.

My mother, who knows a thing or two, says that if something is too easy to come by, then it's not worth having. First came the bank, which I took one step towards and promptly disappeared into a four-foot ditch cunningly concealed by ivy. Pulling the green tentacled creepers off me and spitting leaves I grabbed at the soil to continue my journey upwards, at which a great sod of earth came away, hit me in the stomach and returned me swiftly to the bottom of the ditch. The cat cried again.

The tree was the easy bit. The branch was a little problematic; it gave under my sylph-like weight like a bended yew at Agincourt, at which the moggy jumped onto a higher branch, sensibly. I was left swinging by one arm 12 feet up. I lunged at the kitten. The tree shuddered and the animal fell from its branch.

If a cat's claws are sharp, I can tell you a kitten's claws are sharper. I can also tell you that when you have the latter clinging to your face for dear life, it tends to focus the mind somewhat. Thus, making a noise like Tarzan just missed his rope, together we hit the ground with a most unballet-like thud. The cat ran back up the tree but I was on a roll by this time. I chased after the feline, grabbed it, threw it onto my shoulder and, looking more tree than pilgrim with a particularly fine gouge above my eye, walked back to the road, where Reto was sitting on a crash barrier smoking a cigarette.

'Do you know how much time you wasted?'

He looked at the kitten on my shoulder, mewing. 'What is *that*?'

'It's our cat.'

'And just what are you going to do with this stupid cat?' he shouted over his shoulder.

'Take it to Rome, I guess.' I really hadn't thought this bit through. 'Dick Whittington had a cat', I added, pleased at my quick-witted response.

Into the night we walked, little torches like glowworms held high to warn traffic, while kitty nestled comfortably between my neck and my pack, chewing at the straps. At Terrarossa we stopped for a break; no sooner had I put the cat down than it ran off into the dark. Reto rolled his eyes at me.

Sitting on benches next to the town's new drinking fountain, we drained the last drops from our bottles. I went to push the button that would normally spurt a great jet of water. Nothing. I tried again. Still, nothing.

'You know, this country is so fucked up at times', Reto said, pointing to the pipe that stuck out the ground that presumably would one day be joined up to the water main.

'We'll stop at a restaurant or somewhere, not to worry', I said.

'What restaurant, where? It's gone 11...'

The phone rang; it was the ladies from the Abbazia, where were we? Reto said five minutes away, to which I replied he would surely go to hell.

'I have done far worse.'

'Now why don't I find that hard to believe?' I laughed as we continued on our way once again, me by now walking like I had pooped myself courtesy of a peach of a blister on both feet.

Renata and Patrizia, our two elderly saviours, were patiently waiting outside the Abbazia when we finally found it. As we neared, so they waved. Wrung out, after the best part of 18 hours and 30 miles on the road, goodness we were happy to see them. After some food and a cup of tea, we were shown upstairs to a large airy dormitory. I recognized the boots left outside the next-door room; they were my Polish friend, Andreas's. I poked my head around the door. He was fast asleep, so I tied a note to his laces – he would be long gone before us in the morning.

We left at 11 a.m. the following morning. It was far too late. The day before, however, had taken its toll. Looking at the map and with only about 12 miles to Sarzana, it was going to be a breeze of a walk. The coast was within our grasp and there was a distinct holiday mood in the air. Except one problem, which we would learn to our cost; when it comes to maps, Italians don't really do contour lines. As if they can't afford to print all of them, they just put in the odd one every now and again, such that whole mountains and ranges can sneak up in between the brown wrinkles and no one, except of course the beleaguered pilgrim caught in the searing heat, would ever know.

The first inkling of this was the more than steep heave out of Aulla. In the punishing temperature and the severe gradient our progress fell to less than a mile an hour at one point. It felt like the day before had been but a rehearsal. By the time we reached Vecchietto, we had drunk four litres of water between us. We refilled at the village tap, giving each other wearisome glances. Spurred on solely by the thought of the sea, we grappled with the near-vertical ascent, conversation reduced to little more than an exchange of grunts, groans and pauses for water. And so we pushed on. The slope never-ending. The sun grinding down. On, up, it was the only thing we could do. Eventually, 'as sure as night follows day', we reached the final ridgeline, coming to a halt in an unseemly heap under some trees on the path at the top. It had been the hardest climb of the entire journey.

Most of us think of angels as serene beings of great elegance and beauty with outstretched wings and a halo; and there was Reto, filthy, reeking of the road and soaked in sweat. He was, for once speechless. I looked at my infuriating friend and smiled. 'So, about those bloody mountains you keep telling me the Italians don't have…'

After a few minutes, we carried on, the going easy now that we were coming down off the ridge. Then, about a quarter of an hour later, we came to a natural pause. I remember the wind catching the trees and, as the bough lifted, so a gap appeared through which the cypress-filled plain beyond gave rise to two verdant hillsides. I stared out. There was, however, something different about this view. At first, my eyes couldn't articulate it.

Reto, behind me, fell silent. Between the two hilltops there was a line, so faint that it merged seamlessly with the sky as to be almost indecipherable. It was the sea.

'I...er,...I see you in the *willage* below...'

I nodded. My friend filed past in silence. He didn't look back. All I could do was just stare ahead. Not a vacant gaze but one of total absorption as my eyes drank in this sudden and dramatic change in scenery. A ship hove into view. That anyone – let alone me – could walk 1,124 miles through four countries to the Mediterranean was joyous. I sat down under a shading oak tree, a donkey with large twitching ears leant a comforting head over the fence and for the best part of an hour we just looked at the blue; it was beautiful.

287 miles to Rome.

18

Marina di Pietra Santa to Gambassi

'And God spake all these words, saying ...
Thou shalt not make unto thee any graven image, or any
likeness OF ANY THING that IS in heaven above or that IS
in the earth beneath, or that IS in the water under the earth:
Thou shalt not bow down thyself to them...'
The Second Commandment, Exodus, Chapter 20 vv 1, 4
and 5, *The King James Version of the Holy Bible*, 1611

NOW EVERYWHERE WERE OLIVE groves, pine trees and that
sandy soil of the Mediterranean coast. While here, on the sea
plain, everything suddenly felt affluent; size counting for all –
big cars, big sunglasses, big hair and even bigger houses. It was
Italian flamboyance at its best.

Despite the carnival atmosphere of Sarzana on market day,
we stopped only momentarily – odd, given our cumulative
fatigue, but the siren-esque signs proclaiming '*Mare*' urged us
ever on in a state of excited anticipation. So, we veered off the
Via Francigena for a long-awaited break on the coast.

This phase of the adventure, however, was extended by the
final realization, which had been dawning on us for a few days,
that Italians are incapable of judging distance. Three hundred
yards is invariably always nearer 800 or, in our case, four miles
turned out to be seven. But it didn't really matter – we were off
to the beach.

Arrive at the sea and it is then a simple question of going
either left or right. To ensure we didn't end up walking miles
in the wrong direction, I enquired of a beautifully dressed and
most welcoming young lady from Gabon who, at the time,
was just coming out of the bushes, as to which direction was
Marinella de Sarzana. She stretched her arms out wide, as if

finishing a big number and announced: 'My darlin', everywhere is Marinella...' So we turned left.

There were boats all over the place, in varying states of repair. The strip was a festival of neon and what was so nice was that on every corner there was a young lady who was always pleased to see us and welcome us to the town. I could barely conceal my delight at the sight of giant pulsating lobsters, flashing pirates and illuminated anchors that lit the place up like a mini-Las Vegas. We had two numbers to call for a bed; the first didn't work and the second turned out to be an old people's home – or at least that was what reception felt like when we walked in.

Renata, who was in charge, had, by the look of the photos on the wall, once been blonde and gorgeous but that had been in the previous millennium. Now she ran her hotel like the dictator of a small state from a large wooden palisade affair that was, I suspect, more enclosure than desk to welcome guests from.

'What time do you want to leave in the morning?'

''He wanna leave at six.' Reto was doing the talking as by now I could barely stand.

'Six?! Bloody six o'clock?!!! What does he think I am, a gold medallist at making breakfast?!' she erupted from the corral. 'No, no, no', wagging her finger at me as if I had just excused myself in the middle of the room, 'six is not possible.' Reto gave me a stern look. He could see I was beginning to bristle. A lot was riding on this conversation; get it wrong – as we had been accomplished in doing over the last few days – and we would be out on the street. In our frayed state we were in no condition to go anywhere.

'Besides, 'ow's 'e gonna get out?'

'The door is locked?!' I exclaimed.

'The gate is.'

'I'll climb over it...'

'You can't, the Police will think you're breaking out!'

'What is this place?' I whispered to Reto.

'Your bed for the night so shut the fuck up!'

A compromise was agreed. No breakfast, but the drawbridge would be opened at the appointed hour so that I could head further down the coast, leaving Reto in bed, to make his way on to Pisa later in the day.

I would miss my friend.

The next morning, at six on the dot, Renata greeted me downstairs like a tormented bulldog on too short a lead. Hissing a forced *buongiorno*, she pressed a button, the steel doors opened and, stepping out into the fresh dawn air, I walked to freedom and the sound of waves crashing on the beach.

The Hotel San Marco was special, like unearthing a picture of great value in a junk shop. Set back from Marina di Pietrasanta's main street amid leafy houses, the moment I saw the rusting hotel sign propped up on a balcony, I knew I had discovered a gem. From the look of the garden, with its forlorn lamps that were opaque with dust, rebellious hedging and part-time drive that hankered to be a lawn, the owner had lost interest a good 20 years earlier. A dusty black VW Beetle sat slumped in a far corner under a tree. It was as if Miss Havisham had opened her doors to the tourist trade.

A pair of large, cracked, green oriental jars stood sentry at the front door. The reception was overseen by an enthusiastic statue of a naked Egyptian girl in black marble from *La Belle Epoque*. The desk itself was hidden under piles of unopened post, on the far side of which plumes of smoke rose up like a brooding volcano. I peered over to find a slight but immaculately dressed man sitting there, hunched over his computer. He had a face that was creased like an old tobacco leaf, grey hair drawn into a ponytail and a neatly trimmed goatee beard. He stood up and greeted me in the manner worthy of a grandee with a rough-hewn timbre reminiscent of John Hurt – the effect, no doubt, of many cigarettes and too much partying. Unlike the other hoteliers, however, he did not judge my appearance but more subtly declared that, most sadly, sir, there were no rooms left – except one double. Indeed, he made a bit of an act of it, looking down his ledger and computer screen twice with much raising of apologetic eyebrows. After the faceless marble atria of the many establishments I had already been unceremoniously ejected from that morning, I was beyond caring. Besides, even at the king's ransom demanded, I was so tired that I said 'I'll take it'.

The route up to the fourth floor was a long winding staircase lined with old watercolours of Venice, engravings of St Peter's and sepia photographs in which teams of water buffalo pulled the town's fishing fleet out to sea from jetties that have long gone.

My room, all faded lampshades and summer florals that would have been pride of place in a charity shop years ago, brought back comforting memories of spare bedrooms in my grandmother's house. The bathroom, however, was the pride – a marble sanctuary, which, once flooded by the shower, would remain a permanent wetland for the next two days. The lavatory had been slotted in at perfect right angles to the bidet like a key stone in an archway; indeed so exacting was the craftsmanship that it would have been just the thing for a right leg amputee but, for the rest of us, however, the ingeniously positioned apparatus required a whole new thought process a bit like the conundrum when presented with a bactrian camel to ride – which, if either, of its two humps do you sit on? You can never be quite sure.

The pace of life in the groomed oleander-lined streets of Marina felt relaxed and peaceful like I imagined South Beach, Miami in the 1950s; the perfect place to catch my breath before continuing deeper into Tuscany. The beach, whose crowded promenade was liberally scattered with giant sculptures made from the locally quarried Carrara marble, was a different place altogether – an enormous linear city of multicoloured parasols that stretched almost 25 miles from Marinella di Sarzana in the north to Viareggio in the south, filled to bursting with all shapes and sizes of Italians whose sole interest seemed to be football... and food.

I didn't feel in the mood to swim. Indeed, on the beach, I felt self-conscious, even alien, among so many people. To indulge would have been premature, verging on the celebratory and felt wholly wrong at that moment. Very odd and most unlike me, seeing that in all other aspects of my journey to date I had jumped at any and every opportunity to break free from my peregrinations. So I stared out to sea and strolled long reflective distances in the surf up and down the beach, the water cool on aching legs and the breeze soothing on bare shoulders.

That evening, the air thick with the scent of jasmine, Fabio, who had reached the coast in the morning, came over and joined me for dinner; even in the short five days he had been on the road his transformation was marked – no longer the pasty shop assistant, he had colour and confidence about him.

'To be on the route was freedom, not this', he said disapprovingly, looking about the bar at his overdressed fellow countrymen and women. 'What we did was *extra*-ordinary. If it wasn't, then everybody would be on the Via, but the truth is that it frightens them. The very idea of walking all that way forces people out of their comfort zone; you can see that when you approach them for information – stinking, dirty, stick, pack, they're scared of you. That's true freedom, not the tight t-shirts, cocktails and bright lights of the night.' Later, just as he got up to go, he added, 'it was the best break I have ever had', and gave me a warm embrace, '*buon cammino amico!*'

The mighty barbicans and bastions of Lucca's city walls were once the lynchpin in the tiny republic's hard-won independence. Now they sit resolute and defiant amid parkland splendour, like a venerated dreadnought that has been laid to rest for all to admire. Walking through the massive gateways felt a fitting entrance to Tuscany proper, my home for the next ten days until I would pass beyond the protective gaze of the great watch-tower at Radicofani.

Here, I entered a world where time seemed to have stood still; the cobbled streets, once wandered by Puccini, despite being choked with crowds that shot from sight to sight in the manner of a ball-bearing in a pinball machine, retained an aura of mystery and intrigue – the travails of a city republic that was forever being pawned, sold, seized, ceded, surrendered, invaded or conquered.

It was the *Duomo*, in the corner of the Piazza San Martino, that caught my attention. Its beautifully carved and pillared façade of green and white marble, embellished with medieval wyverns and other such mystical creatures, point more to the antecedents of Christianity than the teachings of Jesus himself. By the main door, on the right-hand pillar, there is a circular labyrinth in the classical style. The size of a large book, it is carved into the marble, beneath which direct reference is made in Latin to the work of Daedalus, who constructed the original on Crete from which only Theseus was able to escape, courtesy of Ariadne's thread. At its centre, now worn away over time by the fingers of the devout, was an image of the Minotaur, the ferocious half-man half-bull – love child of Minos's wife, Pasiphae, and the sacred beast given to the Cretan King by Neptune for sacrifice.

Labyrinths were popular symbols in churches during the Middle Ages; in comparison to the much larger versions at Chartres, Reims and Amiens cathedrals which are laid in the floor, the Lucca maze is relatively discreet. Theories abound as to the significance of these undeniably pagan designs; some think they represent a '*Chemin de Jerusalem*', a pocket pilgrimage for those who didn't have the time, money or inclination to undergo the rigours of the road. Others believe that the maze, a symbolically enclosed space, allowed the mind to contemplate free from external hindrance, while another school has them as a representation that there is only one true path to God. No one really knows.

But the greatest treasure of the *Duomo* that made Lucca a pilgrim destination in its own right lies within. The *Volto Santo*, or 'Holy Face', is a near-lifesize carving of Christ on the cross made from Lebanese cedar, said to be the work of Nicodemus, who was present at the Crucifixion and helped Joseph of Arimathea place Jesus's body in the tomb after His death.

To the cynic, the *Volto Santo* is little more than one of the great advertisements for the cult of relics in the Middle Ages. Its legend is so unbelievable that it must rank in the annals of Christian folklore alongside other such fantastical 'oh look what I've found' tales like the remains of St James mysteriously turning up off Finisterre in a rowing boat, the icon of the Panagia being 're-discovered' through a dream on the Greek island of Tinos and Brazil's patron saint, Our Lady of Aparecida, a clay statue, being caught in fishermen's nets. A crude reminder that behind the toil, sanctity and spiritual purpose of pilgrimage lies a commercial model that such undertakings were, and remain, excellent 'crowd-pullers'. Lucca, right on the Via Francigena as it snakes its way towards the great pilgrim city of Siena, was keen to cash in on the droves of the devoted as they flocked to Rome and the Holy Land beyond.

Today, the *Volto Santo* stands in a colonnaded side chapel protected from prying hands like a prized bird in an ornamental cage. Peering through the grilles of the wrought-iron gates, I stared up questioningly at the statue – the body, taut, rigid, outstretched, hanging there in its full-length robe, darkened by age and candle smoke. There was a simplicity, verging on the plain, that gave the *Volto Santo* great beauty as Christ's wide mournful eyes looked down on me, kneeling below. It is said that Nicodemus awoke from a deep sleep to find that angels had completed the work for him.

The legend of the *Volto Santo* is wondrous. To escape persecution, Nicodemus handed the giant wooden sculpture to a man called Isaacar for safe keeping in a cave. Lost to time, its location was revealed to a mysterious bishop, Gualfredo, in a dream hundreds of years later. The bishop lovingly sealed the statue in tar and placed it on a boat lit from stem to stern with lanterns and candles which he pushed out into the waves; with neither sails nor crew to guide it, the vessel's fate was placed in the hands of Providence.

After drifting across the Mediterranean, the boat finally made land off the western coast of Italy at Luni, near La Spezia, not far from where I too had reached the sea. The year was AD742 and the *Volto Santo*, if legend is to be believed, was roughly 700 years old.

But, every time the people of Luni tried to approach the vessel, it was blown back out to sea. Another dream, in which, this time, Giovanni, Bishop of Lucca is visited by an angel, who informs him of the mystery barque. On waking, the bishop led crowds of cheering Lucchesi two or three days down to the coast, where they found the bewildered Lunis and the recalcitrant vessel. No sooner had Giovanni given thanks to God than the boat immediately came to shore, opening its hatches wide to the cleric. 'Hallelujah!' everyone cried and the *Volto Santo* was loaded onto a cart – with no driver – and the oxen – with no one steering – delivered it straight to the Basilica di San Frediano in Lucca, where a series of frescos can be found telling the statue's story so far. There the *Volto Santo* remained for 300 years until the eleventh century, when the *Duomo di San Martino* was enlarged and elevated to a cathedral. The *Volto*

Santo was then 'miraculously translated' to the shining new *Duomo*, where it has remained ever since.

However, such was the clamour by the multitudes of the faithful for souvenirs that the original was as good as picked to pieces; the current carving is a thirteenth-century replica.

But put the *Volto Santo* in the context of the Middle Ages, when religious belief and observance ruled supreme, and it is easy to understand the power that this venerated wooden image would have wielded in shoring up the faith of the believers and ensuring the ringing of the tills for the Lucchesi. Any conspiracy on the Church's part in talking up the statue's provenance paid dividends handsomely.

Níkulás Bergsson, Abbot of the Benedictine Monastery at Munkathvera in northern Iceland, who travelled all the way to Jerusalem, recording his journey in his twelfth-century itinerarium, *Leiðarvísir og Borgarskipan* (Route and City Guide), noted that the *Volto Santo* had spoken twice: in one case, allegedly insistent that its bejewelled shoe be handed to an impoverished jester, and, in another, in defence of a man who had been wrongly maligned. A hundred years later and a pilgrim from Picardy, falsely accused of murder while making his journey to pay homage to the *Volto Santo*, was rescued from impending death when the executioner's axe blade turned around in mid-swing.

Indeed, so popular was the statue that it gave rise to a plethora of likenesses across Europe, many of which were said to possess their own miraculous powers. In the fourteenth century, the *Volto Santo* spawned a female saint, Wilgefortis or Uncumber in English, daughter of a pagan Portuguese king. It is believed that she prayed to God to rescue her from an arranged marriage. The somewhat dramatic response, which upholds the adage that people should be careful what they pray for, resulted in the poor girl growing a beard and moustache. The suitor, understandably alarmed at this development, changed his mind. Her father, the infuriated monarch, adamant that the hapless princess had grown whiskers on purpose, had her crucified.

So, there I knelt, pondering all this legend, while that meek face stared down. Some nuns came to kneel next to me. I thought on and then thought some more. It was, after all, just a statue. I watched the ladies out of the corner of my eye. I looked up again and concluded that, if there had been a little bit of ecclesiastical skullduggery surrounding the *Volto Santo* over the years, well, what harm? It was a rollicking good story. The statue even at that moment, I could see, was bringing the nuns such joy. I could all too easily imagine the millions upon millions of people to whom it had brought pleasure and happiness over the last 1,400 years. And that is a good thing. I stood up, crossed myself and headed out of town.

Having crossed the River Arno at Fucecchio, I made my way up through the orchards that cling to the steep sloped approaches of the fortified town at San Miniato. It is hard to miss, given the dominating presence of the tower originally built by Emperor Frederick II, which can be seen from miles around, distinct for its extended fingers that stick up like funnels on an ocean liner.

Until 1799, when the last resident, Canon Filippo, died, San Miniato could be considered the ancestral home of the Buonapartes, with the Palazzo Formichini as the family residence for centuries. The Buonapartes had originally settled in Florence and, as minor nobility, had been close to the Medici. Jacopo Buonaparte was an advisor and friend to Pope Clement VII. In 1527, he was witness to the Sack of Rome when the unpaid mutinous troops of the Holy Roman Emperor, Charles V, laid waste to the city. Jacopo's account of this dreadful episode in history is considered definitive. Not long after, however, the family split – one branch to Sarzanna, the other to Corsica. Jacopo's nephews, as Ghibellines or supporters of the Holy Roman Emperor over papal primacy, participated in a revolt against Medici authority over Florence. Centuries later, in 1778, it would still be to San Miniato that the young Napoleon Bonaparte – the French spelling – returned to retrieve the necessary letters and documents from his uncle the Canon, to prove his noble birth for entry to the military school at Brienne-le-Château, where his officer training would begin and so start the dice of history rolling inexorably across Europe once again.

The door of the Convento di San Francesco was large, dark and foreboding. I hung off the bell countless times until, just as

I was about to abandon hope, Paolo, a novice, came panting to my rescue. By the looks of him, he had come a long way to find me which, on entering the building, I soon appreciated, as the thirteenth-century monastery, with six monks clattering about somewhere within, was enormous like an aircraft hangar. It was joined to each of its separate parts by airy corridors whose walls were splashed from top to bottom in avant-garde murals reminiscent of an incomprehensible blend of Dali and street graffiti. Trying to make head or tail of the symbolism resulted in a cricked neck and a headache. I gave up. Pretty colours though.

At supper, in a *ristorante* on the Piazza Buonaparte, I was treated to a visitation from the Florentine Court. Bubbly, elegant and composed, as you would expect a representative of the US State Department, Judith breezed in like a gorgeous summer day, her pretty turquoise dress adding to the moment; complementing her was Antonia, every inch a statement of refined English perfection complete to the diamond brooch and pearls around her neck. Having lived in Florence most of her life, she was a latter-day *Scorpioni*, without the sting; a zealous convert possessed of a knowledge that seemingly knew no boundaries and, above all else, an infectious love of everything Italian. In my off-duty fatigues, sitting opposite the pair who were dressed like they were off to Ascot, it felt like one of those dreadful sinking moments when you walk into a dinner party and realize that you have misread the dress code on the invitation.

Antonia took charge as bottles of white wine from Trebbiano were summoned and plates of *fiore di zucchini fritti*, courgette flowers fried in batter, were ordered to 'keep us going' while the menu was subjected to detailed inspection.

The choices were simple: you could have just about anything you liked, as long as it had *tartufo fresco* – truffle – with it. As a starter I could have had two eggs, *bresaola* or *carpaccio* – all with *tartufo*. For *primi* there was *taglioni, risotto* or hand-made *tortelloni*, liberally laced with the good white stuff, and, if that wasn't enough, for *secondi*, there were *scaloppini* or *tagliata* both '*al tartufo fresco*'. San Miniato is famous for white truffles.

To start, we ordered a little of everything and stole unashamedly from each other until *primi*, when three large steaming barge-like plates of fragrant truffle risotto arrived, their aroma washing through the room on perfumed bow waves.

The girls, who, by comparison to me, had only driven in air-conditioned comfort from Florence, were a picture of restraint, while I, on the other hand, having put in considerable work to reach my dinner that day, began to slobber like a Pavlovian dog at the sounding of its bell. Manners went out the window as I dived in unceremoniously to the deceptively plain-looking dish that was so delicious to the tongue. I eagerly shovelled fork after risotto-piled fork down my throat. In the clumsy mouth-stuffing feeding frenzy, oblivious to all around me, I lost myself to a luxurious food-filled world infused with scent and filled with succulent creamy rice. Meanwhile, somewhere in the background of the gastronomic Elysium I found myself in, Antonia was saying something most interesting about the devastating floods that Florence suffered in 1966 and, I seem to remember, the damage caused by the slicks of heating oil that ringed the buildings with black tidemarks. Nobody batted an eyelid when I ordered a second plate.

I broke my journey up the long winding road that leads to the hilltop town of Gambassi Terme when I received a text message instructing me to pop into the little church at Chianni, just outside. I walked around the building that seemed so at peace with the world in its tranquil setting, until past some large bushes at the rear was a tiny box-like accommodation block, a brand new pilgrim *ostello*. Waiting at the door, arms wide open with smile to match, was LN. How good it was to see my French friend.

But the euphoria of the moment soon passed as LN's face quickly turned sombre. As we went to go inside, I couldn't help noticing the crutch she grabbed at to help her walk. While her companions, Jacqueline and Josceline, a retired couple from Sedan, busied about showering and making good after their day on the road, we sat on her bunk discussing the woes of her journey that had been dogged by injury and pain. Her eyes, filled with tears, said it all: 'A quoi faire Harry? A quoi faire?' The months of anticipation and preparation now seemed in vain as crippling shin splints set to blight her efforts and dreams. Walking to Rome by combination of taxi, bus and train not only defeated the object but was already proving costly. The next day, she would decide if it was time to head back to Reims. We agreed to meet in San Gimignano the following morning.

When I eventually arrived in Gambassi, I found Brian Mooney lounging like Nero on a bench in the Piazza; dressed in olive green with a questionable sunhat perched on his head like a flowerpot, he looked like an old hand-me-down from the Cuban revolution. At his side, dressed in a pretty red frock with straw hat to match was Gail, his wife.

There then followed a ritual, which many serial pilgrims and walkers delight in, without so much as a 'may I?' Like some mysterious rite handed down over the ages, it verges on the primeval and is not dissimilar to baboons inspecting each other in a zoo. Brian almost immediately, after shaking my hand, picked up my rucksack and pulling a face like he'd just got a hernia, exclaimed: 'What have you got in there, Harry?'

'A socket set from Halfords.' I fixed him a glance and rounding on the former Reuters correspondent, added: 'Don't tell me Brian, you haven't packed your dinner jacket?'

'I'm only carrying eight kilos.'

'I can see', I said, looking with some contempt at his quick-dry safari suit with pockets and zips in some very odd places.

There was, however, little coincidence to this Livingstone-esque rendezvous in the middle of the Tuscan countryside; the basic plan had been hatched months earlier over dinner in London when it became apparent that our paths might cross. Brian, for whom there are few corners of the Earth that remain un-walked, had landed in Rome 11 days earlier to make the return journey to London; the wrong way for a pizza, as I told him, given that he had completed the Via Francigena the right way two years previously. Gail had come to join for a few days.

In the short period I had known Brian, he had grown to be more than just a good friend, more like a big brother. He was an inherently kind man, imbued with a great sense of fun, who was always on hand to offer advice which he did, freely, in a constant and hilarious flow of texts and emails. But, unlike the rest of us, Brian's progress was conducted with great style, for he travelled like some Papal Nuncio dispensing indulgences and favours to all around. His was a stately process that only went from comfortable hotel to well-appointed *pensione*. The idea of an *ostello* appalled. Unless the place had a minimum of three stars, the crispest of linen and a pool, it wouldn't see so much as the backstraps on his pack. Indeed, such was Brian's strict adherence to this *coda luxuria* that he must be unique among the pilgrim community for arriving at his final destination almost exactly the same weight and shape as he was when he set out. To see Brian and Gail, however, after all these miles was a special moment to be savoured and celebrated like opening a good bottle of wine.

At dinner, Gail appeared in Indian silk. As soon as I set enquiring eyes on her she started fumbling excuses at me: 'I am only carrying five kilos.'

'So, come on then, where are they?' I asked.

'Where are who?'

'The columns of sherpas that must be hidden somewhere abouts so that you and his Nuncio-ship can travel like you are. We've only been together 20 minutes and you've already changed twice, and that's not including your walking kit. The Prince of Wales travels with less clothes than you...'

Brian produced neatly folded maps that were brown with age and looked as if they had been used by Wellington on a campaign, which, knowing him, was quite possible. Soon a short stubby finger was sweeping over the terrain, pointing out 'interesting thises' and 'don't go there that's' which I would encounter or need to know as I neared Rome. Such was Brian's enthusiasm for his subject that it was almost impossible to keep up with the stream of information that poured from him.

I asked Brian why he was walking back to London.

He joked that when he turned up at the Pilgrim Office in the Vatican, the officials had tried to give him a *Testimonium*, the parchment certificate people receive on reaching Rome. They looked at him in disbelief when he said he wanted the first stamp in his Passport as he was heading north; 'no one walks to London', they said.

How we forget. In the Middle Ages, people would have routinely walked back home after pilgrimage. You couldn't help admiring Brian as he followed the waymarkers and read his guidebook in reverse. For him, this was completion of a journey begun in May 2010. Seventy-six days later, he arrived in Rome to a sudden and abrupt stop – an experience that, in comparison to the enormity of the journey itself, fell very short. Brian's 're-entry' to normal life, as he called it, had, even for someone of his enormous experience, been difficult. He wrote to his fellow travelling companions that he found 'the readjustment very strange and sometimes rather hard', as if 'something big is missing in my life'. Thus, Brian's return to England on foot was a promise to himself, to round the circle and send the demons of his outward journey packing for once and for all. All the same, he couldn't help remarking how strange it felt to walk without the tangible goal of Rome in his sights this time around.

The wine flowed freely until, at 10 p.m., some orange watery stuff was produced which made Gail cough and my eyes water. Brian assured us it would staunch the effects of the evening. I never did catch its name to avoid it in the future.

Even at 5 a.m., we found a baker open in the village for some breakfast. Gail arrived in fuchsia pink. Wisely, she had decided to let Brian do the walking that day; she would take the train once in the valley. Eating a croissant, she looked across at her husband who was dressed most individually and turning to me, said witheringly: 'He will insist on looking like a rambler all the time.' I think I knew the real reason Gail was taking the train.

At the crossroads, we kissed and said farewell. I watched as the couple set off down the hill to San Miniato. I gave a final wave before dropping down a steep cypress-lined *strada bianca* into *chianti* vineyards and oak woods that echoed to the woodpecker's hammer and pheasant's call. I was headed for San Gimignano.

195 miles to Rome.

19

San Gimignano to Monteriggioni

Happening to remark, in looking up at the clouds, which were still bright in the west, that 'what had struck me in Italian sunsets was that peculiar rosy hue'. I had hardly pronounced the word 'rosy' when Lord Byron, clapping his hand on my mouth, said, with a laugh, 'Come d–n it, Tom DON'T be poetical.'

Thomas Moore, *With Byron in Italy*, 1830

To visit San Gimignano in summertime is to take leave of your senses; I would rather dangle my eyeballs in rock salt than ever again have to face the wall of humanity that greeted me the moment I stepped through its massive gateway. Trinket shops, medieval torture museums and drink stalls on every corner; the place screamed 'move on!'

I found LN with a big smile on her face in the cloisters of the Convento di San Agostino where she and her two compatriots were staying for the night.

'I think, you know, that I am a little better today', she beamed, 'if I take it, how you say, *slowly slowly*, a little bus, a little walk, I should be okay.' I noticed the crutch was nowhere to be seen. I was glad; it seemed such a pity that she could have got this far only to have to turn back and, besides, to arrive in Rome without my French friend would have felt incomplete.

We pushed our way into the crowds and struggled up into the town, quickly agreeing that San Gimignano was, at that moment, about as much fun as completing a tax return. A cup of coffee later and I abandoned the tourist cauldron for the calm of the road that would lead me to Colle di Val d'Elsa, my destination that night.

'Where are you?' Signor Christian, the caretaker of the Seminario Vescovile del San Cuore, crackled at the other end of the phone. How did I know? I wouldn't have telephoned if I had known where I was.

The lady in the chemist, when I asked her, replied that she knew of a Via San Francesco in Siena. Helpful. From where I was in '*Bassa*', or the bottom, you could see nothing of Colle '*Alta*' save a lone tower surrounded by trees that gave little away. I prayed to God that the evasive Seminario wasn't 'up there' but, sure enough, 'up there' it was and so 'up there' I laboured, up, up and up until, when I thought I had gone 'up' quite enough, it became obvious I had some more to go 'up' again. Indeed, halfway 'up' it became apparent that there was a lot more of Colle in *Alta* than there was in *Bassa*. Indeed, in *Alta*, there was concealed a whole medieval ridgeline, a magnificent Italian secret, encrusted with churches, piazzas and laced with wonky houses at crazy angles – the whole place draped in bright colour as the townsfolk dried washing and aired bedding in the evening sun.

The only pilgrim in town, I was difficult to miss. Christian was a bit of a dude and not your typical caretaker by a long stretch. He found me lumbering about trying not to be the proverbial bull, as I sought directions – perhaps not very sensibly – in a china shop.

Cats, playing on the giant crucifix outside, scampered off like schoolboys up to no good as we approached the Seminario. When we finally got there, it was enormous, with cloisters, gardens, refectories, dormitories, endless passageways and a 'chapel' that could have passed for a perfectly respectable cathedral in a small city. I was shown to a spacious room with four beds and an ensuite in 1970s brown that was perhaps once the Abbot's quarters, such was the fading splendour. Asking me to put the key through the letterbox in the morning, Christian bid me '*buonasera*' and promptly left. I had the entire complex to myself.

After supper, I lay on my bunk looking out of the window onto the gravel forecourt, in the corner of which grew a towering Christmas tree. There was a half-moon and soon the night became lit by stars. My mind began to wander and it was not long before I thought of the great tree covered in lights with the ghosts of priests and students past gathered around it singing carols. Happy times, I thought – but disused and empty, this magnificent building now felt pitiful and forgotten as if its every brick demanded to be full of life once again.

A picture of medieval perfection, Monteriggioni is a smaller but perfectly formed version of San Gimignano and, void of masses, a peaceful idyll by comparison. How strange a coincidence that Dante in his fourteenth-century poem *'Divina Commedia'* should write of Monteriggioni's 'circular parapets' as he and Virgil approached the ninth and final Circle of the Inferno, reserved for treachery – the most heinous crime of all, in his eyes. Since the sixteenth century, it is treachery that now lies at the heart of the town's history.

The hilltop settlement, fortified as a garrison in the twelfth century, sits on the Via Cassia. For over three centuries it valiantly guarded the approaches to Siena, nine miles to the south, from the attentions of an expansionist Florence a day's march to the north.

By 1554, the Italian War had been under way for nearly three years as the dashing Cosimo I de' Medici, Grand Duke of Tuscany, in alliance with Emperor Charles V sought to smash the Republic of Siena for the furtherment of the Grand Duchy and the greater control of Italy by the Holy Roman Empire.

Leading Cosimo's troops was *Il Medeghino,* the Little Medici, otherwise known as Gian Giacomo Medici. Eldest of 14 children, he was the son of a notary born in Milan to a lesser branch of the Medici family from among whose siblings would also rise Pope Pius IV.

After committing an audacious revenge killing in broad daylight at the age of 16, Il Medeghino would go on to become one of the most noted *condottieri*, or professional mercenaries, of his time. Fighting ran in his lifeblood. He was a merciless thug, renowned for extreme brutality. In battle, Il Medeghino's weapon of choice was an axe and, after capturing a town, he would mark his victory by hanging its defenders from the battlements. If you wanted a job doing thoroughly when it came to war, death and destruction, he could be relied on.

On 27 April 1554, Il Medeghino marched on Monteriggioni, sending forward a delegation to parley with the Sienese garrison commander, a Florentine exile by the name of Giovanni Zeti. He refused to surrender. The delegation retired and, not long after, the fortress came under heavy bombardment from the Grand Duchy's artillery. The town well suffered a direct hit. Without water, Monteriggioni's ability to withstand the siege was now very limited indeed. The Sienese agreed, however, that they would fight to the death rather than ever surrender to Florence.

Zeti, on the other hand, had different plans. Under cover of darkness, he slipped out to the Florentine lines where he found Il Medeghino and cut a deal – for the reinstatement of his citizenship and the return of his lands, he would hand over the keys of Monteriggioni to Florence. When Zeti returned, he was leading Il Medeghino's men.

After the town's surrender, Zeti was shunned by all and sundry, no matter how much he tried to justify his action. To this day, it is said that his spirit, not only abandoned by mankind but Heaven and Hell as well, wanders the tunnels beneath Monteriggioni's streets protesting its innocence. No one pities a traitor.

With croissant, pastries, a large cappuccino and a glass of freshly squeezed orange juice, I was sitting at a table in Monteriggioni's little piazza savouring the moment when from behind, to add to my joy, came the unmistakable voice of LN: '*Bonjour!*'

Over yet more breakfast – one of the many benefits of pilgrimming being that you can eat all you want and some – there followed an earnest discussion on the appearance of multiple and varied signs that had seemingly sprung up everywhere due to the sudden profusion of alternate and competing routes to the Via. This was causing some confusion and grief to other hardened pilgrims, many of whom, like me, had now been on the road for some time. LN was an excellent source of gossip. I finished my third croissant and, not long after, announced it was time to head for Siena, which you could just about see in the distance.

'It's a short hop. Maybe two or three hours at most', I said as I waved my strip of map with bold arrows drawn on it that would skirt me through the forest on La Montagnola Senese, miss out the 'scenic route' by taking the road to San Martino, then hop over the autostrada and reach Siena in time for lunch. *Perfetto*.

We agreed to catch up later and, with a cheery wave, I set off down the hill for the short stretch that would take me due south through the woods to the road on the far side.

It was my eightieth day since leaving London and the map in my hand was the fortieth of the journey; bar the odd minor aberration, I reckoned I had walking to Rome sussed. This was largely because the Via is so well marked. Consistent above all other markings was the red and white flash, little more than stripes of paint, sprayed or stuck discreetly on traffic signs, street lamps, trees, fenceposts, indeed anywhere a pilgrim might need to alter course. They had been my constant companion through England, France, Switzerland and Italy – lovingly and efficiently maintained across the continent by selfless bunches of volunteers who each look after their own section of the route. Red and white, for the last 1,200 odd miles.

And happy in this knowledge, off I set. I may even have been singing, I was that content. I crossed the road, red and white sign, walked up a track, red and white sign, hit the treeline and, at the red and white sign (with arrow), turned left into the forest for Siena. Once in the thick of it, the route began to jig about, but that was okay – as long as the general direction was south, the odd few 100 yards of eastward and westward movement to skirt obstacles or property was just fine. Well of course it was, because it had been for the last 80 days.

It began to get hot and at times there was the odd steep climb which I hadn't been expecting, but that was okay as I had refilled my two litres of water in Monteriggioni – ample for the short distance to Siena.

Blithely I followed the red and white signs and all the while I was heading south-ish but my two-mile leg through the woods, which should have taken all of 40 minutes, showed little hint of ending at all. In thick forest, travelling with strips of map that are the best part of three feet long but only six inches wide, I began to realize that I was walking 'off piste'. Yet still the red and white signs. It was getting hotter and the slopes more severe. But it was okay, I kept saying, I had a litre of water left. Besides, I couldn't be that lost, I kept trying to reassure myself, but equally, starved of any visible reference point, I hadn't a clue how far off course I had strayed. Trees everywhere. And red and white signs. All the while it was getting hotter. And still, red and white signs everywhere as if some sadistic aetheist with a hatred for pilgrims had gone out of his way to ensure that every day he had the pleasure of knowing that some poor soul was staggering for his life up in the baking hills trying to get through to Siena. Half a litre of water now. Then, in the distance, at the bottom of a hill, I spied a man. I jogged down to him.

Klaus, on holiday from Hanover, had taken a break from his wife and two girls to go walking for the day. He was a picture of calm. How beautiful the countryside was, he exclaimed and, oh, you're walking to Rome? Since where have you been walking? From London? No? This is not possible. Little did he know that had I not happened on him, my endeavour was about to be very short-lived. Klaus was my angel – he had a guidebook.

The local walking club, I quickly discovered, had taken to marking not just one route but every single path and trail on that God-forsaken hill in red and white which, to remind you, is the colour of the Via Francigena virtually all the way from Canterbury and indeed most other long-distance footpaths across Europe. Now I was not only well on the wrong side of the hill but even further from Siena than if I had stayed put in Monteriggioni.

The water ran out long before I crested the summit. It was the best part of four hours after I left LN that I walked into a bar in San Martino. Parched, I went straight to the fridge and, to the astonishment of the owner, took out a litre bottle of iced water, downed it in one, slapped a few euros on the counter, took another and walked straight out again.

But the truth is that, while the local walking club had, confusingly, daubed that hill in the colours of the Via, I too had grown complacent. Maybe that third croissant had gone to my head, but whatever it was, in my haste, I misread the signage.

Leaving that wretched hill behind me, which was beginning to look quite pretty over my shoulder, I made my way up to Siena. On the outskirts, I reached a roundabout; overhead was a big blue road sign and, written on it in large white letters, the words 'AREZZO – GROSSETO – ROMA'.

151 miles to Rome.

20

Monte Benichi, San Leolino and Siena

'I wish I could make money by telling stories', I said. 'I want to make a million pounds, like Jeffrey Archer, so that I can buy a little house in Tuscany and withdraw from it all!'
Russell Harty, *Mr Harty's Grand Tour*, 1988

'TOCCA FERRO', RICHARD FREMANTLE said as he touched his groin with the index and little fingers of his right hand, stretched out in the shape of cow's horns, while pouring me a glass of white wine. 'It's ancient Etruscan for good luck.' I looked bemused. 'When you can't find any metal, you touch your balls.'

I had been spirited away for a couple of days to Monte Benichi, a castellated village high in the Tuscan hills with views across the landscape that stretched away beyond the mighty Monte Amiata that rose up out of the haze in the distance.

To look at Richard, with his swept-back white hair and handkerchief in the top pocket of his linen jacket, would be to imagine the embodiment of the archetypal English gentleman – until, that is, he opened his mouth and broad New York tumbled out.

But, despite my host's protestations that he was really just a kid from the Bronx who had played 'stick and ball' in the street and terrorized the neighbourhood on his rollerskates, the inescapable fact is that his family remains a pillar of British society, giving its name to one of our most celebrated theatres with a string of illustrious ancestors who served over the centuries either at sea in the Royal Navy or on land in the Foot Guards, trailing the Duke of Wellington in the Peninsular Campaign or having horses shot from under them at the Battle of Quatre Bras.

Secretly, I suspect, this great muse, writer, art historian and museum curator loved being just that little bit different. There was a hint of mischief in his eyes. But even as 'the American cousin', for whom most sentences rarely escaped a liberal lacing of idiosyncrasies from across the pond, his roots were firmly planted on our side of the Atlantic, as books, military treatises, pamphlets, prints and watercolours were variously produced not only as points of interest and understandable pride but also to make me feel at home. Along with Barbara, his joyous other half from Germany, I couldn't help feeling that the house ran on a great sense of *carpe diem*.

'You know, everybody overlooks the Etruscans. Oh the Romans this, the goddam Romans that – they were a bunch of good-for-nothin' bums who forced their way uninvited to any and every party until eventually they took the place over.'

Barbara paused on her cigarette and looked up from the newspaper. She didn't look so sure.

'It's true', he said, 'the Etruscans laid the foundations for what Rome would become.'

Something tugged at my bootlace. I looked down and at the foot of my bar stool, a tiny black kitten with the brightest emerald green eyes stared up at me. 'Pico!' Richard shouted, at which there was a scurrying noise and a ruffle under a curtain from which an angry tail protruded, twitching back and forth.

'The Etruscans not only had systems of government but they were great soldiers, traders, metal workers, smiths in silver, gold, bronze and, above all, iron – a skill they brought with them from Lydia in western Turkey. It's all in Herodotus', a casual aside he threw in like an onion to flavour bread sauce.

'You see, sir', he carried on, 'Lydia suffered a prolonged famine and King Atys split his subjects into two. He kept one bunch and the other he put in the charge of his son, Tyrsenos, telling him the land couldn't support all these people and to head elsewhere. Virtually overnight around 800BC, they took everything they had in ships and ended up here in Tuscany and further south in Umbria. Hence the Tyrrenhian Sea and the Chianina, the white cattle you see everywhere. That's why in Tuscany and Umbria the old, old families are so dark. They're originally from Asia Minor.'

He paused, as if in thought, then suddenly let out a pained 'Ouch!' Pico had bitten his toe.

'Do you know why female figureheads on square riggers more often than not bare their breasts?' he said.

I shook my head.

'I'll tell ya why. 'Cos the Etruscans believed that to bare the breast warded off evil spirits. It's a good luck thing, a bit like the Gorgon's face.'

That evening, a 20-minute drive away, the village of San Leolino had been turned into a circuit, like a very short marathon for foodies and winos that snaked its way up the hill, past the church, through piazzas, back down the hill, past a band and back to the beginning.

At each food stall, plates were filled and glasses replenished. Once. Initially the locals were disciplined about this – a feature of wine tastings that, to be frank, I have always found afearedly dull; everybody pulling learned expressions and looking overly sincere when deep down all they want to do is guzzle the lot. San Leolino was different however. This was a wine tasting for 5,000.

After a couple of rebuffs, and as the light failed, so the villagers behind the many tables of bottles began to relent, especially when I explained that their help that evening would ensure my speedy delivery to Rome; indeed such then was their alacrity to assist my quest that whereas everyone else had to form as orderly a queue as Italians are capable of, I was granted direct access amid much smiling and waving on.

Richard, Barbara and I progressed around the crowded village, our plates alternately loaded with *bruschetta*, Tuscan sausage with beans, cured meats and pecorino cheese. For pudding, we were served *pane col vino*, which is a simple nursery recipe made of stale bread generously soaked in red wine and smothered in sugar; perfection on a plate unless you happen to be on a diet.

By late evening, the one-glass rule had completely fallen by the wayside – the band, deteriorating to an indecipherable wail, couldn't decide whether it was Chinese opera or Punch and Judy, while the menfolk ended up sitting on one side of the street and the women on the other.

On the way back to the car, I discussed my final approach into Rome, which I had decided would be straight down the Via della Conciliazone rather than the route the Via Francigena follows, which slips into the side of St Peter's Square unnoticed. It didn't feel right after walking all that way.

'You got Musso to thank for that', Richard declared.

'Mussolini?'

'Yeah Musso, it was about the only good thing the crap hat ever did.'

I pulled a face.

'Look', Richard said as he walked up to a dusty car door and, spitting on his finger, marked out a map of Italy along its length. He spat again. In the middle of the outline he drew a lozenge. 'From 1870, when Rome fell, until 1929, this', pointing to the lozenge, 'was technically not part of Italy. The Papal States resisted unifying with the Kingdom resulting in Pio Nono, the Pope at the time, describing himself as "a prisoner in the Vatican". Anyways, Musso comes along and summoned Pius XI to the table. He said this nonsense had to stop and, if it didn't, well they'd seize the land anyway. Take it or leave it. He brought an end to the 50 years or so of paralysis, known as the Roman Question and – *voilà* – the Lateran Accords of 1929, which saw the formal birth of the Vatican State with acknowledged rights and status within Italy. Now, before all this', as we went on up the hill, 'St Peter's was surrounded by slums and chaos and so Musso decided, after literally centuries of indecision, to clear all the rubbish out and build the Via della Conciliazone, the Street of Conciliation – a grand road to link the Vatican and Italian State, which he did in 1936. And that, my friend, is the story of the road down which you will walk your final steps in ten days' time.'

We got into the car, Richard slammed on some Puerto Rican jazz at full volume and, with the windows wound down and the cool night air in our faces, we swung our way across the Tuscan countryside back to Monte Benichi.

Arriving in Siena is like that moment when, as a child, you first set foot in a circus top: it is hot, noisy, full of people, and the air is charged with anticipation and excitement. 'The Antechamber to Paradise', as the city is known, is all about pilgrimage and, just like that circus coming to town, everyone loves to flock to its bosom.

Siena's great rival was Florence. In the Middle Ages the latter, situated on the river Arno, was one of the largest cities in Europe. Home to an enormous wool industry, it was immensely wealthy. The former, lacking water in any great quantity yet located on the Via Francigena, consciously fashioned itself as the City of the Virgin Mary, a New Jerusalem where the full economic benefit from the streams of pilgrims heading to Rome could be reaped; indeed, so great was the spectacle created that, for many, Siena equalled St Peter's in importance.

It was only in 1260, after the city defeated the numerically superior Florentines at the Battle of Montaperti, that the Virgin was formally adopted as its patron saint. The night before the battle, the Sienese paraded through the streets to the Duomo and vowed to hand Siena to Mary if they were victorious. They chose as their standard the colours of the *Terzo di Camollia*, one of the three city districts, whose crest was based on the relic of the Virgin's white cloak, housed in the Duomo. Victory ensued and the Sienese remained true to their word. Mary's image was everywhere to be seen from that day onwards in the shape of enormous frescoes on the main gates to paintings, statues and reliefs in churches, streets, town offices and all public buildings. Siena believed itself to be inextricably wed to the Holy Mother and, in her name, went about creating a metropolitan vision of outstanding beauty.

The city grew to become the embodiment of the urban civic ideal. With the massive influx of people, enormous social, economic and educational opportunities were created. Siena's walls had to be expanded three times in the thirteenth and fourteenth centuries, so rapid was this increase in population.

The walls were built not only for defence but also to define the city's ideological boundary. Within, everything was regulated, from the design, construction and composition of buildings to the width of the streets, the behaviour of its citizens and even mandatory participation in religious events, processions and payment of taxes. Failure to comply resulted in residences being torn down, the confiscation of property and punitive fines.

Duomo di Siena
...a beacon to all Christendom of Sienese loyalty to the
Holy Mother.

To cater for the rising numbers of pilgrims, organizations such as the Knights Templar and the Knights Hospitaller established *ospizi* and *ospedali* alongside numerous similar private institutions run by the wealthy and the prominent. Most famous of these was Santa Maria della Scala, opposite the Duomo.

I took a room in a rundown apartment, which had no curtains. Not a problem normally, except that in a window, across the communal lightwell, a couple made love relentlessly throughout the night with all the gusto of deer during the rut. They didn't have any curtains either.

It was a familiar sound, however, that woke me in the morning. The hair stood on the back of my neck as the streets echoed to that reassuring timbre of beating drums on the march; the music of war that for centuries marshalled troops about the field of battle. The men of the *Contrada di Torre*, traditionally the woolcombers, and one of the 17 wards of Siena, in all their flag-waving pomp and maroon medieval finery were parading through the city, dutifully followed by their women and children.

Visiting the Spedale di Santa Maria della Scala, I was immediately captivated by Domenico di Bartolo's expansive frescoes. Painted in the 1440s with almost photographic precision, they stretch across entire walls that arch into the distance like a never-ending underground railway station. The insight they give of life in fifteenth-century Siena is fascinating.

The panel that particularly caught my attention was a painting called *Healing of the Sick* – a gruesome scene from a hospital ward in the *Pellegrinaio*, the Pilgrim Hall, which for over 1,100 years and until the turn of the millennium had been the city's *ostello*. The detail on the near lifesize picture was revealing; crowded with well-dressed city folk, benefactors on a visit, order was evident throughout, despite a cat and dog bridling for a fight in the foreground. The room was arranged with beds for the sick just as in hospitals today and a portly monk looked on, bored, as he took confession from a patient. The place was busy – physicians pored over a flask of urine while a nurse, in white, ministered to a distressed old man lying on a stretcher, his arms reaching out. On the right, porters brought in a casualty and in the centre, amid the tittle-tattling nobility, a semi-naked man was having his feet washed and back dried.

But what really made me smart was that this man had a deep but very neat gash to his thigh; it was meticulously drawn. I stared intently at the gaping wound, held my hand up to it to judge scale and placed it against my own leg. It was a good six inches across and yet, remarkably, the fellow showed no sign of pain whatsoever – artistic licence, surely. A nice lady from Munich, who saw me wincing, told me that the patient was being prepared for surgery. The news left me greatly relieved.

As I stepped back out into the Piazza del Duomo, the sun now high in the morning sky, I was dazzled by the grandiose white brilliance of the Santa Maria Assunta's façade. The focal point of Siena's piety, the Duomo is built on the city's highest point; this impressive building, faced in alternating stripes of black and white marble, reflects Siena's heraldic colours. It was deliberately designed to shine out as a beacon to all Christendom of Sienese loyalty to the Holy Mother.

Showing my Pilgrim Passport at the door, I was ushered into a world of make-believe, a great cavernous hall of stupefying embellishment that was almost too rich to contemplate. From the lofty blue vaulted ceilings that spangled with golden stars, everywhere I cared to look was fine polished marble, bright gilding, patrician statuary, noble sculptures and exquisite carvings including works by the likes of Donatello, Bernini and Michelangelo – ecclesiastical theatre on the grandest scale.

Clambering over this magnificent testament to medieval artistry was a gawping and gaping multitude who had, just as in yesteryear, travelled from the world over to marvel at this amazing sight; the women were clad in disposable shawls that wafted behind them like ghostly vapour trails. As an onlooker to this religious freakshow of giddying excess where humility had been rigorously swept aside, I felt oddly removed. I became suddenly possessed of an unnerving feeling that most probably the scene before me had 'ever been thus', including the wily Sienese jangling their coffers with glee outside in the shape of knick-knacks and souvenirs for sale. As I left, I thought to myself that pilgrimage in Siena remains good for business

– never mind if the visitor today is more tourist to stare than pilgrim to worship.

In the Piazza once again, I gazed back up at Giovanni Pisano's remarkable west front. Combining elements of the Gothic, Romanesque and Classical styles in a mix of columns, sculptures, pinnacles, adornments and mosaics, it is both indulgent and beautiful; the epitome of Italian craftsmanship.

In 1294, Florence started to build the iconic Basilica di Santa Maria del Fiore to a scale that would dwarf Santa Maria Assunta. The Sienese authorities, realizing this, embarked on a rebuild of such magnitude and scale that their transformed Duomo would become the largest cathedral in the world. A building truly worthy of the Virgin, it would eclipse Constantinople's Hagia Sophia and tower over St Peter's – so limitless was Sienese ambition. The new construction would ensure, of course, that the all-important pilgrim trade, on which Siena relied, wouldn't be diverted elsewhere.

Work started in 1337. However, ten years later, in October 1347, a small fleet of Genoese merchantmen was returning from the Crimean shores of the Black Sea laden with cargo from the Silk Route. By the time the ships reached Sicily, most of the crews were either dead or extremely ill. The Black Death had reached Italy.

The Great Pestilence, as it was known, swept across Europe in the following two years like wildfire through parched forest; a cataclysmic event, its rapacious advance struck not only at the heart of every family but the very fabric of society itself. Nothing would ever be the same again.

To put matters into context, the combined death toll of the First and Second World Wars was roughly 76 million people. The Black Death, it is estimated, killed 200 million in the fourteenth century – half the known world.

Siena was particularly hard hit; its principal source of income, pilgrims, dried up and soon the money ran out. Of a population nearing a 100,000, only about 10,000 survived – many fled but far more died. The rule of law collapsed, the clergy abandoned their communities and, thereafter, Church authority was widely challenged.

Agnolo di Tura del Grasso, the Fat Man, wrote in his journals about this desperate chapter in the city's history: 'Father abandoned child, wife husband, one brother another; for this illness seemed to strike through the breath and the sight. And so they died. And none could be found to bury the dead for money or friendship. Members of a household brought their dead to a ditch as best they could, without priest, without divine offices. Nor did the [death] bell sound. And in many places in Siena, great pits were dug and piled deep with the multitude of dead... and I, Agnolo di Tura, called the Fat, buried my five children with my own hands. And there were also those who were so sparsely covered with earth that the dogs dragged them forth and devoured many bodies throughout the city.'

The Duomo stands as a gruesome testament to that horrendous year. It remains half-completed. The nave of today was meant to be the transept of tomorrow and the unfinished arches that stretch off to the right are witness to the failed Sienese dream. It would take until the twentieth century before the city's population levels recovered.

The Black Death was perhaps the first nail in the Republic's coffin. Florence, by dint of its position if nothing else, grew ever prosperous. It was only a matter of time before its smaller rival was outpaced and ultimately fell. For while Florence embraced the Renaissance with all its might, Siena remained locked in the shadows of the Middle Ages.

151 miles to Rome.

21

Monteroni d'Arbia and San Quirico to Radicofani

The country is wild and lonely: the climate harsh...when the wheat ripens and the alfalfa has been cut, the last patches of green disappear from the landscape. The whole valley becomes dust-coloured – a land without mercy, without shade.

Iris Origo, *War in Val d'Orcia*, 1947

I LEFT SIENA BY the Porta Romana. Once again, Tuscany, a carpet of post-harvest yellow, glowing before me. I was heading into a land once described as 'bare and colourless as elephants' backs' – the *Crete Senesi*.

It was not far down the road when suddenly a gruff voice behind said: 'Eh, English!' Domingo, unbeknown to me, had been in Siena at the same time, with LN; the latter, still not fully recovered, was making her way separately by bus to Radicofani.

Like long-lost brothers, we greeted each other with open arms – it was as if we had never parted. However, the joy of reunion quickly passed as Domingo's expression hardened. Carrying far too much weight, by his own admission, he looked worn out – the journey had exacted its price, and he now sported a large elasticated bandage around his left knee to boot. 'I fell badly down a bank', he shrugged. That carefree morning in Switzerland now seemed far behind, as resentment and anger seemed to leach from every pore of my Spanish friend's body.

'I hate this place', he vented over coffee in Isola d'Arbia, his eyes searching around him.

I looked at him in disbelief, 'Tuscany?'

'For me it is a penitence', he shook his head, 'all these bloody cypress trees everywhere is death. Death! You know, where I come from, they line the paths to the cemetery. I am so depressed by this Via Francigena – these last few weeks have been so hard on the head, man.'

Since we had parted, the solitude and monotony of the rice plains had indeed been punishing for him, the more so carrying injury. But Domingo's situation can't have been helped by the admission that in Italy he was determined to make his way to Rome by waymark alone and without maps. With sections of the Via Francigena now routinely and often confusingly signed by rival walking associations, Domingo risked being led a merry dance around the Italian countryside – compounding his problems further.

I was just embarking on an outpouring of sympathy in a futile attempt to lift my companion's funk when, in the nick of time, onto the verandah flopped two ladies to my rescue. Pilgrims by their packs and clothes, in the lead was Carmen, petite, dark and gorgeous, and behind followed Josephine, an amazon of a woman, carrying a large bough for a staff, complete with branches and leaves, to round off the earth mother look. Josephine was at one with nature, her head almost entirely engulfed by an enormous shock of white hair which seemed to move of its own accord as she walked and gave her the air of a rather grand ornamental chicken. Whether she could see out at all was a matter for discussion and may explain why Carmen walked in front all the time.

Josephine was dressed for comfort in opened-toed sandals and a relatively tight-fitting bikini, which I am sure was practical but a little off-putting when she sat down. This rather startling ensemble merely added effect to their somewhat dramatic entrance as, quite unabashed, they plonked themselves at our table. It was totally in character for the winsome pair who, it seemed to me, had left Dijon with the sole intent of wafting their way to Assisi on a cloud of divine providence. Goodness and beauty, they were convinced, surrounded them in all its glorious and diverse manifestations.

Just like Domingo, they too had elected to walk without maps – except that, in their case, they were adamant that they travelled with the help of angels. That they had got this far, they believed, was evidence that God was indeed their guide. Barking mad was my initial reaction to this, but then, given my own experiences of late and the undeniable fact that the couple were only 75 miles from their destination, their theory, it could be argued, carried some weight.

The joyous pair with their impish sense of humour and infectious spirit had a certain sense of calm and serenity about them. In their refreshing company Domingo relaxed and regained some of his old form. Then, a small cloth bag filled with white feathers was produced.

'What are those?' I asked.

'These are the feathers of angels, left on our path to mark the way', Josephine said. Almost in evidence, she laid them out one by one like delicate white cards in a game of patience. I watched the breeze gently catch the fluffy down at the quill ends as Josephine proceeded to tell us where each and every one had been found. She insisted that Domingo and I should have one each to protect us on our final days to Rome. I smiled but refused on the pretext I really had to go. 'I have to meet friends for lunch where I am staying the night nearby.'

'Meet friends for lunch?' Domingo perked up. 'Oh, lunch now is it? Ha, bloody ladies who lunch! Come on then, who? No, don't tell me, knowing you it's a Duke and Duchess.'

'Well, not exactly', I replied a little sheepishly, 'but seeing as you ask, actually it's a Conte and Contessa.' I think some almond croissants were launched in my direction. I beat a hasty retreat down a bank, shouting over my shoulder that it was nice to meet Josephine and Carmen, *bonne continuation*, while reminding Domingo that his breath still smelt and I would see him the next evening at San Quirico.

It's not every day that you have to wade across a river to get to lunch, which is what happened when I reached the lazing Arbia and got the stepping stone sequence wrong. I walked the last half-mile to Castello di San Fabiano through the fields with my boots squelching, much of my track marked by a trail of drips.

The Castello, an enormous red-brick peel tower built in the thirteenth century, is an enchanting place of arcadian beauty. It is set in rolling hills amid oak and pine, on a rambling estate at the centre of a maze of gravelled drives lined with lemon trees and lavender bushes.

As I approached, I noticed two dogs sheltering from the heat under some oleander bushes. Even 200 yards away I could see their ears prick up. I began to wonder how I would plead with hosts, whom I had never met, to call their charges off. Then I began to fear that, given the place was so enormous, they might never realize, perhaps until the cheese soufflé was overdone, that their guest was late arriving.

'Darling, did you lock the dogs up?'

'No dear, I thought you did', the Contessa's reply.

A pause.

'Oh...'

But I needn't have worried. I prepared my stick at the ready but there was no bare-toothed charge in death-snarling anger; one old boy glanced in my direction while the other slowly lifted himself up and drunkenly zig-zagged across the courtyard to inspect. There was a deep slobbering bark and, sensing little danger, he grunted and returned to the comfort and quiet of the shade.

I rang the bell. Nothing. I tried the door. Locked. I rang again. Still nothing. Just as I was summoning up the courage to ring for a third time, footsteps came hurrying down the staircase and the door flung open. Tall, refined, ruggedly handsome with close-cropped grey hair and effortlessly relaxed, the beaming Conte Andrea Fiorentini welcomed me in. Even with designer stubble, he was every inch the noble. I apologized for being late but explained I had fallen in his river on the way.

He took one look at me in my dripping state and quickly agreed that a shower and change would be the fairest thing all round.

Originally built for defence, everything in San Fabiano happens on the upper floors. I was led up endless flights of stairs lined with sculptures, portraits, banners and suits of armour, down airy corridors hung with shields, halberds and swords, until finally reaching my bedroom.

Restored and looking vaguely civilized, I made my way downstairs. Turning the corner, an enormous dog, part-collie but more wolf, came bounding down the corridor at me. Divested of stick and in a confined space, I was defenceless with little room for manoeuvre. I braced myself, fearing the worst, but just as the hairy monster was about to launch himself at me, he slowed, wagged his tail and, jumping up, licked my face. Relieved, I was none too fussed therefore at being delivered into the drawing room stooped down with my arm in the canine's mouth.

'Hello', I announced, looking up at everyone from my lowly position like Quasimodo freshly sprung from his belfry.

'Oh Fez!' Beatrice, Andrea's wife, cried, 'let Harry go please! I am so sorry, we got him as a guard dog but he is more a pussy cat.' Albeit a rather big one, I thought to myself, as he took up most of the sprawling sofa next to his mistress. The Contessa, with long flowing hair and wearing a pretty cotton dress, was glamour personified. She possessed the intangible magic and sensuality of a fifties film star. The moment she uttered so much as a word in her silken English accent, it was impossible not to fall under her spell.

The chic drawing room was in a state of half-darkness as the awnings had been drawn on the terrace to shield from the searing temperature outside. We were five, the Conte and Contessa, their brother-in-law Jonathan who lived with his wife nearby and a friend, Tim, visiting from London.

Andrea gave me a dry martini. It felt strange to hold the dainty cocktail glass by its stem rather than grab it brutishly as I had grown accustomed of late with mugs, cups and bottles of water. It was like a temporary release, a tantalizing glimpse of a world, lost to me months earlier, that I would regain in a matter of days. Talk was of London. The great city, which had seemed so remote these last few months, now felt like it was just around the corner. Even this far away, it was impossible to escape its reach. A knock at the door and the maid popped her head around to announce lunch.

The dining room was not grand; in fact with its tiled floor and ochre walls it had the simplicity of the refectory about it. As we sat down, Andrea explained that it was 'at this table that Il Duce negotiated the Concordat with the Pope in the late 1920s, leading to the creation of Vatican City as we know it today'. I thought back to my conversation with Richard in San Leolino a few nights earlier.

It was perhaps fitting that the family now owned the piece. In 1919, the Fiorentinis set up a company to import and distribute construction equipment but, as Mussolini's National Fascist Party took hold of Italy, importing goods was restricted or banned altogether in order to revitalize the ailing economy and create work for the unemployed. The company made a clever move into the manufacture of bulldozers, diggers, scrapers and earthmovers – in short, the tools that Mussolini needed to bring his vision of a 'new Republic' to life. At the heart of this dream, both physically and spiritually, was a Rome that would be fashioned as a worthy heir to its imperial ancestor. It was to be the envy of the world.

Throughout this ambitious programme, it was Fiorentini machinery that led the charge as Il Duce's grandiose schemes saw marshes drained, motorways built and slums swept aside for imposing boulevards like the Via della Conciliazione, the authority for which was signed on the table that I was about to eat lunch at.

Over soup, Andrea started to talk about how, in the Middle Ages, pilgrims on the Via Francigena were considered to be a valuable commodity as, by dint of the length of their journey, they carried a lot of money with them, usually in the form of coin. While he explained this, I couldn't help smiling to myself, because that morning I had drawn the last penny from my bank account. Without so much as a bean to my name, 'valuable' was now the last word anyone could use to describe me.

'...which of course is one of the ways the Sienese made money. Pilgrims and people in general moving about the country were encouraged to use the banking facilities provided by Banca Monte dei Paschi di Siena, which, as you remember, is the oldest surviving bank in the world.' Everyone started to nod sagely in collective recall. At that time, this was news to me, so I nodded my head anyway. 'You could deposit your money in Siena, complete the distance to Rome and on arrival present your letter of credit and retrieve the funds. It was, how you say, a "win win" for the bank really' – the Conte was enjoying this – 'because legend has it that the Sienese ran the brigands that controlled the hills around Radicofani, so if your money wasn't taken by the bank, they would receive it via the robbers anyway.'

'You must be referring to *Banda dei Quattro*', I said, thinking of Italy's Robin Hood, Ghino di Tacco who, along with his father, uncle and younger brother, took to the hills and a life of crime because of the punitive levels of taxation forced on them by the Sienese Church authorities. He eventually established himself in the castle at Radicofani. His methods, if not entirely admirable, were novel – students and the poor were allowed to pass free, while anybody else was assessed, relieved of most of their valuables, fed and sent on their way with enough to get by.

Ghino avenged the execution of his father in dramatic style when he marched into the Papal Tribunal in Rome at the head of 400 men carrying a pike. There he summarily beheaded Judge Benincasa, who had sentenced his father to death in Siena years earlier, jammed his head on the pike and took it back to Radicofani, where it was displayed from the tower for all to see.

In a weird twist, the wheel of fortune turned in Ghino's favour when he captured the Abbot of Cluny who, making his way back to France, elected to stop off at a nearby spa to cure himself of the indigestion he was suffering following overindulgence in Rome. Ghino locked the hapless cleric in his fortress and fed him on the unlikely diet of bread, lentils and wine from San Gimignano. Bizarrely, it seemed to have the desired effect. So impressed was the Abbot, he petitioned Pope Boniface to pardon the outlaw. The Pontiff not only obliged but appointed di Tacco a Knight of Saint John and made him Prior of the Ospedale di Santo Spirito in Rome.

But the Conte corrected me. Ghino had been born 200 years before the Banca Monte dei Paschi di Siena was founded in the late fifteenth century. 'But it is wild country that the Via Cassia passes through to Radicofani. Always has been…', he added, passing a plate of cheese.

We assembled for dinner on the terrace; the heat gone from the day, the evening was bathed in a gentle warmth like embers in a fire cradling night into morning. Tuscany seemed to be laid out in neat rows of wheat and vine in every direction and, where it wasn't, the unruly green chaos of ancient woodland lent a perfect balance to the order that reigned in the fields below. The Conte greeted me with an aperitif containing an innocuous brown liquid, which in the wrong bottle could have been mistaken for engine oil. One shot of Andrea's home-made *nocino* or walnut liqueur could fly a rocket to the moon. The ingredients are fairly straightforward, the Conte explained. 'You take 20, 30 or so green walnuts, in their husks, add cloves, cinnamon, lemon rind, sugar and water. We have a tradition here, I don't know why but we do, to pick the walnuts on San Giovanni, the 24th of June, in the evening and then we make the liqueur up that night.' I took a sip from my glass. It was delicious but I spluttered as it hit the back of my throat like I had been involuntarily flown through the sound barrier.

As if suddenly prompted, he added, 'Oh, and did I mention the litre of pure alcohol too?'

'No', I croaked back at him, 'that's 95 per cent proof isn't it?'

'Er, not exactly', holding up a finger in emphasis, 'to be precise 96 per cent...'

Beatrice appeared in a flowing kaftan. She was excited at the prospect of the return of two of her sons, who were driving back from the Bay of Naples where they had been sailing.

The boys, charming, spirited and full of enthusiasm, turned up shortly after and it was not long before we were making happy inroads into the *nocino* again. The atmosphere was beautifully relaxed; the moon cast silvered light over the solemn darkness, the crickets sang while the bullfrogs grumbled and groaned and every now and again an owl's screech would pierce the night. Had not the call of Rome been echoing in my head as it had done every night since early May, we could have easily talked the hours away till dawn, such was the company I had the pleasure to be in.

In the morning, Andrea and Beatrice were insistent that they wave me off, despite the ungodly hour of 5 a.m. We hugged, we kissed and Fez jumped up. I walked out the door, straight down the drive and out into the fields. I daren't look back, so painful did I find the farewell.

In that respect, these days were difficult – at once both charged with great euphoria and deep sadness. For months now, if not years, I had thought of little else save reaching Rome. Now the goal was nearly in my grasp, all I wanted to do was savour every last minute of the journey before all too quickly, like grains of sand in the hand, they were lost for eternity. Never to be replaced.

Not long after I left San Fabiano, I met Carmen and Josephine heading in the opposite direction.

'Aren't you going the wrong way?' I asked.

'No', Josephine replied, showing me the waymark in a battered guidebook which they had correctly identified but completely misinterpreted.

'You should be going east, not north'.

'But we are…' she insisted.

'You can't be', I said, 'look at the sun.'

'But the guidebook says…' Josephine was adamant.

'Yes', I said, studying the guidebook, 'it does say take the marker at the football pitch, but you have read it the wrong way round.'

'It's not possible.'

'Look', I started to fumble for my compass, the second time I had used it the whole journey, 'north is behind me…the way you are headed right now.' The shimmering needle pointed unfailingly over my shoulder in the direction they were headed.

She looked at Carmen, who gazed on with a degree of disinterest. They shrugged at one another.

'But the guidebook…'

'…is right. It is you who went wrong.'

Another look at Carmen. Another shrug. She stared again at the foxed page almost as if betrayed. I watched the computation. A collective, 'aah!' like Archimedes in his bath, the couple declared I was an angel and set off once again, but this time in the right direction.

'May I urge you to buy a map?' I cried after them. I never saw the pair again.

It took an age to reach the pretty village of San Quirico that afternoon, the air sultry and still, Italy still in the grip of a searing heatwave. When I finally arrived, after an arduous grind up a never-ending hill, there was quite a commotion; a large crowd was blocking the street outside the church – a funeral was taking place. I eased my way through the throng to the *ostello* tucked down the back of a side street; with its sandstone buildings and winding streets, the place reminded me of the Cotswolds. There, sitting in a heap on top of his rucksack, covered in sweat and looking very out of sorts with himself, was Domingo, along with two other, equally dumb-faced and exhausted young pilgrims.

'You made it then', he said, hardly looking up at me.

'Yeah', I just about summoned the energy to mutter, grabbing at my shoulder straps for that long-awaited moment when I could at last release myself from the burden of my rucksack. I flung the thing to the ground and immediately started to grab for my water bottle.

'What are you all waiting for? Why can't we go in?'

'The priest says we are to wait here.'

To which I replied, quite bluntly, in short words easily understood in the international vernacular, that I was not in the mood to be treated like a schoolboy. Of course, my state had nothing whatsoever to do with the copious amounts of walnut liqueur consumed the night before. But how was I to know that the two fresh-faced young guys sat with Domingo and witness to my volatile outburst were curates from Poland?

Kuba and Adam were in their last months of training in the Catholic Seminary at Cracow. Not only were they angelic of face, they were angelic of character. From that moment on, their ever-smiling faces would be a constant source of reassurance and joy the moment they turned a corner or came into view for the rest of the road to Rome. They were relieved, I would later learn, to be walking in Italy. If they had attempted a similar journey in their homeland, they would have had to undertake it in full cassock, carrying rucksacks too. Here, they were in 'disguise' and as filthy and fragrant as the rest of us.

It was Kuba who found me nursing a beer outside a bar. 'Don Gianni wants to see us.'

Don Gianni, in his late 30s, was a great bear of a man. It was rare to find a priest so relatively young. He had great charisma and was clearly much loved by his ageing parishioners. Everywhere he went, an enquiring and snuffling bulldog, Diego, followed him. We were called into his office and made to sit down at chairs arranged around his desk. His tone was matter-of-fact, his disciplined manner of imparting information instantly reminding me of briefings before embarking on operations in the Army.

With much gravitas and in great detail, like a general launching his men into battle, he talked us through every stage of the route to Radicofani, including the vital last garage where we could rest and refill water bottles before the final six-mile hike to the top.

'Do not take the signed way', he warned, 'it will add five, maybe eight kilometres to your journey and, in this temperature, you will die'.

Clasping his hands snugly around his belly, he looked us in the eye and summed up: 'Gentlemen, you have a long day ahead of you tomorrow. You will leave early, for on the hill, there will only be you, the heat and God. In fact, sometimes, I am not even sure if God is there at all.'

The air was cool and fresh the following morning and, apart from the odd dog barking, a scurrying hare or bemused pine marten, all was quiet as I left San Quirico. I paused at Vignoni Alto and looked down the steep valley side to the Orcia. The sun was rising and the landscape was wrapped in the comforting softness of dawn. Immediately below, the hillside was punctuated with cypress and daubed with swathes of woodland. But in the far distance, the unmistakable outline of Radicofani lurked menacingly. On top of its ridge, it looked like an upturned bowl but even 20 miles away you could clearly make out the sinister black silhouette of the watchtower. After the river, however, there was nothing; not a house, not a tree – just the bare unforgiving landscape sliced in two by the relentless Via Cassia as it headed south for Rome.

Kuba and Adam caught up with me at the garage, the last stop two hours before the top. Domingo, being Spanish, wasn't really into early starts. He was to be found flailing somewhere around in the heat of the day miles behind. We didn't say much, knowing to save our energy for what was to come. Normally, I would have stopped and waited, but I was on a roll – to linger could risk losing the momentum and legs might start to stiffen.

Radicofani
…in the far distance, the unmistakable outline of Radicofani
lurked menacingly…

Besides, there was no point hanging about; the top of the hill had to be reached and there was no time like the present to get on with it.

Faced with a severe climb, and in order to get the job done as painlessly and quickly as possible, I am quite happy to admit that I took out my iPod, selected *The Best Disco Album in the World...Ever* and plugged the earphones in. Cocooned in my own little world of late 1970s glitter and glamour, serenaded by the likes of Chaka Khan, Village People, Diana Ross and Rose Royce, I quite unashamedly shook my body, jumped to the beat and boogie-woogied all the way to the top. I never stopped once.

102 miles to Rome.

22

Radicofani to La Storta

We are the Pilgrims, master; we shall go
Always a little further...

James Elroy Flecker, *The Golden*
Road to Samarkand, 1913

DOMINGO'S BOOM WOKE US all when he finally reached
the Spedale di San Pietro e Giacomo in Radicofani late that
afternoon on 1 August.

Rest was now out of the question. I decided to clamber up to
the fortress; it had, after all, been the focus of my attentions for
some time. Inside the great tower, I climbed the dark staircase
to the top. There was a pleasant breeze. Far below, I could hear
people in the town, jazz music from a radio and somewhere in
the distance a tractor's labouring whine as it ploughed in the
fields. I paused and reflected on the haul of the last two days,
looking out over the battlements at Ghino di Tacco's one-time
fiefdom. The land seemed washed in that blue haze of high
summer; I traced my progress back to distant Siena, now but
a smudge on the northern horizon. To the south, Rome still
remained tantalizingly out of reach, somewhere beyond the Lago
di Bolsena.

As I took in the hills and woodland around me, it was not
thoughts of thirteenth-century gentlemen bandits that captured
my imagination but events of 22 June 1944 – when 'all the time
the shells were falling...and the planes flew overhead' – the date
when the cold-faced brutality of war finally unleashed itself in
all its horror on Iris Origo, Marchesa di Val d'Orcia. She was
a remarkable woman with a selfless quality who together with
her husband, Antonio, lovingly restored the estate at La Foce.
From 1943, the place became a haven for children, families and
other less fortunates escaping the miseries of conflict. The stark
scenery that had for days preoccupied me now seemed serene,

calm and at peace in the late afternoon sun. It was impossible to conceive that 70 years earlier it had been witness to chaos, death and destruction of a magnitude that thankfully only relatively few of us these days have had the misfortune to experience.

In her enchanting diaries, *War in Val d'Orcia,* Iris recorded how, caught up in the chaos of a full-scale Nazi withdrawal and the might of the Allied advance, a German officer told she and her husband that if they left at once 'they may be able to get out of range ...'. Warned to stick to the middle of roads to avoid mines and to spread out in case fighter planes mistook them for soldiers, they had little time to weigh up their options. And so, in an act of great courage, the couple gathered up the 60 folk who had taken refuge in their buildings, including four babies and 28 children and, often under continuous artillery bombardment, set out 'in a long, straggling line, with the children clutching at our skirts, half walking, half running... down the Chiancino road'. By the end of that terrible day, having made it to Montepulciano, the Marchesa simply wrote: 'We have left behind everything that we possess, but never in my life have I felt so rich and thankful as looking down on all the children as they lay asleep. Whatever may happen tomorrow, tonight they are safe and sound!'

I returned from the battlements to find everybody sitting in a row preparing for the evening ritual of washing of feet – a daily tradition in all hostels run by the Confraternita di San Jacopo di Compostella. I joined the queue. Elvia, a retired hairdresser, who along with her husband, Alberto, a former railwayman, both from Venice, were the volunteer Hospitallers for the week, came to inspect.

'Pilgrim feet', she said, rubbing soothing hands over my calloused soles; she immersed them in a bowl of warm salted water, clasped them in a fresh linen towel, dried and kissed them while Alberto blessed me. Anywhere else this intimate and simple ceremony might have seemed absurd but, there and then, I only felt humility and privilege. After the day we had endured, there was a definite healing quality to the custom, like a spiritual full stop, that left us refreshed and reinvigorated.

Summoned to the dining table for supper, Elena, the cook, had prepared a wholesome feast in vast quantity that included steaming bowls of home-made minestrone and shanks of lamb in thick gravy piled high with casseroled vegetables. We were joined by a couple of local guests and two Italian pilgrims from Montecatini: Pietro, an architect and Antonio, a retired telecoms man with designer stubble and a ponytail. For two weeks every year, the pair had been walking the Via down through Italy. They were now on the penultimate leg of their journey.

With the exertions of the last few days behind us and the final big heave before Rome out of the way, there was a distinct atmosphere of celebration in the air. I forget how the singing started precisely. The table fell momentarily silent and then all eyes suddenly turned on Alberto who, with shaven head and bulging biceps, made the most unexpected tenor. He sat up and, with arms outstretched, filled the room with song as *O sole mio* poured forth from him with great feeling and emotion. When he finished we were all rather taken aback and for a minute or so just blinked and gazed at one another. It was not long however before we joined Alberto in Verdi's *Chorus of the Hebrew Slaves*; even if we didn't know all the words, *la la la* was a very good substitute.

It was Antonio, jester personified, who egged Domingo on. Incapable of refusing a chance to perform, my bull-chased friend from Pamplona jumped up and sang his own version of Carmen Miranda's *'I, yi, yi, like you very much'*, which took him cavorting around the room like a dancing bear, to much clapping, cheering and wolf-whistling. Things improved little when attention turned in my direction. It never fails to surprise me just how many people around the world, let alone around the table that night, know the words to *Roll out the Barrel*; it was, I have to confess, the pitiful sum total of my musical recall that evening. It had been a long few days.

Tired out, the party was over almost as quickly as it had started – for most of us anyway. An hour or so later, asleep in the dormitory, I became aware of movement outside in the hallway; there was, however, an indecisive clumsiness about it.

'I, yi, yi, yi, like you very much' came the faint sing-song whisper as Domingo tried to steal his way into the room

unnoticed. Fumbling in the darkness he made a grab for the ladder that would lead him up to his top bunk. '*I, yi, yi, yo...*' a protracted grunt as the bed above me teetered, then shuddered violently like a ship in a heavy sea as the strength to compensate escaped Domingo and he was rudely thrown to the floor. A pause, followed by a certain amount of floundering around, some poorly suppressed fits of the giggles and the circus act was ready to be repeated again, until someone lobbed a boot which connected with a rewarding thud. Silence.

The next morning, after being blessed that I might know right from wrong and God called upon to protect me on my way, I embraced Alberto, kissed Elena and Elvia, said my goodbyes and, stepping out into the early sun, left Tuscany behind me.

Following the route of the old Via Cassia, now little more than a dusty track down the steep barren ridgeline, I found myself walking in an evocative landscape that was home to no one, except here and there the odd remote farmstead and file upon file of sheep obediently herding themselves across the hillsides towards Lazio. It was like the Northumbrian moor.

The end-of-term atmosphere spilled over into Aquapendente, where we sang and danced some more, this time adding a scout troop to the coterie with whom we found ourselves sharing the rambling old Capuchin convent at the top of the town. The place was run by two splendid elderly nuns, suore Livia and Amelia, who were not the slightest bit fazed by the unexpected tumble of life and humanity that had suddenly descended on their orderly existence. Sensibly, they declined our overtures to join in the revelry.

By comparison, the *ostello* in Bolsena was neither easy nor obvious to find, which was odd given that the address for the Suore del Santissimo Sacramento was unequivocal: Piazza Santa Cristina 4, opposite the basilica in the heart of the town. But there was no number 4 to be found, just a collection of tourist shops selling odd-shaped inflatable toys for children to play with on the lake. Twice the six of us went around the Piazza, Domingo pulling unhelpful confounded faces. Not a sign. Eventually I suggested we ask in the bank, a tall non-descript modern building that was across from the church with opaque windows and a uniform façade of gunmetal bronze. The door was shut so I pressed the buzzer.

After a long pause, there was the noise of distant footsteps, a key turned, and the smiling face of a surprisingly young Suor Stella welcomed us in. It was modern, airy – a bit like the headquarters of a multinational conglomerate. We agreed this was the most unlikely looking *ostello* any of us had set foot in.

After lunch by the *lago*, we ventured into the darkened halls of the Basilica di Santa Cristina, named after the saint who was martyred for her faith in the third century. Among other punishments, Cristina of Bolsena is alleged to have endured being hung from hooks, placed in a furnace, put to the wheel, grilled alive, drowned with a millstone, shot with arrows and attacked by snakes. The instigator of these terrible deeds was said to have been her father, a senior magistrate.

The basilica was a busy place, not unsurprisingly because it was here, in 1263, that the mystery at the very heart of the Catholic faith was revealed to a German priest. Peter of Prague had decided to go on pilgrimage to Rome to reaffirm his faith and, importantly, his wavering belief in transubstantiation – the transformation of Communion bread and wine into the body and blood of Jesus Christ. Arriving in Bolsena, Peter prayed at Santa Cristina's tomb and then celebrated mass in front of it. In accordance with the ritual, at the moment of consecration, as he held the bread over the chalice, blood started to pour from it, dripping onto the *corporal*, the square of white linen beneath. Peter was so overwhelmed that he stopped the ceremony immediately, wrapped the silver goblet in the cloth and retired to the sacristy, on his way spilling yet more blood on the marble floor. Pope Urban IV was so moved, when he heard news of the event, that many believe it greatly influenced him to establish the Feast of Corpus Christi a year later to celebrate the Blessed Sacrament.

The explanation, however, may be more simple. In 1819 an Italian doctor, Vincenzo Sette, discovered the 'microbe of miracles' on polenta that would later be named *micrococcus prodigiosus*. This microscopic organism whose colonies emit a foul smell, produce a brown-red matter not dissimilar to blood. There are cynics who say that some wily clerics in the Catholic

Church may have been wise to the phenomenon much earlier; knowing that the bacteria thrived on damp wafers, there is a suggestion that – perish the thought – they may even have engineered 'bleedings' to religious advantage.

*

Not long after San Antonio, the Via Cassia began to climb gently, passing through olive groves, oak copses and past fields of stubble. Just before a sharp left-hand bend I noticed a sign beckoning to a Commonwealth War Graves Cemetery.

I walked down the path until I reached a headland overlooking the Lago di Bolsena. This tranquil spot was once the site of Field Marshal Alexander's forward headquarters after the fall of Rome in June 1944. How busy it must have been 70 years ago. George VI visited in the August of that year, presenting no less than four Victoria Crosses for bravery in action. But now it was the resting place for 600 Allied sailors, soldiers and airmen killed in the fight to liberate Italy. At the centre of this beautifully tended scene, the spreading branches of an oak tree swayed gently in the breeze that blew off the lake. Laying my rucksack down by the hedge, I made my way down the rows of graves: ranks of Grenadier, Coldstream and Scots Guardsmen stood alongside their Indian, Canadian, Australian, New Zealand, South African and other British comrades in arms. For some time, I am not really sure how long, I just sat among them, at home with my own.

Montefiascone, high on the caldera's edge, is a magnificent sight with its skyline of domes and turrets. For me, as I toiled up the hill, any notion of magnificence ended abruptly after a milestone that announced 100 kilometres to Rome. Home for the night was an airy garage next to a large church that was part-warehouse and part-dormitory. It had doors that opened wide enough to fit a small lorry. Adam and Kuba, the first to arrive, laid out their bedding over two mattresses on the floor while I got a sort of camp bed contraption and Domingo, who, as usual, arrived last, ended up on a sofa that would not have looked out of place on a public tip.

The room was stacked to the rafters with pallets of EU longlife milk, spaghetti and biscuits, all stamped in authoritarian red 'FOR AID RELIEF'. Kuba and Adam said 'we shouldn't' – however, with biscuit in one hand and carton of milk in the other, I announced that 'we should', and no sooner had he walked through the door than Domingo was in complete agreement with me.

For a bit, he and I just ate biscuits and drank milk until by about the second packet and third carton we began to feel, as a growing sensation of nausea wore on, that the novelty had worn off and started to contemplate the spaghetti with interest.

'How much money you have?' Domingo blurted out.

'Ten euros.'

'I too...how about you boys?'

Between them Adam and Kuba had 30, so it was quickly agreed that we would head into town, buy food and cook on the electric ring that had been thoughtfully provided.

With a diameter of 27 metres, the dome in Montefiascone's cathedral is one of the largest in Italy; custom dictated that we had to visit. But, once inside, a curious thing happened; instead of wandering about, Domingo and I simply sat down. For a good five minutes we stared ahead motionless.

'What are you thinking?' I said.

'Nothing, absolutely nothing.'

'Same here.'

'I think I have church indigestion.'

The baroque carvings, the wonders of the architecture by now stood for little. We were churched out.

So we left, bought some mandatory bottles of the local wine, *Est! Est!! Est!!!* and returned to our garage. In the car park outside, we rigged up a table using some crates and dined *en famille* and *al fresco* by the light of street lamps. It was Adam who summed up the evening perfectly when he declared that for all its simplicity and with the few cares we had in the world, we were at that moment probably the happiest people on earth. He was right and we drank to our good fortune more than once.

Until, that is, it was time for bed. I was just about to turn the light off when something in the glass cover attracted my attention.

'Oh my God!'

'What?' Domingo replied.

I pointed in silence. A large scorpion was scuttling up and down the casing directly overhead. I couldn't kill it, as I couldn't reach it and, besides, Domingo was adamant the scorpion should live. I reminded him that was all well and good as it wasn't his head that the creature would land on unannounced in the night. Equally, the consensus in the room – namely Kuba and Adam – was that it would be impossible to sleep with the lights on and there wasn't room, thanks to the food aid piled around us, to manoeuvre the bed out of the way either. Domingo then demanded to have a closer look. He climbed up onto a chair and tapped the cover with his stick. He tapped again, this time with a little more vigour.

'Careful', I remonstrated, worried that scorpion might escape; at least in the current situation we knew where it was.

'It's dead, you blood English fool!' he pronounced as he jumped down onto the floor.

'You sure?'

'Yes, course I am sure.'

'It could just be sleeping', I added, 'nice and warm in that light.'

'You try and make it move then. It's been fried!'

I tapped my stick against the light. The scorpion had indeed seen happier days. I went to bed very quietly.

*

We split after Viterbo, Kuba and Adam to Vitralla, Domingo to Sutri and me to Capranica. Following a long dawn walk through the woods and streams of the Valle Mazzano, I caught up with my Spanish friend the morning after on the busy road leaving Sutri.

'How are you?' I asked.

'Okay', he grunted, 'well, as good as can be expected when you have slept on a desk and had Andreas snoring next to you on a table.'

'Andreas the Pole?'

'*Si*! I said him you were about but he told me he is still

recovering from the week he spent with you after Vercelli; besides, he is having a day off. I brought you breakfast though.'

'Really?'

'*Sì*', he growled, at which he produced a miserable-looking excuse for a plastic bag within which was the remains of a crescent-shaped object that looked as if it had just been run over.

'How old is that?'

'This morning', he protested.

'Did you sit on it?'

'Not exactly', he replied looking sheepish, 'it kinda got stuck in the vending machine door.'

By now there was hardly a need for maps. On every gate, lamppost and stile there was a commendable array of arrows in every shape, form and size imaginable pointing the way to Rome. Like homing pigeons we knew where we were headed. We watched as a British Airways flight bound for Fiumincino airport flew in overhead, its undercarriage already down for landing. Vying for space alongside the traffic-choked roads filled with freight lorries and juggernauts thundering towards Rome, the Via was squeezed to a trickle as the landscape softened to a featureless undulation of paddocks, market gardens and nut orchards. In silence we limped along, until Domingo suddenly shouted from behind: 'Did you know *After Eight* mints are kosher?'

For an hour or so, the chocolate became the subject of much debate – did the mint filling come first then the chocolate, or was it the other way around? We couldn't decide.

*

With only 21 miles to walk before journey's end, Domingo and I went our separate ways again the next morning as we left Campagnano for La Storta. Nothing was said; we just knew that for our last full day on the road we wanted to be alone with our thoughts. It was a bewildering sensation, as the world we had grown so comfortable in, which we were an indelible part of, was about to unceremoniously eject us.

The cars got bigger, the clothes more expensive and the

houses grander as Rome drew ever closer. I was picking black-berries in a shady lane, the sun catching on the bracken behind me, when a man drove past in a large blue Mercedes with the roof down, his little boy in the passenger seat beside him. He stopped and reversed back.

'Where are you from, sir?' in broad New York.

'*Londra.*'

'*A piedi?*'

'*Si a piedi, novantatré giorni*', his eyes bulged in disbelief.

'Alfredo, this gentleman has walked all the way from London', he said, turning to his son, 'ninety-three days!'

'May I ask where you are going?'

'*A Roma.*'

'*Complimenti, complimenti* indeed, Sir'. He shook his head, slipped the car into gear and drove off.

10 miles to Rome.

23

A Roma!

They walked on, thinking of This and That, and by-and-by they came to an enchanted place...
A. A. Milne, *The House at Pooh Corner,* 1928

SET BACK FROM THE busy Via Cassia, the Istituto Suore Poverelle at La Storta, a modern complex in a large garden, was an ungainly marriage of barrack block, hospital and 1950s holiday resort complete with marble chip flooring, concrete parterres and a surplus of Scouts. St Peter's Square was now only ten miles away but, despite the traffic's roar all around us, it was a good place to hole up for the night before the final stretch.

LN was already *bien installée* by the time Domingo and I walked in through the enormous automatic gates. Suor Pina, a smiling nun of advanced years dressed in white, showed us to a room in a basement. As every evening since early May, I set about washing my kit. Except that on this evening of all evenings, everything got an extra scrub. I polished the brass keys that hung off my rucksack, cleaned the cover and sponged down the Union Jack sewn on the back. The t-shirts that were once dark blue had faded to lavender, my bright red Edmiston baseball cap now frayed peach and the boots that had carried me since Gray, white with dust, all went under the tap.

In the corner, the ID discs and crucifix that went around my neck by day were hanging off my thumbstick, just as they did every night; I looked at them, the St Christopher, given by my friend James Keatley, once shiny and bright had lost its sheen all together. I cradled the stick in my hands, running them up and down the ash shaft; the base above the ferrule battered and chipped while the bark at the top was polished black with sweat and the crook smooth to the touch from day after day of wear. That stick was like an unbreakable extension of me now.

I took my Pilgrim Passport out from its red plastic bag. The orderly collection of stamps on the first page, Rose's post office frank, St Nicholas's Church Childe Okeford, St Paul's and Canterbury Cathedral had soon given way to a chaotic assortment of red, blue, green and black markings of all shapes and sizes, indeed anywhere space permitted on both sides of the now foxed-edged document – except for one final square at the end. Rochester, Dover, Calais, Wisques, Camblain l'Abbé, Reims, Bar-sur-Aube, Mouthier, Lausanne, Aosta, Vercelli and Pavia were all distant memories, some so far off I could hardly remember where or when, just the names, but nonetheless stop-offs that had got me to this night, all of which led to the morrow and Rome. Had I really walked all that way? A prospect which, five years earlier, seemed quite inconceivable.

I dug into my pack, took out the forty-seventh and final map; it was an ugly-looking thing, more brown than green, the route disappearing into a lattice-like spider's web of yellow, at the top of which was written '*CITTA' DEL VATICANO*' – words that represented the chequered flag. I placed it in my map case along with the compass that I had had so little use for. Tidied up, smartened up, I was ready to go. LN put her head around the door: 'Let's picnic on the terrace.'

Domingo had found a marble table in the garden, shaded by three large cypress trees. It was a simple supper, sardines, bread, tomatoes, cheese and some apples with a bottle of red and a bottle of white wine. We were oddly subdued, contemplative. It was as if 9 August was some sort of day of reckoning. I suppose in a way it was. We would all be back in the real world before noon.

LN, her foot resting on a garden chair, announced that she was going to take the train in, and walk from Monte Mario. Domingo said he would join her, having read in a guidebook that it was quite acceptable to let the railway do the penultimate seven miles, given that the road was such a dog's dinner of a route. I smiled, saying that it was such a pity he hadn't felt up to walking all the way to Rome, especially as he had only started halfway at Canterbury, unlike those few of us who had set out from the City of London. But he was adamant and, of course, in true Spanish style, it afforded him more time in bed too.

'What does it matter?' he snapped back. 'We can't even go into San Pietro because we have walked all this way in shorts. Does God really care what we wear? It's the other guys on foot that made the road for us, not the Church. The Church couldn't give a damn. Besides, our journey is as good as over now, so who cares if we take the train or not.' His sudden outburst took me aback.

LN said she was looking forward to tomorrow. 'For me, this has been a difficult journey. I never foresaw such problems with my foot and my leg in all my life. So, to reach the end means a chance to go home, sort things out and get better. It will be good to see my Alain and the dogs. Had it not been for you two, thank God, I would have gone home a long time back.'

Domingo, who was strangely quiet, said that he too was looking forward to seeing his girlfriend and that perhaps 'now it's the time to settle down once I get back', and then added, rather ominously, 'whenever that is...'.

As LN and I started to clear up, Domingo excused himself to go to the room. Once finished, I kissed LN on both cheeks, gave her a hug and holding her in my arms looked her in the eye, '*A Saint Pierre!*'

When I returned to the accommodation, I found Domingo with his back to me, hunched against the bed, his head in his hands. 'Do you think people will care what we've done?'

'Of course not', I replied. 'Sure, they'll say "wow" for a moment, but then they'll be talking about last night's movie, the new restaurant in Chelsea or the latest play in the West End. It's not that they don't care, it's that they haven't got time to care; everybody these days is too caught up in their own lives.'

He kept his back to me, his head hung. 'I don't want to get like that again.'

'You can't live all your days, running and hiding. You have to go back to the real world sometime.'

'But what if all this is nothing?'

'It will be "nothing" if you choose it to be. It's you who make it something. After all these miles, the days on the road, the solitude, the sweat, the tears and the pain, has all that hard work been for nought? You've got this far, don't you dare give up now!'

'My girlfriend said she was proud of me, but I have done nothing', his words muffled by the pillow.

'Most people can only dream of such achievement. Not many folk have the determination to walk all those miles. For the everyday Joe, what you've done, seen and experienced is something to be proud of, so live up to that, for Joe's sake if nothing else', I said. 'We've had the best of times, but now you have to take what you've learnt and apply it to life with renewed oomph. That's what you came for, wasn't it?'

'I guess. I have my homework tomorrow. I promised to pray for so many people along the way. I have a list.'

'Me too.'

'There was a homeless man in Péronne who I shared the night with in a church. You know, so often I felt like a tramp on the Via – uncared for, discarded, of no use. And in Pamplona...' he gave a big sigh and wiped his eye, 'oh my God, with the current *crise*...it's my fear.'

I couldn't bear to see my friend like this. I went up, grabbed his arm and turned him around, his enormous frame shuddering uncontrollably in my embrace. 'Pilgrims don't give in.'

It was dark the following morning when I crept out of the room – La Storta was in total silence as I padded down to the gate. When I got there, I soon realized that I didn't know how to open it. In the excitement of arrival, I had forgotten to ask. I got my torch out. There must be a button somewhere, I thought. I found a keypad on the right, pushed it in vain. It bleeped and flashed but I stopped, worried I might wake a nun when an intruder alarm sounded in some far-off vestry. I considered climbing over, but what if I was arrested by the Police in the process? There must be a way out. I pressed some more buttons. Nothing.

I stepped back and sat down for a minute to have a think. I was locked in. With my chin resting on the crook of my stick I sat there, and then, as the dawn came, I noticed by my right a little metal stake sticking up with an enormous yellow button on it. Like something out of *Alice In Wonderland*, you could hardly miss it really; all it lacked were the words 'Press Me'.

I pressed it. The hydraulic arms gave a satisfying wheeze and '*abracadabra*', the doors parted and out I shot into the morning.

The markings were clear as I turned onto the Via Trionfale. The pavements were strewn with broken glass, plastic bottles, cigarette packets and discarded shoes as I walked past festering municipal bins and under fizzing pylon lines. It was the most untriumphal road I had been on. Then the pavement disappeared altogether and I was just another soul fighting for air in the exhaust and noise of Romans racing to work.

I watched with envy as a train shot past. I was beginning to think that maybe Domingo and LN had the right idea. Then I checked my map. I was the wrong side of the railway line. Up ahead I could see an *autostrada*, blue signs indicating the airport. I am on the wrong road I thought, convincing myself that, unable to get off it, I would be forced onto the highway and end up like a cheap airline flight, not in Rome but almost Rome. I fumbled for my compass, laid it on the map grid and checked. The compass never lies. Seemed OK. I carried on – not that escaping the road was easy, given the tall chain-link fence I would have to get over. I kept my eye open for a break; vandals were sure to have made a hole somewhere – they had had a good go at everything else.

Mercifully, the rubbish and traffic gradually relented, giving way to trees and boulevards; a semblance of order returned, coiffed ladies walked coiffed dogs on dainty leads. With time in hand, I stopped in a café for coffee and some breakfast. Standing at the bar, I watched the barrista's poetic ballet while he prepared the two cappuccinos I ordered. Turning and pirouetting on his heel, first saucers were laid out, then spoons were polished and placed down together facing the same way left and right of the cups, before the final froth was added with ever such a sleight of hand and '*prego, signor*!' I texted progress to my sister, Kate, in Cumbria.

Further on, to my left I found the stone arch in the wall that I had been looking for. I walked through and started up a long set of gravelled steps; like a dog on a scent, I knew where I was headed. I turned right, now racing up to Monte Mario – a gate and then, among the olive and pine on a bald sandy patch, I spotted the unmistakable silhouette of LN in a soft linen shirt and walking trousers.

'You made it uh?' she said, as I put my arm on her shoulder. 'Yeah.'

We looked through the gap in the trees and, staring in silence, nodded. Below us stretched a kaleidoscopic pattern of mansion buildings, monuments, offices, bridges, churches, the snaking Tiber, shops and ancient ruins. Rome, in all her magnificence. And, towering above everything else, shining in the morning sun, St Peter's Basilica; the tallest dome in the world. Beautiful.

Of course, Domingo shattered the moment when he came clumping along.

'Oh, the pedestrian finally arrived then!'

How we jigged, danced and laughed in jubilation while cameras were produced and passersby accosted to take photographs.

I looked at my watch. 'Heavens, I am going to be late!'

'Now who? Not another count?'

'No, a doctor of climatology if you must know. I'll see you down there!' With which I grabbed my kit and charged off, running all the way down the steep-sided slopes until, through the car park, I picked up the Viale Angelico. Even in my rush, the name got me thinking. Had this whole escapade, from the moment my laptop was struck by lightning, been some bizarre form of divine intervention? I hadn't the time to consider, but, for sure, God had truly held me in the palm of His hand, just as He had been asked in May when I set out from our village church in Dorset.

Three months earlier, I had arranged to meet Dr Iarla Kilbane-Dawe, who had been on a teaching assignment with the European Space Agency, at 10 a.m. in St Peter's. I was hanged if I was going to be late. I usually am for most things. Everywhere there were buses, cars, people and touts, all of whom insisted to a man, and a woman, that I purchase cheap tickets to the Vatican. If only they knew. I ran on and turned left down towards the great bulk of the Castel Sant'Angelo. It was all happening too quickly. I stopped, gathered myself and, hesitantly at first, with my head bowed, turned onto the Via della Conciliazione. For a moment I faltered. I couldn't bear to look at the great basilica, the very sight of which meant the end of the road, completion of the adventure and return to reality. Then, remembering my words to Domingo the night before, I lifted my head. There, filling the great avenue before me, stood the mighty St Peter's.

I drew a deep breath, pulled my shoulders back and began to march towards my destination – all the time thinking of the *Libro d'Oro* that I had thumbed through the evening before; Americans, Chileans, Russians, Chinese, Koreans, Belgians, French, Swedes, New Zealanders – in short, someone from every nation of the world seemed to have written in that book as they too prepared to make good their entry to the Eternal City. The message was the same throughout, that of thanks for the generosity and warmth of welcome they had received along the way.

And as I took the final steps of the 1,411 miles I had walked since London, so I too concluded that in this modern age when all too often life just rushes us by, there is nothing on this Earth, neither wealth nor material gain, rank nor privilege that matters more than man's kindness to man and the love of family and friends.

And, suddenly, there I was in a swirl of humanity, like a tramp, like a pilgrim, one of thousands; it was not important how any of us had got there, that we had got there at all was what counted. An arm shoved out from behind a column with a glass of champagne. 'You're late, Major!' the good doctor's voice bellowed in deep Irish brogue.

'When have I ever not been?' I smiled as I downed the glass.

Then, almost as if in celebration, the mighty bell of St Peter's sounded. I looked up and there, perched on high, was a blackbird, singing his heart out.

'Shall we walk to the hotel?' Iarla said.

I shot him a look and, raising my hand high above my head, shouted: 'TAXI!'

FINE

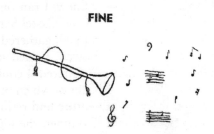

Epilogue

Bring me my bow of burning gold!
Bring me arrows of desire!
Bring me my spear! O clouds, unfold!
Bring me my chariot of fire!

William Blake, *Jerusalem* from the preface
to *Milton a Poem*, c 1804

THERE FOLLOWED AN 11-HOUR lunch, which started in the Piazza Navona and ended up, I think, in the lee of the Pantheon, the words *M Agrippa L F Cos Tertium Fecit* forever etched on my mind.

The next morning, feeling remarkably chipper and civilized, dressed in 'normal clothes', I returned to the Vatican, queued for an hour and, after being searched, was led through a warren to the basement where, in a side office not dissimilar to a doctor's waiting room, I found Andreas, Kuba and Adam. A smiling lady asked us to fill out some forms and after more smiling she stamped our Passports and gave us a computer printout to say we had walked to Rome. Leaving, we were taken to see St Peter's tomb. We never saw a priest.

Domingo and LN joined us for the Pilgrims' Mass, taken by a visiting French clergyman, assisted by Adam and Kuba. We all made it, but perhaps the saying really is right: it is the journey not the end that matters.

It was Reto, with whom I crossed the Cisa Pass, who said that a pilgrimage is made up of two parts: the first, penance, while you order your thoughts; and the second, absolution, when you walk with a clear head. But I believe there is also a third part, and that is grief for the hole in life that the completed undertaking leaves. And what of the others?

Sylviane, in her wheelchair, I heard made it to Rome a few days earlier. Reto still teaches in Switzerland. Every now and then he threatens to come to England during the holidays.

Carmen and Josephine made it safely to Assisi and back again without the aid of maps, while Brian Mooney walked through his garden gate in Essex to be met by his wife, Gail on 16 September 2012. Alain, with whom I set out from Canterbury but who had to return home, finally reached St Peter's later in the year on 26 October, while Pietro and Antonio, at Radicofani, completed the last section of their pilgrimage on 5 August 2013.

LN hung up her panier and sold her balloon in February 2014, after 40 years in the sport. She is still dusting off pilgrims on the road to Reims and plans to walk to Assisi and Rome, once again, in the coming months.

St Spyridon of Corfu worked his charms for Carole Thomson in Martigny; she beat cancer and is now making a full recovery.

After, I took off to the Greek Islands. When I eventually returned home, some people asked if I had changed at all. Changed in what sense I wondered? I am still 15 minutes late for everything, if that was what they were asking, but perhaps I do feel a little more content to let the wheel of life turn at its own pace.

And Domingo? He is yet to settle, as he said he would, but he is happy and that is all that matters. We stay in touch from time to time; the last I heard of him he was somewhere in France.

But returning to that map in the *ostello* at Costa Mezzano and my conversation with Oliver, the trattoria owner in Chapter 17 – what I didn't tell you was that the dotted line continued south from Rome through Corfu, Crete and Rhodes to Cyprus, Acre and ultimately Jerusalem. So I apologize, dear reader, for while I may have reached my stated destination, ever since that moment I have had the worrying notion that possibly this is the story of a journey only half-told. Maybe, who knows?

Once the mass was over, our work done, we all went in search of a bar and, sitting outside at a long table, ordered drinks. I proposed a toast, 'Happy Endings'. We all laughed and, just as we raised our glasses, so LN chipped in, 'no, Happy Beginnings!'

Grazie.